Haiti and the Haitian Diaspora in the Wider Caribbean

New World Diasporas

UNIVERSITY PRESS OF FLORIDA

Florida A&M University, Tallahassee
Florida Atlantic University, Boca Raton
Florida Gulf Coast University, Ft. Myers
Florida International University, Miami
Florida State University, Tallahassee
New College of Florida, Sarasota
University of Central Florida, Orlando
University of Florida, Gainesville
University of North Florida, Jacksonville
University of South Florida, Tampa
University of West Florida, Pensacola

New World Diasporas

Edited by Kevin A. Yelvington

This series seeks to stimulate critical perspectives on diaspora processes in the New World. Representations of race and ethnicity, the origins and consequences of nationalism, migratory streams and the advent of transnationalism, the dialectics of homelands and diasporas, trade networks, gender relations in immigrant communities, the politics of displacement and exile, and the utilization of the past to serve the present are among the phenomena addressed by original, provocative research in disciplines such as anthropology, history, political science, and sociology.

More Than Black: Afro-Cubans in Tampa, by Susan D. Greenbaum (2002)

Carnival and the Formation of a Caribbean Transnation, by Philip W. Scher (2003)

Dominican Migration: Transnational Perspectives, edited by Ernesto Sagás and Sintia Molina (2004)

Salvadoran Migration to Southern California: Redefining El Hermano Lejano, by Beth Baker-Cristales (2004)

The Chrysanthemum and the Song: Music, Memory, and Identity in the South American Japanese Diaspora, by Dale A. Olsen (2004)

Andean Diaspora: The Tiwanaku Colonies and the Origins of South American Empire, by Paul S. Goldstein (2005)

Migration and Vodou, by Karen E. Richman (2005)

True-Born Maroons, by Kenneth M. Bilby (2005)

The Tears of Hispaniola: Haitian and Dominican Diaspora Memory, by Lucía M. Suárez (2006)

Dominican-Americans and the Politics of Empowerment, by Ana Aparicio (2006)

Nuer-American Passages: Global Migration in the Twentieth Century, by Dianna J. Shandy (2006)

Religion and the Politics of Ethnic Identity in Bahia, Brazil, by Stephen Selka (2007)

Reconstructing Racial Identity and the African Past in the Dominican Republic, by Kimberly Eison Simmons (2009)

Haiti and the Haitian Diaspora in the Wider Caribbean, edited by Philippe Zacaïr (2010)

HAITI AND
THE HAITIAN DIASPORA
IN THE WIDER CARIBBEAN

Edited by Philippe Zacaïr

University Press of Florida
Gainesville/Tallahassee/Tampa/Boca Raton
Pensacola/Orlando/Miami/Jacksonville/Ft. Myers/Sarasota

15 14 13 12 11 10   6 5 4 3 2 1

Library of Congress Cataloging-in-Publication Data
Haiti and the Haitian diaspora in the wider Caribbean / edited by Philippe
Zacaïr.
p. cm.—(New world diasporas)
Includes bibliographical references and index.
ISBN 978-0-8130-3461-4 (alk. paper)
1. Haitians—Caribbean Area—Ethnic identity. 2. Haitians—Caribbean Area—
Migrations. 3. Haitians—Relocation—Caribbean Area. 4. Haiti—Emigration
and immigration. 5. Caribbean Area—Emigration and immigration. I. Zacaïr,
Philippe.
F1930.A1H35 2010
305.896′972940729—dc22
2009034725

The University Press of Florida is the scholarly publishing agency for the State
University System of Florida, comprising Florida A&M University, Florida
Atlantic University, Florida Gulf Coast University, Florida International Uni-
versity, Florida State University, New College of Florida, University of Central
Florida, University of Florida, University of North Florida, University of South
Florida, and University of West Florida.

University Press of Florida
15 Northwest 15th Street
Gainesville, FL 32611-2079
http://www.upf.com

To Éric Calpas

Contents

Preface and Acknowledgments

I find it quite difficult to point to the genesis of this book project. The more I try to refresh my memory, the more I have the feeling that it has always been in some corner of my mind. I cannot help but remember watching carnival in the streets of Pointe-à-Pitre as a young child with my cherished grandmother. She loudly applauded every group until the Haitian band passed by, after which her mood completely changed for a short period. I remember being puzzled by her sudden, surprisingly negative, and almost violent reaction to the Haitian group. I had only noticed that they sounded a little different from the Guadeloupeans, but I did not bother to ask her any questions and I did not think about it any further. Some pieces of these childhood memories resurfaced from time to time as I encountered disturbingly similar prejudices against Haitians or other Caribbeans living in Guadeloupe. Over time I began to develop a deep interest in inter-Caribbean relations which probably inspired my subsequent professional choices. Meeting many years later with Cécile Accilien was without a doubt a decisive moment leading to the idea of this book. As we became friends, we held endless long-distance phone conversations on the relationship between our respective island societies: Haiti and Guadeloupe. These conversations directly led me to propose and chair a panel entitled "So Similar and Yet so Foreign: Haiti and Haitians in the Wider Caribbean" at the Latin American Studies Association meeting held in Puerto Rico in 2006. The panel was very successful and the audience appreciated the juxtaposition of very diverse interpretations of the Haitian experience in the Caribbean and the United States. The decision to create a book based on the model of the panel came out immediately.

This project would never have come to fruition if I had not counted upon encouragement and generous help from a number of colleagues and friends. First, I would like to thank Kevin Yelvington for expressing from the outset his strong interest in this project and for recommending that I submit it to the University Press of Florida. Many thanks also to the outside reviewers for their constructive comments and suggestions for improvement and to the editorial staff of the University Press of Florida. I am also indebted to Paul Brodwin who generously allowed me to reprint in this collective volume his seminal work, "Marginality and Subjectivity in the Haitian Diaspora," originally published in *Anthropological Quarterly* 76, no. 1 (2003). I would like to express my deepest gratitude to Odile Ferly, Cécile Accilien, Maud Laëthier, Pierre Minn, Sharon Clarke, Catherine Reinhardt, and Marc Lony for their willingness to be part of this adventure and for their hard work. I feel especially indebted to Catherine Reinhardt who co-wrote the introduction of the book and generously offered to translate into English Maud Laëthier's article which was originally written in French. Reinhardt also put me in contact with Myrtha Désulmé. Désulmé, the president of the Haiti-Jamaica Society, not only allowed me to tell her family story but also provided me with much help and encouragement. Many thanks also to Colin Keavenney who took over the translation of Marc Lony's article. Finally, I would like to thank Bill Haddad, chair of the History Department and Tom Klammer, dean of Humanities and Social Sciences at California State University Fullerton for allowing me to reside in the Caribbean for an extended period of time to pursue my research projects.

Introduction

PHILIPPE ZACAÏR AND CATHERINE REINHARDT

On July 11, 2003, the Costa Rica–based Inter-American Court of Human Rights began examining a case brought against the Dominican Republic by several human rights organizations such as the Movimiento de Mujeres Domínico-Haitianas and the International Human Rights Law Clinic on behalf of Dilcia Yean and Violeta Bosico, two young girls of Haitian origin born in Dominican territory.[1] The organizations claimed that the Civil Registry of the Dominican Republic had refused to issue the young girls birth certificates and, thus, to recognize their Dominican citizenship. Yet, as they argued, the Dominican constitution that established the principles of jus soli entitled Yean and Bosico to Dominican citizenship. Deprived of a legal existence by the Dominican state, the girls were forced into permanent lawlessness and social vulnerability.

Three years after their initial consultations with the contending parties, the five members of the court ruled in favor of Yean and Bosico. The judges concluded that the Dominican Republic had indeed violated the fundamental rights of the plaintiffs, including the right to a nationality, to full equality before the law, and to a legal existence. The court instructed the Dominican State to publicly apologize to the young girls, grant them financial compensation, and take adequate measures designed to curb what appeared to be routine discriminatory practices targeting the sons and daughters of Haitian migrant workers.

The ruling, however, was met with vehement protests in Santo Domingo. In December 2005, the Dominican Supreme Court rejected the recommendations of the Inter-American Court of Human Rights. The Dominican justices claimed that children born on Dominican soil to undocumented foreigners or temporary migrant workers—two categories into which virtually all Haitian immigrants fall—do not have an automatic right to Dominican citizenship. Since the 2005 ruling of the Inter-American Court of Human Rights, the standing of Haitian migrant workers and their Dominican-born descendants has steadily deteriorated. For thousands of Dominico-Haitians, full recognition as Dominicans remains unattainable. Worse, anti-Haitian violence has increased since 2005 due to massive expulsions of Haitians by the Dominican government. Many have been physically assaulted, their houses burnt down by angry Dominican mobs. Some have even been killed (Paulino 2006).

The political debates, legal disputes, and rising violence associated with a large presence of Haitian immigrants are not, however, unique to the Dominican Republic. In the wider Caribbean, such debates have inflamed the island of Guadeloupe—a French overseas *département*—since the summer of 2001. At that time, Ibo Simon, the host of a popular television show, began portraying Haitian immigrants as "curs," "vermins," and "scums." Ibo called upon Guadeloupeans to defend themselves against the invasion of "bloodthirsty" Haitians. Subsequent events proved that Simon had been heard. Several Haitians were physically assaulted in the streets of Pointe-à-Pitre after being identified as Haitians. Groups of Ibo admirers began attacking and burning down Haitian houses.

In November 2001, several Guadeloupe-based Haitian associations as well as antiracist and human rights organizations successfully brought Simon and Michel Rodriguez—the director of private television channel Canal 10—to justice.[2] The court found Ibo and Rodriguez guilty of inciting to discrimination, hatred, and violence against one or more individuals because of their ethnic origin. Nevertheless, the interethnic tensions unleashed by Ibo and Rodriguez have far from subsided. As more and more impoverished Haitians risk their lives to reach the shores of Guadeloupe, many Guadeloupeans' perceptions of Haitian migrants have gone from bad to worse. Following Simon's lead, populist politicians rarely hesitate to use the media to target Haitians as the unique source of every evil in Guadeloupean society. However, contrary to the Dominican example mentioned above, violent prejudice against Haitian migrants seems to go hand-in-hand with admiration for and adoption of many elements of Haitian history and culture by Guadeloupeans. This paradox exemplifies the complexity of the relationship between Haiti, Haitians, and other peoples of the contemporary Caribbean.

Many other examples of anti-Haitian violence can be found in French Guiana, the Bahamas, or Venezuela (Charrier 2000). This violence is by no means new in Caribbean history. The 1937 massacre of approximately 15,000 Haitians on the Haitian-Dominican border is one of the most tragic outcomes of the Haitian migrants' journey (Derby and Turits 1993; Turits 2002; Castor 1983; Derby 1994). What makes the Dominican and Guadeloupean examples mentioned above particularly fascinating are the similarities of the verbal and physical expressions of violence against Haitian migrants in such vastly different Caribbean territories. The imagined terrestrial, linguistic, religious, and racial boundaries with Haiti that characterize Dominican national narratives do not apply in the case of Guadeloupe. Sharing a comparable colonial trajectory until 1804, similar racial characteristics, and analogous linguistic origins, most Guadeloupeans cannot seriously consider the Haitians' blackness or use of the Creole language as foreign.

If Guadeloupeans reject a people who resemble them in many ways, what is their violent prejudice founded upon? What characterizes the common thread of anti-Haitianism in Guadeloupe, French Guiana, the Dominican Republic, and the Bahamas? Can one speak of a unified anti-Haitian prejudice that has played a role in the construction of national narratives and given rise to these mechanisms of prejudice in the wider Caribbean?

Stuart Hall's (2003) distinction between two different ways of thinking about cultural identity proves helpful in exploring the violent rejection of a people so similar to other Caribbean populations—in particular in the French Caribbean—as the Haitians are. One way of thinking about cultural identity proposes an essential, true, collective "Caribbean" self. Within this definition, cultural identity reflects the common historical experiences and cultural heritage as expressed by the Caribbean or black diaspora (234). Following this perspective, the current antagonism toward Haitian migrants by people of the Caribbean cannot be accounted for. Hall's second view of cultural identity does, however, provide a perfect tool of analysis to further explore this violent prejudice. According to this second way of thinking, there are deep and significant differences which constitute what the people of the Caribbean have become. With the intervention of history, the cultural identities of Caribbean people have become transformed as they have been subjected to the "continuous 'play' of history, culture, and power." As a result, it is now impossible to speak of "one" Caribbean experience or "one" Caribbean identity (236). Hall elaborates on this "doubleness" of similarity and difference in relation to the West:

> Vis-à-vis the developed West, we are very much "the same." We belong to the marginal, the underdeveloped, the periphery, the "Other." We are at the outer edge, the "rim," of the metropolitan world—always "South" to someone else's El Norte. At the same time, we do not stand in the same relation of the "otherness" to the metropolitan centers.

Each has negotiated its economic, political, and cultural dependency differently. And this "difference," whether we like it or not, is already inscribed in our cultural identities. (238)

Haitians have developed an entirely different relationship to the United States and Europe than have Guadeloupeans, Bahamians, Jamaicans, French Guyanese, or Dominicans. Intra-Caribbean relationships superimpose themselves on these former or current colonial relationships, adding a level of complexity that is not always welcome in the receiving society.

Focusing on the specific example of Haitian and Dominican migrant workers in Guadeloupe, Laënnec Hurbon (1983) analyses how the struggle for self-preservation in the face of colonial violence leads to the creation of an imaginary Guadeloupean space, a symbol of purity and authenticity. Perceived as an "invasion," the massive influx of Haitian and Dominican migrant workers threatens the imaginary Guadeloupean space and endangers the sought after homogeneity (Hurbon 1983: 1998). Augmenting the tensions inherent in colonial and postcolonial relationships, migrant workers are not recognized as kin sharing a common historical past, and in the case of Guadeloupe and Haiti, the French and Creole languages, music, and magic/religious practices. Instead, these migrants become scapegoats upon which Guadeloupeans project their own feelings of alienation, having themselves been victims of colonial violence (1997).

In the preface to the first volume of the U.S. journal *Diaspora*, in which he announced the birth of the concept of diaspora, Khachig Tölölyan (1991) examined the ways in which nation-states imagine themselves as sites of homogeneity. In order to achieve this, they must assimilate and destroy differences, assign them "to ghettoes, to enclaves demarcated by boundaries so sharp that they enable the nation to acknowledge the apparently singular and clearly fenced-off differences *within* itself, while simultaneously reaffirming the privileged homogeneity of the rest" (Tölölyan 1991: 6). The problem with Haitian migrants is that they often do not demarcate themselves clearly from the receiving society, thereby blurring the differences. Based on these reflections Tölölyan concludes that the idea of a homogeneous nation is now being replaced by a vision of the world as a "space" continually reshaped by cultural, political, technological, demographic, and above all economic forces (6). To be sure, the massive movements of peoples from one nation to another—in which the Caribbean is to some extent a crucible—has fundamentally challenged the possibility of maintaining homogenous nation-states. The xenophobic and often violent reactions to Haitian immigrants within the Caribbean basin, however, exemplify the difficulties faced by those who have pushed the boundaries of nation-states to become "traveling cultures" according to Robin Cohen (1997: 128), or "nations unbound" to use Basch et al.'s term (quoted in Cohen 1997: 136).

Recent literature on diaspora and other related concepts is wide ranging (Catanese 1999; Conway 2003; Fabre and Benesch 2004; Laguerre 1998; Laguerre 2006 etc.)[3] However, rather than discuss the different theories about diaspora, (Cohen 1997; Tölölyan 1991), transnational communities (Gowricharn 2006), transmigrants (Glick Schiller and Fouron 2001), deterritorialized nation-states (Basch 1994), transnations, and transnational nation-states (Appadurai 1996), we prefer to focus on the way in which "movement" is an essential component of the diasporic phenomena. It is the continuous movement of Haitians across the geopolitical boundaries of the wider Caribbean that brings their similarity with other people from the Caribbean head-to-head with their simultaneous and profound foreignness. The encounters between Haitian migrants and host societies are in turn reflected in the ever-changing perceptions that the different cultural groups have of one another. Kevin Yelvington speaks of diaspora as an "interactive phenomenon" which cannot be reified (quoted in Richman 2005: xiv). No label can capture the continually evolving relationships within which diasporic groups find themselves engaged. Their "production" of identity (to use Hall's terminology) is never complete and always in process (Hall 2003: 234). "The ruptures and discontinuities which constitute, precisely, the Caribbean's 'uniqueness'" are fundamental components of the Haitians' diasporic experiences (236).

Cohen engages the notion of movement to observe how the creation of diasporas has moved margins to the center, bringing marginal groups suddenly into close proximity and shared spaces. (Cohen 1997: 134). As Haitian migrants coexist with host societies, they are often stigmatized, despised, and assigned to the lowest level of the social hierarchy. "An pa Ayisyen a-w" [I am not your Haitian] has become a common insult in Guadeloupe (Hurbon 1983: 1999). And yet, the interactive attribute of diasporic exchange also encompasses a paradoxical fascination with the rich cultural patrimony of the Haitian people who seem to have emancipated themselves from an obsession with the "white," "colonial" gaze (2000). The Guadeloupeans' desire for their own original culture, with its contours clearly defined and unaltered by outside influences (2000) is foiled by the force of cultural exchange and the gradual reappropriation of Haitian music, Vodou practices, and Creole as common patrimony (2002). For Hurbon this is the base of a "true Caribbean community" (2002). Hall would call it the "doubleness" of similarity and difference (Hall 2003: 238).

In view of their tragic consequences in the Caribbean past and present, understanding the complex expressions of anti-Haitianism from a comparative perspective is a matter of urgency not only for human rights advocates but also for social scientists. Yet, the perceptions/receptions of Haitian migrants among Caribbean communities have not been studied from such a comparative perspective (Allman 1982; Perusek 1984). The historiography of Haitian migrations in the wider Caribbean remains both linguistically and geographically fragmented. While the conditions of Haitian migrants in the Dominican Republic have received the attention of scholars across disciplines, this is not the case in other Caribbean territories.

From the infamous 1937 massacre orchestrated by Rafael Trujillo to the slave-like working conditions of sugar workers in Dominican *bateyes*, the Haitian question in the Dominican Republic has been thoroughly studied by historians such as Richard Lee Turits and Lauren Derby, as well as by other social scientists (Paulino 2005; Duany 2006). For the Bahamas however, beyond pioneering works by Dawn Marshall, Michael Craton, and Gail Saunders (Marshall 1979; Craton and Saunders 1992), recent investigations regarding the complex process of the integration of Haitian migrants into their new societies remain scant (Sears 1994). This relative absence of research is even more pronounced for the Eastern Caribbean. There is still a complete lack of scholarly investigations in English for French Guiana. Similarly, scholarly works on Guadeloupe are rare despite the size of its Haitian migrant community and the complex relationship existing between Guadeloupean natives and Haiti (Brodwin 2000; Brodwin 2001; Johnson 1982).

Investigating Haitian migrations and anti-Haitianism in the wider Caribbean raises numerous legal, cultural, economic, and political issues which call for an interdisciplinary approach. For this purpose, this book brings together contributors from diverse disciplines including history, anthropology, literary studies, and sociology. In addition to the academic perspectives explored in the first part of the book, the second part is dedicated to personal reflections on present-day lived experiences of Haitians in diaspora.

Part 1 explores the Haitian diaspora in Guadeloupe, French Guiana, the Dominican border region, and Jamaica. It begins with a reprint of anthropologist Paul Brodwin's seminal article on the Haitian diaspora in Guadeloupe. Brodwin traces the marginalization of Haitians living in Guadeloupe. Haitian diasporic subjectivity is fashioned by the experience of marginalization and by the ways in which Guadeloupeans imagine these migrants. Brodwin's article sets the stage for Philippe Zacaïr's study of the trial of television show host Ibo Simon, who was charged with inciting racial slander and violence against the Haitian community. Zacaïr discusses how popular media played a significant role in simultaneously spurring and condemning anti-Haitian violence. The relationship between Guadeloupeans and Haitians through their "literary confrontations" is the focus of Odile Ferly's contribution. Ferly argues that unlike their male predecessors, such as Aimé Césaire and Édouard Glissant, French Caribbean women writers more readily focus on the reality of contemporary Haiti with its political and economic upheavals and consequent diaspora. Ferly analyses the figure of the Haitian immigrant in Guadeloupe in Maryse Condé's novel *Traversée de la mangrove* and Simone Schwarz-Bart's play *Ton beau capitaine*. She compares these figures to a Guadeloupean character settled in Haiti in "Seeing Things Simply," a short story by Haitian-American Edwidge Danticat. Maud Laëthier's article on Haitian migration in French Guiana concludes the first series of contributions on the French Caribbean. Laëthier explores the ways in which Guianese society has imprisoned Haitian immigrants in fixed social stereotypes. Although Haitians make up approximately 30 percent of the immigrant population, their host society is almost entirely ignorant of their cultural specificities. Perceived as a representation of the clandestine, Haitians are associated with the idea of invasion. Laëthier shows how such stereotypical portrayals are interiorized by many Guianese-born Haitians and shape the image they present of themselves.

The experience of Haitian migrants is further extended to Jamaica and the Dominican border region. Haitians moving back and forth between Haiti and the Dominican Republic in search of healthcare in the Dominican border town of Dajabón is the focus of Pierre Minn's article. Minn examines the discourses and practices that accompany the provision of medical services to Haitians in the Dominican border region. Drawing from extensive research conducted in a Dominican government hospital, Minn finds "two coexisting but contrasting rhetorics" at play: health as a human right and medical humanitarianism. Together they shape the very complex dynamic of Haitian-Dominican relations. In the next contribution, Sharon Clarke turns her attention to the arrival of Haitian refugees in Jamaica following Haitian president Jean-Bertrand Aristide's ouster in February 2004. Using an anthropological case study approach from the perspective of international human rights, Clarke discusses the Government of Jamaica's response to the refugees. Departing from an initial favorable stance, the Government of Jamaica quickly considered the burden of Haitian refugees to be unsustainable and turned increasingly against them.

Part 2 begins with a conversation between Philippe Zacaïr and Jamaican citizen of Haitian descent Myrtha Désulmé. Désulmé, the president of the Haiti-Jamaica Society, talks about the particular trajectory of her family in Jamaica and her relentless work to raise Jamaicans' knowledge of and appreciation for Haitian history and culture. Following Zacaïr's conversation with Désulmé, Cécile Accilien offers a free spirited account of her experience as a Haitian in diaspora. An immigrant to the United States at the age of twelve, Accilien grew up in New Jersey before pursuing an academic career on the Pacific coast and now in Georgia. Accilien expresses her uneasiness at finding her place in American society and disputes commonly-held representations of Haiti and Haitians in the U.S. She especially challenges common associations between Haitians and the AIDS epidemic. She believes that the overwhelmingly negative depictions of Haiti and Haitians lead to continuous discrimination and unfair immigration practices.

Finally, Part 2 ends with a dialogue between two residents of French Guiana—Mr. Jacques and Dieula—and Francophone studies specialist Marc Lony. Dieula, a Haitian woman working as a maid in Cayenne talks about her personal journey from the southern Haitian town of Aquin to French citizenship. Dieula's account is set against that of Mr. Jacques, a Guianese who married a Haitian woman and reflects on the relationship between Haitians and his fellow Guianese. He offers his vision of the transformation of the Haitian population in French Guiana. The interviews are introduced by Lony's philosophical reflections on the migrants' experience of "time."

Notes

1. Corte Interamericana de derechos humanos, *Caso de la niñas Yean y Bosico: Sentencia de 8 de septiembre de 2005*.

2. These associations include: la Coordination haïtienne Tèt Kolé, le Centre Haïtien d'Information et de Documentation, les Amis d'Haïti, la Ligue des Droits de l'Homme, le Mouvement contre le racisme et l'anti-sémitisme, le Groupement d'Information et de soutien des Travailleurs Immigrés, and SOS Racisme.

3. In his preface to the first volume of *Diaspora* Tölölyan defines the purpose of the journal as follows: "*Diaspora* is concerned with the ways in which nations, real yet imagined communities (Anderson), are fabulated, brought into being, made and unmade, in culture and politics, both on land people call their own and in exile (Tölölyan 1991: 1)."

References

Allman, James. 1982. "Haitian Migration: 30 Years Assessed." *Migration Today* 10, no. 1: 6–12.

Appadurai, Arjun. 1996. *Modernity at Large: Cultural Dimensions of Globalization*. Minneapolis and London: University of Minnesota Press.

Bash, Linda and al. 1994. *Nations Unbound: Transnational Projects, Postcolonial Predicaments, and Deterritorialized Nation-States*. Basle: Gordon and Breach.

Brodwin, Paul. 2000. *Pentecostalism and the Production of Community in the Haitian Diaspora*. Milwaukee: University of Wisconsin CLACS.

———. 2001. *Marginality and Cultural Intimacy in a Transnational Haitian Community*. Milwaukee: University of Wisconsin CLACS.

Castor, Suzy. 1983. *Migración y relaciones internacionales (el caso haitiano-dominicano)*. México: Universidad Nacional Autónoma de México.

Catanese, Anthony. 1999. Haitians: Migration and Diaspora. Boulder: Westview Press.

Charier, Alain. 2000. *Le Mouvement Noir au Vénézuela*. Paris: L'harmattan.

Cohen, Robin. 1997. *Global Diasporas*. Seattle: University of Washington Press.

Conway, Dennis. 2003. "The Caribbean Diaspora." In *Understanding the Contemporary Caribbean*, edited by Richard S. Hillman and Thomas J. D'Agostino, Boulder: 333–354. London: Lynne Rienner.

Craton, Michael and Gail Saunders. 1992. *Islanders in the Stream: A History of the Bahamian People*. 2 Vols. Athens and London: University of Georgia Press.

Derby, Lauren. 1994. "Haitians, Magic, and Money: Raza and Society in the Haitian-Dominican Borderlands, 1900 to 1937." *Comparative Studies in Society and History* 36, no. 3: 488–526.

Derby, Robin and Richard Lee Turits. 1993. "Historias de terror y los terrores de la historia: la masacre haitiana de 1937 en la República Dominicana." *Estudios Sociales* 26, no. 92: 65–76.

Duany, Jorge. 2006. "Racializing Ethnicity in the Spanish-Speaking Caribbean: A Comparison of Haitians in the Dominican Republic and Dominicans in Puerto Rico." *Latin American and Caribbean Ethnic Studies* 1, no. 2: 231–248.

Fabre, Geneviève and Klaus Benesch. 2004. *African Diasporas in the New and Old Worlds. Consciousness and Imagination*. Amsterdam and New York: Rodopi.

Glick Schiller, Nina and Georges Eugene Fouron. 2001. *Georges Woke Up Laughing: Long-Distance Nationalism & the Search for Home*. Durham/London: Duke University Press.

Gowricharn, Ruben. 2006. *Caribbean Transnationalism: Migration, Pluralization and Social Cohesion*. Boulder/New York: Rowman & Littlefield.

Hall, Stuart. 2003. "Cultural Identity and Diaspora." In *Theorizing Diaspora*, edited by Evans Braziel et al., 233–246. Oxford: Blackwell.

Hurbon, Laënnec. 1983. "Racisme et sous-produit du racisme: immigrés haïtiens et dominicains en Guadeloupe." *Les Temps Modernes* 39, no. 441–442: 1988–2003.

Johnson, Kim. 1982. *Report on Migrant Workers in Guadeloupe*. Trinidad: Caribbean Conference of Churches.

Laguerre, Michel. 1998. *Diasporic Citizenship. Haitian Americans in Transnational America*. New York: St. Martin's Press.

———. 2006. *Diaspora, Politics, and Globalization*. New York: Palgrave Macmillan.

Marshall, Dawn. 1979. *The Haitian Problem: Illegal migration to the Bahamas*. Mona: University of the West Indies.

Ong, Aihwa. 1999. *Flexible Citizenship: The Cultural Logics of Transnationality*. Durham and London: Duke University Press.

Paulino, Edward. 2005. "Erasing the Kreyol from the Margins of the Dominican Republic: The Pre and Post-nationalization Project of the Border, 1930–1945." *Wadabagei* 8, no. 2: 35–71.

———. 2006. "Anti-Haitianism, Historical Memory, and the Potential for Genocidal Violence in the Dominican Republic." *Genocide Studies and Prevention* 1, no. 3: 265–288.

Perusek, Glenn. 1984. "Haitian emigration in the early twentieth century." *The International Migration Review* 18, no. 1: 4–18.

Richman, Karen. 2005. *Migration and Vodou*. Gainesville: University Press of Florida.

Sears, Alfred. 1994. "The Haitian question in the Bahamas." *Journal of the Bahamas Historical Society*, 16 no. 1: 10–20.

Tölölyan, Kachig. 1991. "The Nation-State and its Others: In Lieu of a Preface." *Diaspora: a journal of transnational studies* 1, no. 1: 3–7.

Turits, Richard Lee. "A World Destroyed, A Nation Imposed: The 1937 Haitian Massacre in the Dominican Republic." *Hispanic American Historical Review* 82, no. 3: 589–635.

I

Haitian Diasporas

1

Marginality and Subjectivity in the Haitian Diaspora

PAUL BRODWIN

What forms of subjectivity emerge in contemporary diasporas, and can anthropologists discern them through single-site ethnography? Diasporas are defined, of course, by the cultural connections and flows that knit together a single geographically dispersed group. The Jewish historical experience, regarded by many as an ideal type, involved a sprawling social world of interlinked practices, families, travel circuits, and dreams of return to the homeland. Contemporary diaspora groups, especially refugees or immigrants living in expatriate minority enclaves, constitute themselves through non-local configurations of people, media, capital, information, and political ideologies (Appadurai 1996, Rouse 1991). The phrases which appear again and again in this literature—the cultural bifocality of displaced and mobile collectivities, spread across a variety of sites and maintained by multi-stranded social relations—imply two separate analytics about diasporic subjectivity.

According to one influential viewpoint, the tension of "living here and remembering/desiring another place" (Clifford 1997: 255) determines how people construct the identity of their diasporic group: how they map its boundaries, invest in it materially and emotionally, and construct its difference from other groups. Collective identity depends on the politics of location, and the location of diasporas is (by definition) plural, fragmented, dynamic, and open. In these circumstances, the structures of feeling about group affiliation differ fundamentally from those arising in geographically bounded settings. If culture is regarded as the property of a spatially localized people, its collective self-representation seems to emerge out of bounded, everyday, face-to-face interactions.

By contrast, people leading non or supra-local lives organize their sense of collective identity in fundamentally different ways. They may cultivate a myth about their lost homeland, and on that basis generate the criteria for ethnic inclusion and exclusion (Safran 1991). They may travel back and forth in a transnational family network, pursue parallel life strategies in two (or more) places at once, and thereby refigure older notions of national identity (Glick Schiller and Fouron 2001). They may find themselves thrown on the defensive by shifting politics in their homeland and forced to craft entirely novel and hybrid tropes of self-definition (Gross et al. 1996).

The second analytic about diasporic subjectivity situates it in people's response to their present and immediate surroundings, instead of their glo-balized exchanges, memories, and desires. It grows from the general insight that subject formation depends on processes of both exclusion and agency, both "othering" and self-fashioning. "There are two meanings to the word subject," Foucault wrote, "subject to someone else by control and depen-dence, and tied to his own identity by a conscience or self-knowledge" (1983: 212, see also Gupta and Ferguson 1997). The two meanings are intimately related to each other, since we arrive at self-knowledge through (and even in the same terms as) particular experiences of external control. Stuart Hall makes a similar argument in his parsing of the word "identity." Dominant discourses and practices interpellate us—hail us into place as particular so-cial subjects—and thereby produce our subjectivity. Identities are not the pure products of self-fashioning, but instead positions that we are obliged to take up in a determinate social world. We may know or suspect that they are representations constructed by others, but nonetheless we invest in the particular position, recognize ourselves in it, and identify with it (Hall 1996).

Members of a given diasporic enclave within a larger dominant soci-ety are both agents with the capacity to author their (dislocated) lives and "subjects" fixed into place by surrounding structures and discourses (see Mankekar 1994). Privileging their agency leads to the usual emphasis on globally-circulating signs and practices as the medium of diasporic subjec-tivity. (At worst, it leads to celebrations of hybridity and dislocated identity as ipso facto resistant.) By contrast, privileging the way people are forced to occupy determinate subject positions highlights the experience of mar-ginality and exclusions where a particular group currently (if temporarily) resides. The first analytic about diasporic subjectivity is attractive because it promises a clean break with anthropology's myopic focus on the local. It regards the production of subjectivity as itself a work of agency and imagi-nation, which all members of a particular diaspora carry out in roughly the same way. According to the first analytic, Haitians in Guadeloupe, Santo Domingo, New York, or Montreal constitute themselves as a single social formation in supra-local terms. Their subjectivity emerges out of the same set of globally-circulating rhetorics, musical forms, religious practices, political projects, etc. The second analytic, however, enables a different ethnographic analysis of diasporic subjectivity. For people who travel from resource-poor societies to the metropolises of the developed world, collective self-definition is often a practical response to concrete, near-at-hand experiences of subordination and marginality. It emerges in a particular place, even as it accommodates their global conditions of life (cf. Olwig 1997). Undoubtedly, the vehicles of diasporic subjectivity are ideas, people, money, and media that circulate in transnational space. But people weave them into a singular rhetoric about their group's identity chiefly when they confront the situation immediately at hand, and it is often a harrowing situation of marginality and racialized stigma. According to the second analytic, Haitian migrants living in separate national societies develop significantly different notions of their groups' essential characteristics.

This article follows the second analytic of diasporic subjectivity sketched above. I argue that the collective identity of Haitians living in Guadeloupe, French West Indies, emerges less from their travel across borders than from their daily experience of marginalization on the streets of Pointe-à-Pitre (the island's main commercial city) and in the imagination of their literal neighbors, Guadeloupe's Black French citizens. Recalling that identity is a relationship of difference, I site the collective identity of this diasporic enclave in the ways Haitians engage Guadeloupean society and conceptualize their place in it. Viewed from the other direction (the standpoint of the dominant society), Guadeloupeans fabricate their own collective self-representation by using Haitians as a foil. The Afro-Caribbean residents of Guadeloupe alternate between admiration and contempt as they discuss the attributes of the Haitians living in their midst. But in either case, they employ the category "Haitian" as an imagined locus of the cultural authenticity and pride which they are afraid of losing in their rapid assimilation to French norms. This article uses ethnography in single location to trace the origins of diasporic subjectivity in local processes of structural and symbolic marginalization. The conclusion demonstrates the local production of subjectivity by contrasting the discourses of identity developed by Haitians living in Guadeloupe, the Dominican Republic, and the United States.

Marginality of Haitians in Guadeloupe

About 24,000 Haitians live in Guadeloupe, an overseas *département* of France located in the eastern Caribbean (INSEE 1999).[1] They constitute a small minority enclave that is subject to economic and legal discrimination. As non-citizens, they remain vulnerable to arrest and deportation under French immigration law. The constant threat affects their use of urban space, and it produces their residential and economic exclusion. Moreover, Haitians are stigmatized because of the place they occupy in the local social taxonomy: what they are made to represent in the collective imagination of Guadeloupeans. Their experience of state-imposed and discursive marginality is the grounds for their collective self-representation. At one level, they press claims to full legal incorporation as citizens or documented residents. At another level, however, they self-consciously reinforce the position of cultural outsider in order to defend against their symbolic denigration and to criticize the dominant exclusionary norms. Although Haitian migrants wish to obtain the proper residency papers, they also stereotype their own cultural distinctiveness in order to underscore the cultural weakness of Guadeloupe and its dependency on France, and many Guadeloupeans agree with their critique. Out of these multiple responses to marginalization emerges a distinctive subjectivity in this node of the global Haitian diaspora.[2]

The importance of marginality to my argument demands a brief genealogy of the term. By definition, marginal groups occupy an unequal and disadvantaged position within common fields of knowledge and power (Tsing 1993: xi). They are excluded from full participation in social life despite their normative claims of equality and sentiments of belonging (see Germani 1980). The classic literature begins with the predicament of ambiguous belonging, but it then develops general models of marginality that are based on quite specific cases or historical types. For Simmel (1908/1950), traders who settle in a foreign society provide the core example of marginality: fundamentally mobile persons who are not "organically connected through established ties of kinship, loyalty or occupation" with members of the surrounding society (404). From this single illustrative case, Simmel builds his theory of categorical strangers, their enlightened objectivity, their tendency to be treated as generic outsiders, and their vulnerability to scapegoating. Robert Park (1937/1950) favors a different definitional example: groups who live on the margins of two (often antagonistic) societies. His typical case is the hybrid individual (in his words, Eurasian, Mulatto, or partially assimilated Jew), a historical product of large-scale migration or imperialism, who is not "willing to break, even if he were permitted to do so, with his past and his traditions, and not quite accepted, because of racial prejudice, in the new society in which he now [seeks] to find a place" (354). This ideal type underlies Park's characterization of the generic marginal man as a sophisticated cosmopolitan who is gripped by inner turmoil and distressing self-consciousness.

Mid-twentieth-century American social science featured debates over another influential ideal type of marginality: traditional enclaves within modernizing cities which yet remain unintegrated with urban institutions and whose residents are politically apathetic, anomic, and socially disorganized (as evidenced by violent crime, family breakdown, etc.). Perlman (1976) criticized this "myth of marginality" by reference to poor rural-to-urban migrants living as squatters in Rio de Janeiro. Based on her intensive case study, Perlman argued that marginality in general is a form of material domination: a dependent position within hierarchically-ranked groups which is enforced by active rejection from the labor market and other opportunities of city life. Several contemporary studies also rely on case studies of Latin American urban squatters to build general theories of marginality as enforced inequality and dependence (e.g., Vélez-Ibañez 1983; Byrne 1999 provides a recent restatement of his view). Marginality clearly refers to several distinct but overlapping social conditions, some of which describe the Haitian diaspora in Guadeloupe. This group is the product of large-scale migration; Haitians are urban dwellers who do not benefit from local opportunities and are treated as disloyal outsiders; and they occupy a liminal position between their homeland, Guadeloupe, and the United States, the preferred next stage in their transnational trajectory. However, in the classic literature about settled traders, hybrid individuals, and urban squatters, marginal and mainstream groups belong to the same nation-state. Fundamental questions of citizenship or a shared future in the same national space are rarely raised, and therefore the classic models cannot fully account for the predicament of current-day transnational diasporic groups, especially migrants from developing societies now living in North American or European cities. Such groups are marginalized precisely because of their chronic state of divided allegiance, and their experience differs according to their histories of migration and incorporation into new societies. The current global diaspora of Haitians began in the early 1960s with the exodus of the political enemies of "president for life" Francois Duvalier along with other members of the middle and upper classes. By 1972, a broader cross-section of Haitian society had begun to leave due to worsening economic deprivation and political repression.[3] The second wave of migration has continued until today, waxing and waning in accordance with political events at home as well as immigration policies abroad. Haitian migrants typically face poverty, formal and informal discrimination, and outright hostility in the societies where they settle (Lawless 1992). Like other transnational groups, Haitians do not resemble immigrant minorities which have permanently ruptured with their collective pasts or labor migrants with ticket in hand for the return home (Basch et al.: 4). They establish new enclaved communities at a symbolic distance from the receiving society and organize new forms of connectedness with kin, friends, and business and political partners throughout the diaspora. The enclave in Guadeloupe resembles other Haitian transnational communities (see Stepick 1998, Laguerre 1998). Of the approximately 25,000 Haitians now living in Guadeloupe, almost all were born in Haiti, the majority hope to move eventually to the United States or Canada, and those holding current visas and work permits travel in a wide circuit between Guadeloupe, Haiti, other Caribbean nations, France, and the United States.[4] The Haitian community in Guadeloupe has an ephemeral, unstable quality and a range of possible futures (cf. Glick Schiller et al. 1987). It may persist in its present form as a loosely organized group of undocumented workers, continually replenished by new arrivals from Haiti. Segments of this population may eventually gain French citizenship or disappear over time through individual resettlement in the United States or deportation back to Haiti (the fate in 1995 of the former Haitian community on St. Martin, an offshore dependency of Guadeloupe).[5]

The marginalization of Haitians in Guadeloupe dates from their arrival on the island in the mid-1970s. Haitians originally came as cane cutters in the midst of a bitter struggle over unionization in the declining Guadeloupean sugar industry (Hurbon 1983). Without their knowledge, Haitian men were used as strikebreakers by the owners of sugar plantations, and in 1975 they became the target of violent opposition (including lynch mobs) led by pro-union Guadeloupeans. Although the violence was quickly quelled by progressive politicians and Catholic activists, it left an enduring image of Haitians as opportunistic foreigners opposed to the interest of the ordinary citizen of French Guadeloupe, while also making many Haitians reflexively distrustful of Guadeloupeans. In the 1980s, Haitian immigration increased from the relatively controlled deployment of poorly paid agricultural workers to a wave of small merchants and unskilled laborers who came without documentation or who remained after their visa expired. The majority of today's Haitian community in Pointe-à-Pitre belongs to this migration wave.[6]

Most of the men work in the construction industry as masons or laborers and most women become *commerçantes* (in Haitian Creole, *madan sara*): traveling vendors of agricultural produce, clothing, and household goods.

All the Haitians I spoke with in Guadeloupe would prefer to have their papers in order, but the twists and turns in French immigration policy create enormous difficulties (see Hargreaves 1995). Their first decade on the island gave Haitian migrants a false sense of security. The sugar workers of the mid-1970s had legitimate short-term labor contracts, and up until 1981, any Haitian with a valid passport and return ticket could legally enter Guadeloupe simply by leaving a cash deposit at the airport immigration office. They received a one-month visa, and through timely visits to the Sous-préfecture in Pointe-à-Pitre, they could eventually renew it for periods of three months or one year. During this period, Haitians benefited from Mitterrand's general amnesty for immigrants who had illegally settled in France. Those with a steady job and proven date of entry could easily obtain ten-year residence permits. However, exclusionary rhetoric started to rise in metropolitan France in the early 1970s, and when the center-right took control of the government in 1993, Interior Minister Charles Pasqua promptly announced the goal of "zero immigration." The "Pasqua laws" tightened entry requirements, increased identity checks, and sharply restricted access to residency permits. They also authorized deportations without judicial review on the broad grounds of threats to public order. In Guadeloupe, these deportations involve strong-arm tactics such as arrests at night and forced entry into private homes (GISTI 1996: 133).

How Haitians try to become regularized thus depends on how and when they entered Guadeloupe. Those who arrived before 1981, recalling Mitterrand's amnesty policy, feel entitled to legal residency. They carefully guard their Haitian passports and their receipts for visa renewals and asylum applications. With these documents in hand, they continue trying to apply for residency cards at the immigration office in Pointe-à-Pitre, but are almost invariably turned away. Immigration officials tell them that an expired passport is insufficient, or that they must obtain their visa first from the French embassy in Haiti, or that a labor contract is needed, or that periods of undocumented residency disqualify them for regularization, etc. Haitians who arrived after 1981 or with false papers often follow up another provision in French law. They try to obtain a family residence card by marrying or having a child with a French citizen or convincing a citizen to adopt a child born in Haiti. Several people referred to this strategy with the popular saying 'Every Guadeloupean has his Haitian.' Guadeloupeans not only employ

Haitians as domestic or manual laborers; they may also protect Haitians through marriage and kinship ties. Nonetheless, I knew of only a handful of Guadeloupean-Haitian marriages. Most Haitians told me that their poverty makes them unattractive partners.

State-Imposed Marginality: Ethnography of an Immigration Raid

For the above reasons, between 60 percent and 80 percent of Haitians in Pointe-à-Pitre lack proper citizenship or residency papers according to Haitian priests and activists as well as Guadeloupean lawyers and social workers. Their uncertain legal status creates a fundamental insecurity in everyday life, and it drives their political, economic, and residential marginalization. An immigration sweep I witnessed one evening suggests how such threats are the grounds for the group's diasporic subjectivity. During research I joined the Church of God of Prophecy, an all-Haitian Pentecostal church in Pointe-à-Pitre (see Brodwin 2003). I attended worship services and frequently traveled to revivals cosponsored with other local Haitian congregations. Arriving after dark at one revival in June 1996, our van pulled into a long gravel driveway already cluttered with parked cars and trucks. Members of three Haitian churches milled about in front of the revival tent waiting for the service to begin. The area was poorly lit by a single weak street lamp, and most people, preoccupied with greeting friends and watching over their children, did not initially notice the two Guadeloupean men, each with a sidearm and a vest emblazoned "Police," moving quietly but briskly through the crowd. They talked quickly to several people chosen randomly in the crowd, before beginning to interrogate Claude Antoine, a member of the Church of God who had driven with us. After a few questions, the police led Claude away, pushing to one side someone who tried to speak with him, and escorted him to the back of an unmarked car where two other Haitian church members were already sitting.

The police worked unobtrusively for a few more minutes, with no one raising their voice in question or protest. After they returned to their car and backed it onto the main road, one of the police got out and confronted the driver of our van, another church member in his mid-twenties named Marc Doricent. Speaking sharply in Guadeloupean Creole, instead of the official and more respectful French, he demanded Marc's papers. Without emotion, Marc reached into his briefcase and handed over the passport, but then the police demanded his residence card. Marc gave it to him, and the policeman, still dissatisfied, asked to see his driver's license and told him that it was out of date and that he did not have the right to drive. At this point, Marc's deference vanished and he started to argue, but the police simply raised their voices and repeated that he could not legally drive in Guadeloupe and must come to the police headquarters in two days at 8 A.M. Confiscating his license, the police drove away with the three Haitians they had arrested still sitting in the back.[7] Extremely shaken, Marc returned to the small group of us still standing by his van, where one middle-aged woman was repeating that she had no idea what was happening until it was nearly over. Another said that this was the first time she had seen such a thing with her own eyes, and then urgently asked a series of questions in rapid succession: Why did the police decide to ask Claude for his papers? Why did they conduct their raid tonight? Did someone in the neighborhood tip them off? A young man related that a few days ago, the French immigration service had stopped Claude from boarding a flight to Montreal. He had a valid visa for Canada, but his Haitian passport was outdated and he was forced to return to his house. Did the police put Claude's name in a computer and then follow him here? In lieu of an answer, the first woman simply said, "I always carry my papers with me! I never forget them!"

Marc and I left the heated discussion and joined the Haitian pastors standing with a few others on the edge of the crowd. Their mood was pained and dismayed as they struggled with people's concerns. Would the police return Claude?

"Probably not," Pastor Cantave, the head of the Church of God of Prophecy, answered ruefully, "the guy's not legal" (*msyé pa an règ*). Will the police come back after the service, now that they know where to find us? "No," said another pastor, "they've already had their full" (*yo deja pran manje yo*). The congregation vehemently objected to Marc's treatment, asserting that the police could make him renew the license, but could not confiscate it outright. ("But you know, this is France," said one pastor, shaking his head from side to side.) Arresting people in front of their revival group rankled the pastors even more. "They don't have the right to enter the church," said Cantave, "so instead they come right up next to it."

"Yes," one woman bitterly agreed, "they do this in front of the door of the house of God."

The speculations and anguished debates about these events ultimately lasted several weeks. To begin with, people were shocked that the raid targeted a meeting of Haitian Pentecostal churches. About half of all Haitians in Guadeloupe have become Pentecostal. These congregations offer the only formal institutional affiliation available to undocumented migrants. The pastors are all legally resident Haitians, and their churches are registered at the Préfecture. The pastors therefore have the right to visit their congregants who wait in jail before deportation, an opportunity denied to family and friends. Besides boosting morale, these visits address practical concerns about the return of money and belongings. Moreover, because of the residential dispersal of migrants, Pentecostal churches are the only all-Haitian spaces in the city, and they offer a place to speak Haitian Creole freely and a source of job tips, friends, and even marriage partners. Because their parent denominations have implanted similar churches throughout the Caribbean and North America, Haitian missionaries and pastors routinely travel from Guadeloupe to Haiti and other transnational communities (For example, the Church of God of Prophecy has congregations serving Haitians in Miami, New York, and Boston). The regional Pentecostal network offers a low-cost and trustworthy conduit to circulate money, cassette tapes, and letters between dispersed friends and families and hence to maintain transnational linkages (see Richman 1992a: 67ff).

Launching an immigration raid at a Pentecostal revival thus threatens one of the major staging grounds of the Haitian transnational community (see Brodwin 2003 and Stepick 1998: 85).

People's reactions to the raid were also shaped by their broad personal experiences with legal marginalization. Most Haitians I spoke with know a relative, friend, or neighbor who has been deported.[8] People often described the difficulties faced by those without papers: the reluctance to seek official aid or even to enter a government office and the pervasive anxiety that makes them "sleep with one eye open." The threat of deportation also alters how people inhabit urban space. The immigration police typically raid areas with a high concentration of Haitians, such as construction sites and outdoor markets.[9] Consequently, Haitian migrants do not linger to socialize after work, and some people without jobs prefer never to leave the alleys near their home. Some people try to move every few months to avoid arrest. Summing up the situation, one man told me "It makes you never want to go outside," and he illustrated his point by squeezing his shoulders together, arms held tightly to his sides, and glancing around him in a caricature of a hunted animal. Haitians deeply resent their treatment, but they do not assert a blanket claim to rightful residence in Guadeloupe. I heard no one argue that their hostile reception in the 1970s incurred a moral obligation to grant them citizenship, or that the sheer wealth of the French Antilles compels it to welcome migrants coming from a far poorer nation. People usually denounce not the injustice of deportations in the abstract, but rather the particular way they are carried out. The police take those arrested to a detention center at the central Raizet airport and then expel them within two days.[10] Leslie Adrien, a twenty-three-year-old Haitian man, describes the most common scenario: "They take you right to the airport, and you're forced to leave in your dirty clothes. They don't let you go back to your house to recover your belongings or to ask your boss for the money you're owed." Pierre Salnave, a forty-two year-old Haitian with a valid French ten-year residence card, explains the resulting stigma:

> Haitians feel shame when they're sent back from Guadeloupe. They arrive with an old pair of pants, a dirty shirt, they don't have anything with them, and this is how they return to their family. What is their family thinking? That they spent so much time in the other country, and have only this to show for it?

The stigma of dirty clothes and meager belongings figured in every conversation about deportation because it threatens an important diaspora ideal. Deportation destroys not only one's own economic prospects, but also one's reputation as a solid provider and a bridgehead for other family members to move abroad. In the ideal migration trajectory, one leaves the country poor but ambitious, finds work and supports dependents back home, and returns to Haiti for a visit with the visible marks of financial success (expensive clothing and gifts). Returning as a ragged and penniless deportee demolishes this scenario; hence, virtually everyone singles out being denied showers and a change of clothes as the most objectionable aspects of deportation.

Depending on their economic circumstances, Haitians do not necessarily fear returning to their homeland. Leslie Adrien explained the situation to me as we sat in his sparsely furnished one-room home in a popular neighborhood wedged between a busy road and a newly built apartment complex. The neighborhood, a remnant of early twentieth-century Pointe-à-Pitre, consists of a few narrow alleyways lined by the wooden colonial-era *cases créoles*, a once-ubiquitous housing style occupied now by only the poorest Guadeloupeans and migrants from Haiti and Dominica. The city already plans to raze this area and construct concrete public housing blocks (the Habitations à Loyer Modéré or HLM), typical of urban zones in metropolitan France. Without citizenship papers, Leslie will not qualify for an apartment in the HLM, and he will probably move to another part of the city or to a squatter settlement in the abandoned sugar fields on the city's edge. Arriving in Guadeloupe during the economic downturn of the mid-

1990s, Leslie had never been able to count on construction work for more than a few days per week (let alone a long-term labor contract), and undocumented workers like him did not dare protest low or withheld wages. After recounting his options, Leslie told me plainly that he would rather be in Haiti. He had entered a downward spiral of economic and residential marginality that benefited neither him nor his dependents in the homeland. In his case, structural marginality had become de facto extrusion, and no personal loyalties or dreams of assimilation impelled him to stay in Guadeloupe.

To survive the interwoven forms of marginalization, Haitians learn how to gauge their vulnerability in different arenas of everyday life. The immigration raid at the Pentecostal revival confirmed people's impression that police target them when their guard is down. In the summer of 1996, I heard of several Haitian men arrested as they arrived at construction sites in the morning or as they left after a full day's work. Police also interrogate people on the streets near their homes, and those who have lived in Guadeloupe since the early 1980s seem especially at risk. Such individuals have grown less vigilant over the years, and many of them (wrongly) believe that they are entitled to legal residence. Like the people arrested in front of the revival, they assume a level of protection they do not actually enjoy. The Haitian transnational community here has not entered the middle class; hence it does not have its own legal advocates or mass media outlets to educate people about immigration law. A state-regulated mutual assistance agency occasionally helps undocumented Haitian members gain residency cards, but only a few Haitians are willing to pay the membership fees. In the mid-1990s, Tèt Kolé, an advocacy organization founded in Haiti by supporters of then-President Aristide, had a small office in Pointe-à-Pitre, but many Haitians regarded its political activities as too remote from their daily lives. The need for concealment creates a pervasive anxiety about personal security in everyday life. Migrants compared their plight to being caught in a well-laid trap. They know that despite all precautions, they can easily be arrested and deported without appeal, and they describe the risk in tones of resigned inevitability. In the weeks following the arrests at the Pentecostal revival, church members privately criticized the police's surreptitious methods and their habit of bending the law as they please. For these reasons, most people do not bother to contest expulsions. Occasionally, however, people do protest less extreme types of harassment and disrespect. For example, Haitian market women verbally resist the municipal police who force them to move the makeshift stalls they set up on the sidewalks in the downtown shopping district. One woman described what she typically tells police: "I say, give me a place to sell! I live here, I had my children here, now they're at school. They [the police] say they can't give me a place to sell my things. But if they let us in the country, they should let us work." Her complaint not only makes the limited claim to pursue her livelihood in peace, but also points out the contradictions of the Guadeloupean immigration policy that invited Haitian workers during the labor shortages of the late 1970s and 1980s but then hounded them out in the tight economy of the 1990s. Indeed, Haitians have developed a good sense of the local and supra-local processes that maintain their marginality. Most people connect the shifting climate for undocumented migrants to both local economic forces and the policies of successive French administrations. They recall the immigration crackdown when Jacques Chirac took office in 1993 and compare their own situation to the widely reported expulsions of undocumented Maghrebian and black Africans in metropolitan France in the mid-1990s (Freedman and Tarr 2000).

The French administrative apparatus in Guadeloupe interpellates Haitian migrants as disposable non-citizens who deserve neither a future nor a comfortable present on the island. Haitians' collective self-representations are calibrated to this particular form of marginality. They diagnose their predicament through striking images of abject subjectivity: a hunted animal, caught in a well-laid trap, or the failed transnational migrant who is sent back home dirty and shamefaced. The images recall one aspect of the definition of subjectivity from Foucault and Hall: the social position one is forced to occupy in dependence upon a dominant power. In response (but using largely the same political framework of identity as the French state), Haitians argue that they deserve citizenship because of their years of residence and productive labor. Even in resistance, therefore, Haitians remain in the subject position of immigrants to France. They draw the analogy between their marginality and that of north and sub-Saharan immigrants deported by police in Paris. Taking up this position recalls the other aspect of subjectivity: agency and self-fashioning which nonetheless partially accepts the imposed representations.

Discursive Marginality: The Dilemma of Guadeloupean Subjectivity

The marginalization of Haitians is produced by the French state as it inserts them into the category of non-citizen and then extrudes them. But it is also produced by the collective imagination of Guadeloupeans as they insert Haitians into the local social taxonomy (cf. Derby 1994). Guadeloupeans construct the essential characteristics of Haitian migrants in the context of the political impasse and cultural malaise within Guadeloupe itself. Their denigrating stereotypes of Haitians emerge from the ambivalence over their own collective identity and the rapid social transformations on the island. The collective self-portrait held by the majority residents of Guadeloupe combines the colonial history of racial hybridity with the present ambivalence toward metropolitan France. The current-day population includes descendents—in various combinations and mixtures—of African slaves, the French planter aristocracy, poor French indentured laborers, the nineteenth-century mulatto middle class, East Indian cane workers imported after abolition in 1848, Middle Eastern trading families, and French civil servants (Abénon 1992). When Guadeloupe became a *département* of France in 1946, the entire population automatically became French citizens. As a result, the collective self-image of Guadeloupeans involves both a formal, juridical equality and the explicit acknowledgment of racial *métissage* [mixture]. Contemporary residents refer to each other without malice as *bata-zendyen* or *bata-nèg* (the Creole words literally mean bastard-Indian and bastard-black), and individuals openly discuss racial mixing in their family lines. Even members of the white elite (the *béké*) say they are more comfortable in the presence of black Guadeloupeans than white Frenchmen (Besson 1989). Leading intellectuals elaborate the same theme. The author Maryse Condé has declared that all of the island's ethnic communities are "equally Guadeloupean," and also that the typical islander resident is not racist (Condé 1989). According to the sociolinguist Dany Bébel-Gisler, the authentic culture of Guadeloupe will be created by individuals representing all possible combinations of class and race (Bébel-Gisler 1989: 14).

Haitians, however, remain locked out of this open-ended, syncretic, and definitionally "Creole" mixture, and the reasons lie in the deepening contradictions of departmentalization. Metropolitan administration paved the way for the penetration of Guadeloupean society by French products, media, educational practices, and, of course, the French language itself (Schnepel 1993; 1998). Residents have become eager consumers of French goods and dependent clients of the French welfare system, but they have also become enrolled in a new politics of difference. Departmentalization has valorized French identity more than ever before in the history of the island. By the 1990s, the local social taxonomy involved an intricate series of differentiations favoring French norms. For example, residents of Pointe-à-Pitre told me that the population of Marie-Galante—a nearby rural island where remnants of the old sugar economy still survive—was darker and more backwards than city-dwellers. They instructed me (a white American) to speak only French, not Creole, in downtown banks and government offices. A working-class Guadeloupean woman who I knew lamented that she was the only member of her family never to visit France, and parents routinely urge their talented teenage children to seek higher education and professional training in France.

Departmentalization both intensified the cultural hierarchy of the colonial period and pushed it into a new, more dangerous phase. The longstanding hierarchy of the French Antilles split the society into a valorized French stratum and a rejected Afro-Creole stratum, and it gave the greatest esteem to the practices which were the most foreign to the majority population (Burton 1993, Benoist 1972). However, the old elitist system at least allowed Creole practices (language, family organization, housing styles, etc.) to survive relatively undisturbed in the lower echelons of colonial society. By contrast, the post-1946 policy of assimilation, with its mass consumerism and urbanization, has left the majority of Guadeloupeans complaining of being cut off from the perspectives and habits of their Antillean past (Suvélor 1983: 22–23). Middle-class Guadeloupeans openly discuss the dislocation and its effects in daily life. People complain about having to live in apartment complexes built by French firms and designed for a cold northern European climate. They recount the loss of neighborhood grocery stores and butcher shops, driven out by competition from the *grandes surfaces* and *hypermarchés*, the ever-growing shopping malls and supermarkets. They report that their children feel uncomfortable speaking Creole after a few years of higher education or job training in France. Speaking about such losses led people to more general comments about divided identity such as the following: "We Guadeloupeans don't know who we are;" "We don't know whether we are French or ourselves." Renée Gilles, a Guadeloupean social worker, explicitly connected people's ambiguous and uprooted identity to the process of cultural assimilation.

People identify with what they see on television. There could be a weather report about snow in a certain region of France, and people start to get really interested in it. There is a whole generation of children here named Krystal and Bobby, after the characters in Dallas [the syndicated American series] that everyone watched on television. . . . Assimilation is still going forward, and we in Guadeloupe don't have any grounding. We are facing something that is moving very fast, but we are not in control at all.

The status of spoken and written Guadeloupean Creole encapsulates the problem. Various nationalist and pro-independence groups, fearing that the French language would eventually extinguish Creole, championed its use at labor rallies, in left-wing publications, and even a few schools from the 1960s through the 1980s (Schnepel 1993). But the reign of Creole as an anti-colonialist symbol was short-lived. While television and radio now feature more Creole than before, it is mostly for commercial jingles and folklore programs. As actually used in the media and public sphere, the language now carries Guadeloupeans' nostalgia for their lost past; it threatens to become a commodity which island residents consume, but do not themselves produce (see Miles 1995). (In a parallel development, Marie-Galante has become a tourist destination which markets its sugar plantation and local rum distilleries to vacationers from Pointe-à-Pitre.)

The pressures for Guadeloupeans to assimilate to metropolitan norms consign Haitians to a particularly disempowered position. Insofar as Guadeloupeans embrace French identity and opportunities, Haitians are devalued according to the dominant axis of difference. Many Guadeloupeans told me that Haitians resemble the residents of Marie-Galante: physically darker and more African-appearing than themselves. Most people know that Haitians entered the island as sugar cane workers, the quintessential slave's occupation that is geographically and socially distant from the urban, French-oriented worlds of business and administration. Haitian Creole is far less Gallicized than Guadeloupean Creole, and people often parody the Haitian accent. Even the homes of Haitian migrants announce their distance from French ideals. For decades, municipal authorities in Pointe-à-Pitre have systematically demolished the neighborhoods of tight-packed wooden *cases créoles*, the vernacular architecture of the French Antilles, and erected multi-story concrete apartment blocks in their place. As mentioned above, undocumented Haitians cannot rent the new apartments, so they by necessity occupy the remnants of the older Antillean city. Urban renewal has created a moral topography which separates the national modern from the colonial past, metropolitan from local architecture, and even the healthy from the sick. The first urban area to be transformed was a malarial, swampy zone that is still called "l'Assainissement" (the "cleaning up"). Almost all Haitians in Pointe-à-Pitre live in the socially low (and disappearing) spaces left over by urban renewal.

Having constructed Haitians as the symbols of their repudiated colonial past, Guadeloupeans are afraid that Haitians will disrupt their proud achievement of French modernity. According to one middle-class Guadeloupean woman:

> There is a fear of Haiti. People see it and they think it is like Africa. It can make us regress—that is people's fear. 'We have already been emancipated from Africa, from savagery, and we should continue to move towards France': this is people's attitude.

Such sentiments capture the fear of Haitians who, in the Guadeloupean imagination, will undercut their own tenuous European cultural citizenship. The same cliché enters discussions about Guadeloupe's future. The possibility of independence from France continues to generate debate, and a violent pro-independence movement enjoyed popular support in the 1960s and 1970s. The opponents of independence still invoke Haiti as the best reason to remain a French *département*. They raise the rhetorical question: What will we become as a sovereign nation? The typical response is, another Haiti: poor, disorganized, and politically corrupt; independent but at an unacceptable price. In the Guadeloupean imagination, therefore, Haitians threaten what Guadeloupeans hope they have achieved.

However, insofar as people regard assimilation into France as a species of culture loss, Guadeloupeans envy Haitians as bearers of a more potent Afro-Caribbean authenticity. For example, Guadeloupeans who parody Haitian Creole for amusement have also told me that they are shocked when they hear Haitians use words that fell out of use many decades ago in Guadeloupe.[11] People recall that Haitian bands were the first musical groups billed as "local programming" on radio stations in the 1960s and 1970s, before the current wave of zouk and other Antillean popular styles. Haitians thus represent to Guadeloupeans a past phase of their own society, and they provoke an anxious self-recognition because they remind Guadeloupeans of the Caribbean identity they have discarded. In the words of Renée Gilles,

> If we had something of our own to preserve, it would be better. The Haitians have that. They want to preserve their history, their language. Every Haitian that I met knows the history of their country, its battles, and so on. . . . So, when faced with Haitians, they are the mirror that we don't want.

Haitian migrants elicit envy and resentment because they embody what Guadeloupeans feel they have lost in the process of assimilation. They are an unwanted mirror because they reflect back not the Frenchified Guadeloupean culture of today, but the richer, more Antillean-based culture of the past. Guadeloupean attitudes towards Haitian healing power exemplify the same interpellation. Many Guadeloupeans believe that the Haitian *houngan*, or Vodoun practitioner, is more powerful than local folk healers, called *gadezafè*, and I heard many stories of local residents who consult Haitian Vodoun practitioners: e.g., a university administrator who traveled to Haiti in order to rid himself of a chronic illness caused by a curse and a politician who sought a *houngan*'s help in winning an election. Some people explicitly ranked the spiritual potency of various types of healers. They placed Africans first, followed by Haitian *houngans* (who, as one friend explained, are more powerful because Haiti has preserved its African culture longer than the Antilles) Guadeloupean *gadezafès*, and finally folk healers from Martinique—the nearby overseas French *département* which people assert is even more assimilated to metropolitan norms than Guadeloupe.

Cultural Intimacy and the Play of Stereotypes

Haitians and Guadeloupeans rarely interact with each other outside the relation of laborer to boss or itinerant merchant to customer. Nonetheless, Haitians explain their symbolic marginalization in terms parallel to those of the Guadeloupeans quoted above. They know quite a bit about the layering of defensiveness and nostalgia in Guadeloupeans' stereotypes of them. Haitian migrants argue that their dishonor and marginality are an effect of local residents' confusion over their own identity as both black Caribbeans and French citizens. Guadeloupeans always try to imitate the French, Haitians believe, and hence they are both intimidated by and jealous of Haitians' cultural autonomy and obvious national pride. This argument rests on a particular stereotype of the over-assimilated Guadeloupean who cannot quite shake off his Caribbean past. The stereotype pinpoints the "sore zone of cultural sensitivity" among Guadeloupeans (Herzfeld 1997: x). Haitians claim that their very presence disturbs the official ideology of French superiority by forcing Guadeloupeans to acknowledge that they acquired French citizenship at a high cultural cost.

Haitians believe that Guadeloupeans actually do recognize their commonality with Haitians, but are embarrassed by it because it belies their formal identity as French; in the end, they disrespect and marginalize Haitians as a defensive maneuver. The most elaborate version of this argument concerns Guadeloupeans' surreptitious use of Haitian Vodoun healing. In Haiti, people who suffer from humanly caused illnesses must seek out the healing power of neo-African Vodoun practitioners; Western biomedicine is regarded as ineffective in such cases (Brodwin 1996, Brown 1991). Haitian migrants assume that Guadeloupeans follow the same logic of medical decision-making. For example, I asked a Haitian friend in Pointe-à-Pitre what would happen if Guadeloupeans were afflicted with an illness sent by a human enemy (a pathogenic attack caused by jealousy or hatred). He replied, "They go to an houngan. They find one here or they go to Haiti." Surprised, I asked whether Guadeloupeans believe in this sort of healing power. "They believe in it more than we do! But they won't tell you. You can ask them, but they keep it hidden."

The same theme appears when Haitians discuss the Guadeloupean *gadezafè* whose practices overlap with those of Vodoun specialists. Like the *houngan*, these local healers perform exorcisms, lead prayer groups, and specialize in illnesses caused by social conflict (see Bougerol 1993, Ducosson 1989, Benoit 2000). They emerge from the same historical matrix as Haitian Vodoun: plantation slavery, the centuries-long intermixing of West African and French Catholic religious practices, and suppression by the Catholic clergy. The folk healers of Guadeloupe are, in a historical sense, cognates of those in Haiti. However, Haitian migrants dismiss them as far weaker than their Haitian counterparts, and they also state that local *gadezafè* learn their trade through apprenticeships with Haitians.

The conviction that Guadeloupeans secretly acknowledge the superior power of Haitian Vodoun enters Haitians' criticism of their employers. Certain wealthy Guadeloupeans, I was told, owe their fortune to a Faustian bargain with a Haitian Vodoun practitioner. Furthermore, the same Guadeloupean boss who cheats Haitians on the job or disrespects them in the street will run to a Haitian *houngan* when biomedical treatments fail. As one Haitian man put it, Guadeloupeans "know that Haiti is the original. They know Haitians are born with it. They know it's the African rite which is the strongest." Set against the negative clichés attached to Haitians, this is a resistant and cynical counter-image which migrants hold of the dominant society. It asserts that despite their European Community passports and French cultural fluency, Guadeloupeans have ready recourse to Haitian healers with their neo-African practices.

What do Haitian migrants accomplish by such arguments? First and foremost, Haitians claim cultural intimacy with Guadeloupeans. Cultural intimacy refers to "the sharing of known and recognizable traits that not only define insiderhood but are also . . . disapproved by powerful outsiders" (Herzfeld 1997: 94). Haitian migrants claim that they are the secret sharers of Guadeloupe's deep cultural essence. Moreover, the traits that the two groups share undercut the Guadeloupeans' preferred, formal self-presentation, and Haitians criticize the hypocrisy of Guadeloupeans who, on these grounds, deny commonality with Haitians. Through the caricature of Guadeloupeans who secretly consult Vodoun healers and acknowledge their superiority, Haitians not only assert their own cultural vitality but point out the embarrassing self-recognition of Guadeloupeans and the ambivalence over their joint (European) French and (neo-African) Caribbean allegiances. After all, Haitians have many opportunities to learn the everyday dimensions of ambivalence as they observe, with an outsider's eye, how the local society operates. The Creole language is still largely suppressed in schools and offices; the local media features endless debates over sovereignty while a large percentage of the island's population depends on the French welfare system, and sanitized presentations of Antillean folklore on television are sandwiched between programming from metropolitan France or the United States.

Noting Guadeloupeans' ambivalent participation in French society, Haitians encapsulate the cultural politics of the island in their stereotype of its black French residents who both repudiate and long for their Antillean past, and hence both denigrate and covertly envy the (Creole-speaking, politically independent, and culturally autonomous) Haitians in their midst. Stereotypes are discursive weapons of power, and Haitians use their stereotype of local residents to invert the power relations between them and the dominant society (compare Herzfeld 1997: 13). The caricature allows migrants to imagine their place in Guadeloupe on more favorable terms. It negates the clichés of Haitians as rapacious, intrusive foreigners and substitutes an (equally essentialized) image of Haitians as more authentic and culturally self-assured Caribbeans. Haitians thus use their stereotype of Guadeloupeans in two ways: as a form of discursive resistance (an accusation of hypocrisy aimed at the group that denigrates them) and as the grounds for their collective self-regard.

Conclusion: Comparative Perspectives on Diasporic Subjectivity

Contemporary diasporas are typically defined as novel social formations constituted by signs and practices that circulate in transnational space. It is tempting to take the next step and assume that their supra-local orientation forms a fundamental aspect of their subjectivity, i.e., that the same global exchanges that produce a given diaspora are also woven into its self-definition and the way it marks its difference from other groups. The situation of Haitians in Guadeloupe, on the contrary, suggests that diasporic subjectivity is finely calibrated to the experience of marginalization in a specific time and place. Comparing the community in Pointe-à-Pitre to other Haitian expatriate groups reveals how subjectivity—as both a structured and structuring response to marginality—differs across several nodes of the same diaspora.

In the 1920s, large numbers of Haitians left their homes to seek work in Cuba and the Dominican Republic. This wave of labor migrants shared certain traits with today's Haitian transnational movement. For example, Haitians living in the Dominican Republic could easily travel back and forth to their homeland, and they pursued economic and social advance by drawing on opportunities in both places. Moreover, they occupied a fragile position on the margins of an inhospitable dominant society. In October 1937 they suffered the landmark case of violent extrusion in the history of Haitian expatriate communities when over 20,000 Haitians residing in the Dominican borderlands were massacred (Plant 1987). Derby (1994) has examined the precursors to the massacre in the micropolitics of the border region, and some of the qualities attributed to Haitians at that time resemble the stereotypes in present-day Guadeloupe. Dominicans construed Haitians as holding a monopoly on dangerous sacred power. They regarded Vodoun magic with awe and deference, and considered the Dominican *curandero* as weaker than the houngan. Dominicans imagined that Haitians' control of Vodoun forces allowed them to produce unlimited wealth and enjoy supernatural abilities.

In plural societies throughout the world, individuals project a nefarious sacred power upon ethnic others whom they perceive as monopolizing productive forces (see Taussig 1980). Haitian Vodoun is a prime target for such projections in Caribbean societies where African cultural practices are branded as dangerous and suppressed, since Vodoun contains the greatest number of explicit African components of all Afro-Caribbean religions. Consequently, attitudes toward Vodoun often serve to marginalize expatriate Haitians throughout the Caribbean, whether migrant laborers in the early twentieth century or in more recent transnational communities. However, the details and consequences of their marginalization are not the same in all places, and the stereotyped projections about Vodoun differ significantly in the Guadeloupean and Dominican imagination.

In the Dominican borderlands of the 1930s, Haitian market-women and moneylenders actually did hold more economic power than local pastoralists. The mixture of awe and resentment of Haitians' spiritual potency dovetailed with Dominicans' fear of the new cash-based, competitive economy that was disrupting their lives. As a result, Haitians were perceived as quintessential strangers consumed with self-interest, and they easily became targets of fear and envy (Derby 1994: 525 and Passim). By contrast, Haitians in Guadeloupe clearly occupy the bottom rung of the island's economic hierarchy. Guadeloupeans regard Haitians not as interlopers endowed with mysterious economic advantages, but as strangely familiar avatars of their own past, possessed of purely cultural potency. In both the Dominican Republic of the early twentieth century and present-day Guadeloupe, stereotypes about Vodoun have perpetuated widespread and uncontrollable social transformations, yet Haitians have been inserted into fundamentally different roles in the local social taxonomy of each society. Dominicans regarded Haitians as the harbingers of new cash-based productive relations, and Vodoun as the source of their resounding economic success. Guadeloupeans, however, regard Haitians as possessing what departmentalization explicitly devalues, especially in symbolic terms. Sugarcane workers speaking the old-fashioned Creole and practicing an "African" religion symbolize the disruptive transformation of Guadeloupe, but Haitians are interpellated as representatives of an earlier cultural epoch, and not (as in the Dominican Republic) the vilified agents of change. Many Guadeloupeans, in their nostalgic imagination, also consider themselves to be left behind, so the transformation is especially poignant, and the essentialized image of Haitians all the more likely to endure. Contrasting the Guadeloupean and Dominican cases shows that the symbolic marginality of transnational Haitians depends on the local contradictions and historical junctures in the particular dominant society where they reside.

The lived experience of marginality, and the subjectivity that Haitians craft in response, also differs between Haitians in Guadeloupe and the United States. In Guadeloupe, state-imposed marginality begins with the denial of French citizenship or other types of legal residence. Haitians' non-regularized status creates the more immediate types of marginality: their clandestine occupancy of condemned buildings, their exploitation on the job, and the everyday anxiety about deportation. Migrants claim the right to stay in Guadeloupe not by elaborating their Haitianness, but by portraying themselves simply as hardworking, law-abiding individuals. In the face of state-imposed marginality, they have nothing to gain by drawing attention to their cultural distinctiveness.

In the larger and more well-established Haitian enclaves in the United States, state-imposed marginality takes a different form, and so does the response. Once they arrive on U.S. soil, even Haitians without proper documentation enjoy a higher level of security, including the right to legal counsel and to appeal deportation orders (Smith 1995). Their marginality arises not because they are threatened daily with arrest, but because they are popularly and bureaucratically defined as black, the nation's most dishonored ethnic category. Haitians respond by elaborating their homeland identity and connections, a strategy that would not work for migrants in Pointe-à-Pitre. Many Haitians in New York City interviewed by Charles (1992), among other researchers, refuse to identify themselves as black Americans because the category symbolizes to them an unacceptable degree of subordination. They reject the lowest position in the U.S. racial hierarchy, and instead privilege their Haitian nationality and particular class or political loyalties rooted on the island, or their similarities with other West Indian immigrants. Moreover, during the time of my fieldwork, Haitians in the United States were interpellated by influential organizations in their homeland as the "Tenth Department," an offshore extension of Haitian political space (the country is divided into nine departments). Beginning in the early 1990s, the populist leader and two-term president Jean-Bertrand Aristide aimed messages of inclusion at Haitians in New York, Miami, and Boston: by far the largest segments of the diaspora. He appealed to them to support the homeland with their remittances, to contribute to Aristide's Lavalas party, and to visit for patriotic tours of the Haitian countryside (Richman 1992b). Many Haitians willingly enrolled themselves in such long-distance nationalism (Glick Schiller and Fouron 2001), even after Aristide was forced to leave the country and the term "Tenth Department" fell out of use. This framing of their diasporic membership fundamentally conditions their membership in families and hometown associations as well as and their reaction to American racism. This sort of subjectivity heightens homeland-based assertions of Haitian identity, even as it transforms conventional meanings of nationalism. For Haitians in Guadeloupe, however, long-distance nationalism is essentially out of reach. Their group is too small and too poor to attract the same level of interest, and their undocumented status prevents most of them from traveling back home. Haitians there are more subject (in all senses of the word) to France's policies toward its offshore dependencies (especially its efforts to tighten their borders and assimilate their residents) than to Haiti's patriotic appeals to its diaspora. These brief comparisons show that the marginalization of the same transnational group differs remarkably from site to site, in line with the historical contradictions and nationalist projects in each. The dialectic of subjectivity thus operates differently and with a different outcome in the separate communities of the same diaspora. It may still make sense, in order to break with the disciplinary fetish of spatially-bound identities, to speak of an overarching transnational social field encompassing all expatriate Haitians. But to explain how they counteract their marginality, we must also delineate the specific practices, calibrated to local processes of marginality, which produce distinctive subjectivities. After all, transnationalism does not occur in an abstract "in-between" or thoroughly delocalized space, but instead in particular places and social relationships (Guarnizo and Smith 1998). Diasporic subjectivity, as well, is locally inflected. Depending on how states control the terms of citizenship, and how local social taxonomies assign value to newly-arrived outsiders, transnational diasporic groups will be simultaneously included and excluded in distinctive ways, and they will embellish or resist their exclusion with different results. Their subjectivity, therefore, will depend as much on the states and societies that immediately surround them as on dislocated transnational processes.

Acknowledgments

Research in Pointe-à-Pitre, Guadeloupe, was carried out over six months in 1994 and 1996 in Haitian Pentecostal churches as well as in the homes and neighborhoods of French Guadeloupeans and Haitian migrants. Individuals interviewed included Haitian pastors and church members as well as Guadeloupean lawyers, priests, and social workers (their names have been changed to protect confidentiality). Fieldwork was supported by the Wenner-Gren Foundation for Anthropological Research and the University of Wisconsin-Milwaukee (Graduate School and Center for Latin American and Caribbean Studies). I am grateful for advice from Ken George, who invited me to present this work at the University of Wisconsin-Madison anthropology colloquium, Kalman Applbaum and Thomas Malaby at UW-Milwaukee, Michel-Rolph Trouillot, Richard and Sally Price, Richard Grinker, Susan Bayly, and several anonymous reviewers. Crucial guidance in Pointe-à-Pitre came from Serge Souffrant, Jacques and Marlène Gilles, Ruddy Nannette, Albert Flagie, and Didier Bernard.

Notes

1. 1946: France's three remaining Caribbean colonies (Guadeloupe, Martinique, and French Guiana) become overseas *départements* ("Départements d'Outre Mer" or DOM). In administrative terms, they are near-equivalents to the departments in metropolitan France; their residents are fully French citizens and now members of the European Community with EC passports.

2. By subjectivity, I mean how people portray their group's essential characteristics, how they identify with such portrayals, and how they accommodate or resist the images imposed upon them by others. Subjectivity comprises both collective representations and personal sentiments of identification with (or rejection of) such representations. At the formal and public level, subjectivity is evidenced by self-conscious statements about group essence, its distance from other groups, its favored self-image, etc. At less formal levels, it emerges from bodily displays, practical choices about how to engage with dominant institutions, whom to befriend or shun, etc. (see Lave et al. 1992).

3. The structural origins of Haitian migration in the twentieth century are analyzed in Lundahl (1983) and Trouillot (1990). For the specific political and economic background of post-WW II migration, see Fouron (1993) and Catanese (1999), among others.

4. The 1990 census lists 12,000 Haitians out of the departmental total of 387,034 (INSEE 1992). However, most Guadeloupean and Haitian officials—social workers, lawyers, and pastors—estimated the real number as twice this official figure by the mid 1990s, and in 1999, the official number of foreigners in Guadeloupe (almost all Haitians) was 26,000 (INSEE 1999).

5. Most studies of the Haitians in the French Antilles, primarily Guadeloupe and French Guiana, focus on their arrival and the first decade of settlement, and hence do not discuss their present adaptations and likely future. See Céleste (1989), Bébel-Gisler and Hurbon (1987), Hurbon (1983), and, for French Guiana, Chérubini (1989).

6. A sizeable number of Haitians also live in rural Guadeloupe, principally around Sainte Rose and Lamentin on the island of Basse-Terre, the site of most commercial sugar, pineapple, and banana plantations. For logistical reasons, I limited my research to the Pointe-à-Pitre area, the commercial and industrial center of the *département*. About 125,000 people (35 percent of the entire population of Guadeloupe) live in this metropolis (which includes the communes of Pointe-à-Pitre, Les Abymes, Baie-Mahault, and Le Gosier). This is the most densely inhabited region in the French Antilles (Atohoun and Cazenave 1994:20).

7. The police apprehended a total of eight Haitians—three in one car and five in another. One was later released when a friend brought his identity papers to the detention center. The rest deported to Haiti.

8. Although most Haitians in Guadeloupe do not personally experience the violence of deportation, it nonetheless helps constitute diasporic subjects in several ways. People

easily recalled to me their relatives who have been sent back to Haiti; they must deal with the deportees' personal effects and obligations left unfulfilled in Guadeloupe, and their stratagems to avoid their own deportation structure how they inhabit urban space (see Axel 2002).

9. Immigration raids are conducted by the federal and municipal police as well as the PAF (Police de l'Air et des Frontières [Air and Border Police]), a service connected to the National Office of Immigration (n.a. 1987). In the mid-1990s, consistent with the anti-immigrant mood of President Jacque Chirac's administration, the PAF was renamed the CILEC (Contrôle de l'Immigration et de Lutte Contre l'Emploi Clandestin [the Service for Immigration Control and the Struggle against Clandestine Workers]).

10. At the time of fieldwork, Haitians in Guadeloupe did not have the right to appeal or even legal counsel (Amar and Milza 1990: 119).

11. Guadeloupeans cited the Haitian Creole word *rad* [clothes] which was replaced by the French-derived *linge* in the local Creole, and the Haitian *kapon* [cowardly] which in Guadeloupe gave way to *lâche*.

References

Abenon, Lucien-René. 1992. *Petite Histoire de la Guadeloupe*. Paris: Harmattan.

Amar, Marianne and Pierre Milza. 1990. *L'Immigration en France au XXe Siècle*. Paris: Armand Colin.

n. a. 1987. "Immigration Clandestine: Huit-Cents Expulsions en 1986." *France-Antilles*. Pointe-à-Pitre, Guadeloupe. (March 7: 1).

Appadurai, Arjun. 1996. *Modernity at Large: Cultural Dimensions of Globalization*. Minneapolis: University of Minnesota Press.

Atohoun, Richard and Jacques Cazenave. 1994. "De la Pointe vers l'Intérieur." *Antiane Éco: La Revue Économique des Antilles Guyane*, no. 24: 20–24.

Axel, Brian Keith. 2002. "The Diasporic Imaginary." *Public Culture* 14, no. 2: 411–428.

Basch, Linda, Nina Glick Schiller, and Cristina Szanton Blanc. 1994. *Nations Unbound: Transnational Projects, Postcolonial Predicaments, and Deterritorialized Nation-States*. Amsterdam: Gordon and Breach.

Bébel-Gisler, Dany and Laënnec Hurbon. 1987. *Cultures et Pouvoir dans la Caraïbe: Langue Créole, Vaudou, Sectes Religieuses en Guadeloupe et en Haïti*. Paris: Harmattan.

Benoist, Jean, ed. 1972. *L'Archipel Inachevé: Culture et Société aux Antilles Françaises*. Montréal: Les Presses de l'Université de Montréal.

Benoit, Catherine. 2001. *Corps, Jardins, Mémoires: Anthropologies du Corps et de l'Espace à la Guadeloupe*. Paris: CNRS Editions.

Bougerol, Christiane. 1983. *La Médecine Populaire à la Guadeloupe*. Paris: Karthala.

Brodwin, Paul. 1996. *Medicine and Morality in Haiti: The Contest for Healing Power*. Cambridge Studies in Medical Anthropology. Cambridge: Cambridge University Press.

———. 2003. "Pentecostalism in Translation: Religion and the Production of Community in the Haitian Diaspora." *American Ethnologist* 30, no. 1: 85–101.

Brown, Karen M. 1991. *Mama Lola: A Vodou Priestess in Brooklyn.* Berkeley: University of California Press.

Burton, Richard. 1993. "Ki Moun Nou Ye? The Idea of Difference in Contemporary French West Indian Thought." *New West Indian Guide,* no. 67: 5–32.

Byrne, David S. 1999. *Social Exclusion.* Buckingham: Open University Press.

Catanese, Anthony V. 1999. *Haitians: Migration and Diaspora.* Boulder: Westview Press.

Céleste, Chérubin. 1989. "Dix Années de Pastorale en Guadeloupe (1974–1984)." In *Le Phénomène Religieux dans la Caraïbe,* ed. by Laënnec Hurbon, 193–206. Montréal, CA: Les Éditions de CIDIHCA(Le Centre Internationale de Documentation et d'Information Haïtienne).

Charles, Carolle. 1992. "Transnationalism in the Construct of Haitian Migrants' Racial Categories of Identity in New York City." In *Towards a Transnational Perspective on Migration: Race, Class, Ethnicity, and Nationalism Reconsidered,* ed. Nina Glick Schiller et al., 101–123. New York: The New York Academy of Sciences.

Clifford, James. 1997. *Routes: Travel and Translation in the Late Twentieth Century.* Cambridge: Harvard University Press.

Derby, Lauren. 1994. "Haitians, Magic and Money: Raza and Society in the Haitian-Dominican Borderlands, 1900 to 1937." *Comparative Studies in Society and History,* no. 36: 488–526.

Ducosson, Dany. 1989. La Folie, les Esprits et Dieu. In *Le Phénomène Religieux dans la Caraïbe,* ed. Laënnec Hurbon, 241–262. Montréal: Les Éditions de CIDIHCA (Le Centre Internationale de Documentation et d'Information Haïtienne).

Fouron, Georges. 1993. *Dependency and Labor Migration: Haiti in the Fold of Global Capitalism.* Durham: Duke University Press.

Freedman, Jane and Carrie Tarr. 2000. "The Sans-papières: An Interview with Madjiguène Cissé." In *Women, Immigration and Identities in France,* eds. J. Freedman and C. Tarr, 29–38. Oxford: Berg Press.

Germani, Gino. 1980. *Marginality.* New Brunswick: Transaction Books.

Glick Schiller, Nina and Georges Fouron 2001. *George Woke Up Laughing: Long-Distance Nationalism and the Search for Home.* Durham: Duke University Press.

Glick Schiller, Nina, Linda Basch and Cristina Szanton Blanc. 1995. "From Immigrant to Transmigrant: Theorizing Transnational Migration." *Anthropological Quarterly,* no. 68: 48–63.

Glick Schiller, Nina, Josh De Wind, Marie Lucie Brutus, Carolle Charles, Georges Fouron and Luis Thomas. 1987. "Exile, Ethnic, Refugee: Changing Organizational Identities Among Haitian Immigrants." *Migration Today,* no. 15: 7–11.

GISTI 1996 (Groupe d'Information et de Soutien des Travailleurs Immigrés). *Rapport du Mission en Guyane et à Saint-Martin: Des Étrangers Sans Droits dans une France Bananière.*

Gross, Joan, David McMurray and Ted Swedenburg. 1996. "Arab Noise and Ramadan Nights: Rai, Rap, and Franco-Maghrebi Identities." In *Displacement, Diaspora, and Geographies of Identity,* eds. Smadar Lavie and Ted Swedenburg, 119–155. Durham: Duke University Press.

Guarnizo, Luis and Michael Smith, 1998. "The Locations of Transnationalism." *Comparative Urban and Community Research*, no. 6: 3–34.

Gupta, Akhil and James Ferguson, eds. 1997. *Culture, Power, Place: Explorations in Critical Anthropology*. Durham: Duke University Press.

Hall, Stuart. 1996. "Introduction: Who Needs 'Identity'?" In *Questions of Cultural Identity*, ed. Stuart Hall and Paul du Gay, 1–17. London: Sage Publications.

Hargreaves, Alec. G. 1995. *Immigration, "Race" and Ethnicity in Contemporary France*. London: Routledge.

Herzfeld, Michael. 1997. *Cultural Intimacy: Social Poetics in the Nation-State*. New York: Routledge.

Hurbon, Laënnec. 1983. "Racisme et Sous-Produit du Racisme: Immigré Haïtiens et Dominicains en Guadeloupe." *Les Temps Modernes* 39, no. 441–442: 1988–2003.

INSEE (Institut National de la Statistique et des Études Économiques) 1990. *Recensement Général de la Population de 1990. Population, Activité, Ménage: 971, Guadeloupe*. Paris.

———. 1999. *Recensement de la Population: Exploitation Principale*. (INSEE web-site: www.recensement.insee).

Kivisto, Peter. 2001. "Theorizing Transnational Immigration: A Critical Review of Current Efforts." *Ethnic and Racial Studies*, no. 24: 549–577.

Laguerre, Michel. S. 1998. *Diasporic Citizenship: Haitian-Americans in Transnational America*. New York: St. Martin's Press.

Lundahl, Matts. 1983. *The Haitian Economy: Man, Land, and Markets*. New York: St. Martin's Press.

Lave, Jean, Paul Duguid, Nadine Fernandez, and Erik Axel. 1992. "Coming of Age in Birmingham: Cultural Studies and Conceptions of Subjectivity." *Annual Reviews of Anthropology*, no. 21: 257–282.

Lawless, Robert. 1992. *Haiti's Bad Press*. Rochester: Schenkman Books.

Mankekar, Purnima. 1994. "Reflections on Diasporic Identities: A Prolegomenon to an Analysis of Political Bifocality." *Diaspora* 3, no. 3: 349–371.

Olwig, Karen F. 1997. "Cultural Sites: Sustaining a Home in a Deterritorialized World." In *Siting Culture: The Shifting Anthropological Object*, eds. by Karen Olwig and Kirsten Hastrup, 17–38. London: Routledge.

Park, Robert E. 1950. "Cultural Conflict and the Marginal Man." In *Race and Culture*, ed. Robert E. Park, 372–376. Glencoe: The Free Press.

Perlman, Janice E. 1976. *The Myth of Marginality: Urban Poverty and Politics in Rio de Janeiro*. Berkeley: University of California Press.

Plant, Roger. 1987. *Sugar and Modern Slavery*. London: Zed Books.

Richman, Karen. 1992a. "They Will Remember Me in the House: The Pwen of Haitian Transnational Migration." Doctoral dissertation: University of Virginia.

———. 1992b. "A Lavalas at Home / A Lavalas for Home: Inflections of Transnationalism in the Discourse of Haitian President Aristide." In *Towards a Transnational Perspective on Migration: Race, Class, Ethnicity, and Nationalism Reconsidered*, eds. Nina Glick Schiller, Linda Basch, and Cristina Blanc-Szanton, 189–200. New York: The New York Academy of Sciences.

Rouse, Roger. 1991. "Mexican Migration and the Social Space of Postmodernism." *Diaspora* 1, no. 1: 8–23.

Safran, William. 1991. "Diasporas in Modern Societies: Myths of Homeland and Return." *Diaspora* 1, no. 1: 83–99.

Schnepel, Ellen. 1993. "The Creole Movement in Guadeloupe." *International Journal of the Sociology of Language*, no. 102: 117–134.

———. 1998. "The Language Question in Guadeloupe: From the Early Chroniclers to the Post-War Generation." *Plantation Society in the Americas* 5, no. 1: 60–94.

Simmel, Georg. 1950. "The Stranger." In *The Sociology of Georg Simmel*, ed. by G. Simmel. New York: The Free Press.

Smith, Jennie. 1995. "Politics of Protection: The Interdiction, Repatriation and Treatment of Haitian Refugees Since the Coup d'Etat of September 1991." *Journal of Haitian Studies*, no. 1, 57–74

Stepick, Alex. 1998. *Pride Against Prejudice: Haitians in the United States*. Boston: Allyn and Bacon.

Suvélor, Roland. 1983. "Eléments Historiques pour une Approche Socio-Culturelle." *Les Temps Modernes* 39, no. 441–442: 2174–2208.

Taussig, Michael. 1980. *The Devil and Commodity Fetishism in South America*. Chapel Hill: University of North Carolina Press.

Trouillot, Michel-Rolph. 1990. *Haiti, State Against Nation: The Origins and Legacy of Duvalierism*. New York: Monthly Review Press.

Tsing, Anna L. 1993. *In the Realm of the Diamond Queen: Marginality in an Out-of-the-Way Place*. Princeton: Princeton University Press.

Vélez-Ibañez, Carlos G. 1983. *Rituals of Marginality: Politics, Process, and Culture Change in Urban Central Mexico, 1969–1974*. Berkeley: University of California Press.

2

The Trial of Ibo Simon

Popular Media and Anti-Haitian Violence in Guadeloupe

PHILIPPE ZACAÏR

On September 5, 2001, the court of justice of Pointe-a-Pitre, Guadeloupe's largest urban area, became the main center of attention on the island. On that day, the court began examining the case of Ibo Simon a former singer turned politician and popular television show host. In an atmosphere filled with tension, Ibo was charged with repeatedly calling for racist hatred and violence against Haitian immigrants and other Afro-Caribbeans residing in Guadeloupe (Alvarez 2001: 6; J. C. 2001: 4; Chanlot 2002a: 15).

For several months before his indictment, Ibo had used his daily television show to systematically portray Haitians as "scum," "vermin," and "dogs" which Guadeloupeans ought to rid their island of (Lesueur 2001: 16; P. L.: 2001). Ibo's fiery speeches and unabashed calls for violence had not gone unnoticed and some had taken his words seriously. In late July 2001, an angry mob of eighty to one hundred Ibo admirers armed with machetes and sticks assaulted the house of an immigrant family from Dominica (E. R. 2001). Ibo had previously directed the attention of the assailants toward this family for allegedly not paying their rent and lacking respect vis-à-vis their Guadeloupean landlord. A woman and her many Guadeloupean-born children were thrown into the street in a display of unspeakable brutality broadcast live on Ibo's show. In a similar manner, Ibo's supporters began harassing Haitian street vendors while arsonists attacked small businesses belonging to Afro-Caribbean immigrants.

During the three days of his trial, about 3,000 individuals gathered around the tribunal in support of Ibo. Guadeloupeans of every social background passionately debated the growing presence of Haitian immigrants in their midst. Forgetting all restraint, many voiced extremely negative views of Haitians. In fact, such denigrations did not cease after the court found Ibo guilty and ordered the cancellation of the show. For the last seven years, Ibo's violent diatribes have been revived and disseminated widely in popular media. In 2005, radio host Henri Yoyotte took over from Ibo, warning his listeners against an upcoming invasion of disease-ridden and bloodthirsty Haitians on the island. Although barred from hosting television shows, Ibo's shadow loomed larger than ever.

Interestingly, Haitians were the targets of almost all negative representations, while other immigrants from Europe, East Asia, the Middle East, and Africa residing in Guadeloupe seemed to miraculously escape Ibo's and Yoyotte's condemnation. Although Haitians are more numerous and perhaps more visible than other groups, Ibo's daily televised vilification of Haitians cannot be seen merely as typical anti-immigrant politics. The almost exclusive targeting of Haitians and the fierceness of the attacks against them testified to the existence of a strong anti-Haitian sentiment among Guadeloupeans. Haitians seemed to be rejected less for being immigrants than for being Haitians.

Yet, during the same period, while many Guadeloupeans deflected blame on Haitians for virtually every evil in their society, they have shown remarkable interest in Haitian history and in many elements of Haitian culture. One must live in Guadeloupe, for instance, to be aware of the extraordinary popularity of Haitian artists and *konpa* music among the people of the island. In addition, the commemorations in 2004 of the bicentennial of Haitian independence resonated in Guadeloupe and gave rise to cultural manifestations, publications in news magazines, and special radio programming on the history and culture of the Haitian people. Unquestionably, popular representations of Haiti and Haitians in contemporary Guadeloupe have been multifaceted. Guadeloupeans have combined rabid anti-Haitian prejudice with admiration for and borrowing from elements of Haitian cultural expression.

This phenomenon is neither surprising nor new for social scientists. Writing in 1983 in a special issue of *Les Temps Modernes*, sociologist Laënnec Hurbon argued that such ambiguity lies at the heart of the relationship between Guadeloupeans and Caribbean foreigners living in their midst (Hurbon 1983). For Hurbon, this ambiguity is the very expression of the Guadeloupeans' own uncertain identity. As they are summoned by the French colonial power to assimilate fully into the French nation, Guadeloupeans have tried to draw the contours of an imagined "Guadeloupean space" that is conceived as authentic and pure (1997). Haitians and other Afro-Caribbean populations are violently rejected as undesirable foreigners as they threaten this supposedly unique and homogenous Guadeloupean space. At the same time, Hurbon added, this desperate attempt to differentiate themselves from other Afro-Caribbeans hides a "fascination" with the Haitians' apparent liberation "from the obsession of the colonial or 'white' viewpoint" (2000).

Anthropologist Paul Brodwin made a comparable observation of this ambiguity after conducting research in Guadeloupe in the 1990s. Brodwin argues that Guadeloupeans view Haitians as "symbols of their repudiated past" in their forced march toward assimilation (Brodwin 2003: 396–399). They reject Haitians as threats to their achievement of French modernity. At the same time, however, recognizing and bemoaning the cultural loss that comes with assimilation, Guadeloupeans "envy Haitians as bearers of a more potent Afro-Caribbean authenticity" (399). Haitians, Brodwin contends, "provoke an anxious self-recognition, because they remind Guadeloupeans of the Caribbean identity they have discarded" (400).

In this article, I discuss how popular media helped ignite anti-Haitian violence while simultaneously combating its ravages from the trial of Ibo in 2001 to the present. As mirrors of Guadeloupean society, radio and television channels reflected the Guadeloupeans' ambivalence vis-à-vis Haiti and Haitian immigrants. Indeed, Ibo's television show turned into an authentic "Guadeloupean space" in which Guadeloupean men and women defined the growing Haitian diaspora as a threat to the very survival of their island society. At the same time, popular media have helped recognize the presence of many popular Haitian cultural elements in the fabric of Guadeloupean society while incorporating new ones. In doing so, they have outlined a different "Guadeloupean space" that extends to the wider Caribbean and acknowledges its strong Haitian component. As they reach a large audience across Guadeloupe, popular newspapers and radio and television programs have exerted a powerful influence in shaping discourses and attitudes toward Haitians residing there. For instance, the burning down of Haitian shops in Pointe-à-Pitre before and during the trial of Ibo was an enactment of popular media discourse.

The period between 2001 and the present is particularly critical for my analysis. In the first place, it coincides with a dramatic influx of new immigrants into Guadeloupe from other Caribbean territories, especially from Haiti. Debates over Afro-Caribbean immigration took center stage during this period. Radio and television programs, popular newspapers, and information magazines focused extensively on immigration and gave strong resonance to the trial of Ibo. From anticolonial *Les Nouvelles Étincelles*, to pro-French *France-Antilles*, popular media also provided ordinary Guadeloupeans with many opportunities to share their impressions of the perpetually changing face of their island. At the same time, the commemorations of the Haitian bicentennial in 2004 dramatically expanded the presence of Haiti and Haitians at the forefront of popular media. The story of the Haitian Revolution inspired Guadeloupeans to reflect on their own history of slavery and resistance to colonialism.

Historians of contemporary Guadeloupe and the French Caribbean have published on neither Haitian immigration nor the relationship between Haiti and the French Caribbean territories. The lack of historiography in regard to Haitian immigration may be explained by the recent development of this phenomenon. So far, only statistical data is available for brief but limited historical overviews. A French overseas *département* since 1946, Guadeloupe became a destination of choice for Afro-Caribbean immigrants in the 1970s. Census data reveals that the pattern of Haitian migration to Guadeloupe over a period of thirty-five years—with arrival peaks and slow-downs—often correlates with both Haitian and Guadeloupean political and economic events. On one hand, the continuous economic degradation of Haiti, combined with regular outbursts of political violence as well as natural catastrophes, translates into immigration peaks. On the other hand, social conflicts in the Guadeloupean banana industry in 1976 prompted banana industrialists to call on immigrants from Haiti and use them as strike breakers (Delachet-Guillon 1996: 34). In like manner, Guadeloupe's housing boom in connection with major investments in the sector of tourism in the 1980s sparked a call for immigrant workers in the construction industry.

In 1974, immigrants still made up less than 1 percent of the island's overall population. By 1999, on the eve of Ibo's virulent anti-Haitian campaign, Guadeloupe counted 5 percent immigrants among its 422,500 inhabitants. The majority came from Haiti (38 percent of the immigrant population), with the citizens of Dominica making up the second largest group (INSEE 2006: 12). Unlike Dominicans (from Dominica) who have the advantage of being Guadeloupeans' closest geographical neighbors, hopeful Haitian immigrants must go on a much longer and often hazardous journey. One major immigration route typically runs from Port-au-Prince to Santo Domingo, then from Santo Domingo to Roseau before reaching Pointe-à-Pitre or the banana-growing region of Capesterre-Belle-Eau. Another route usually takes the migrants to the French half of Saint Martin, which was administratively tied to Guadeloupe until February 2007. (Reno 2008: 137; INSEE 2006: 17). By 1999, Haitians worked more often in the agricultural and construction industries than any other immigrant group residing in

Guadeloupe. Concurrently, women were becoming more numerous among the overall immigrant community, rising from 49 percent of the immigrant population in 1974 to 56 percent in 1999. This signaled the growing importance of family reunifications in the migration processes leading to Guadeloupe. These data are indicative of the fact that Haitian and other Afro-Caribbean migrations to Guadeloupe were evolving in size and nature and were transforming the face of the Guadeloupean economy and society.

Popular media was critical in spreading Ibo's violent anti-Haitian discourse. Canal 10, a private television channel, offered Ibo the necessary platform. Canal 10 was founded in 1986 and was the first in a stream of "pirate" television channels that blossomed at the end of the 1980s in Guadeloupe.[1] Canal 10 quickly gained much popularity among television viewers as it broke the longstanding monopoly enjoyed by state-owned Radio France Outre-Mer (RFO). The new channel broadcast crowd-pleasing films as well as musical and sports events borrowed from North American television networks. In spite of its controversial debut, Canal 10 was duly legalized after the French authorities made efforts to regulate television offerings on the island. Canal 10 maintained a strong following among Guadeloupeans as it marketed itself as a channel with an undisputable local identity, focusing on Guadeloupean events rather than metropolitan French ones, and providing extensive free speech time for the common Guadeloupean folk. Hence, Canal 10 stood in opposition to state-owned channels that primarily broadcasted programs tailored for a metropolitan French audience irrespective of Guadeloupean taste. Hence, Guadeloupeans watched Canal 10 as it offered them a deeply satisfying sense of the "authenticity" discussed by Hurbon.

Ibo's personal background made Canal 10's claim of providing an authentic Guadeloupean voice unquestionable. Born and raised in the underprivileged neighborhoods of Basse-Terre, Guadeloupe's *chef-lieu* [administrative capital], Ibo shared the same life experiences of many Guadeloupeans in his generation. Beginning his career as a singer in popular balls in the 1960s, Ibo temporarily migrated to metropolitan France, leaving behind an island that provided few economic opportunities to its population. Returning to Guadeloupe a few years later, he gained some popularity as a singer as well as an actor in local cinematographic productions. Ibo quickly became an easily recognizable public figure. Using a new African-like name, Waka Danaka, he usually wore colorful African style clothes, cultivated a "rasta" style, and liked to publicly stress the darkness of his skin and other "African" features. At this time, his attitude challenged the "acceptable" behavioral codes dictated by the culture of assimilation into the French nation.

Ibo's show "Tous les jours 13 heures" [Everyday 1:00 P.M.] became the "Guadeloupean space" par excellence. In this show, Ibo met with ordinary Guadeloupeans in their homes, public plazas, and markets alike. In very little time, the show became extraordinarily successful as Ibo joked, laughed about daily local news, but also ferociously discussed every evil in Guadeloupean society. Nothing seemed to escape Ibo's daily commentaries such as the island's pervasive political corruption, the disturbing rise of juvenile delinquency, or its persistent high unemployment (J. C. 2001: 4). Guadeloupean viewers avidly followed Ibo's show at least as much for the content as for the form of his discourse. He avoided the usually polished French language used by local politicians when speaking on television. Instead, he consistently expressed himself in Creole at a time when the Guadeloupeans' popular language was only timidly accepted on state-owned channels.[2] Guadeloupean viewers felt particularly at ease with a dark-skinned, Creole-speaking man who carefully cultivated a "popular" style.

Many also felt at ease when, using traditional colonial rhetoric, Ibo sometimes criticized Guadeloupeans as lazy Negroes, at least partly responsible for their inability to build a true, French-like modern society (Alvarez 2001: 6). Ibo surfed on the feelings of "shame" and "self-hatred" identified by Frantz Fanon as typical of French Caribbeans and of all colonized people (Fanon 1952: 14). Some Guadeloupeans bowed to Ibo's words as they had internalized and accepted as truth French colonial discourse on their alleged natural inferiority. Without a doubt, Ibo embodied the very contradictions of the Guadeloupean people; torn between the demands of French assimilationist policy and the search for an elusive Guadeloupean authenticity.

On his show, Ibo directed his most violent attacks against Haitian immigrants. His portrayals of Haitians encompassed multiple subjects. First, he presented Haitians as profiteers, shamelessly taking economic advantage of good-willed Guadeloupeans: "they do not pay their rent;" "they do not spend a penny;" "they do not bring anything to Guadeloupe;" "they use hospital beds on taxpayers' money;" "they do not pay taxes;" "they get together to take homes away from Guadeloupeans afraid of their evil magic." This last accusation of potent magic with malevolent intentions was another major issue brought forward in Ibo's depictions of Haitians. According to him, "they practice Vodou," and "they cast satanic and machiavelic spells" against Guadeloupeans. As Brodwin points out, "attitudes toward Vodoun often serve to marginalize expatriate Haitians throughout the Caribbean," where African-derived religious practices are often seen as powerful and dangerous (Brodwin 2003: 404). By attributing potent supernatural powers to Haitian immigrants, Ibo presented them as threatening to defenseless Guadeloupeans. Haitians appeared all the more threatening because they were represented as "scum" and "vermin" always on the verge of engaging in the worst treacheries.

According to Ibo, Guadeloupeans needed to be ready to respond: "Guadeloupeans, when a Haitian attacks a Guadeloupean, you must react, you must fight . . . they are bloodthirsty. . . . Haitians will put shit in your mouth . . ." (Ligue des Droits de L'Homme 2002).

In fact, many Guadeloupeans found Ibo convincing. On the week of his trial, popular magazine *Sept-Magazine* interviewed ordinary Guadeloupeans. They were asked if Ibo's controversial television show should be cancelled. A baker declared: "I do not think that Ibo Ibo should be prevented from speaking on television. Many Guadeloupeans share his views. Personally, I do not think that he is delivering a xenophobic and racist message. He only says the truth" (quoted in Chanlot 2001: 8). A taxi man fully agreed: "[Ibo] says what all of us think: there are too many foreigners in Guadeloupe and I believe that it is not by mistake that so many people support him" (quoted in Chanlot 2001: 8). Only three among eight interviewees featured in the magazine issue believed that Ibo's portrayal of Haitians as vermin or rubbish was totally unacceptable and that his television show should be cancelled.

Another proof of Ibo's capacity to successfully reach out to other Guadeloupeans was his transformation from an entertainer to a politician. Usually dismissed as a clown by members of mainstream political parties, Ibo founded "Gwadloup Doubout" [Guadeloupe Standing Up], a political movement that aimed at pushing forward his anti-immigrant agenda. Building on his popularity, he made remarkably good showings in a stream of local elections, even winning seats in Guadeloupe's Regional Council, the island highest representative body.

Why did so many Guadeloupeans support Ibo? Popular media tried to provide an answer. Newspapers and magazines opened their columns to Haitians and gave them the opportunity to talk about their experiences as immigrants and their relationships with Guadeloupeans (Grugeaux-Etna 2000a: 16; n. a. 2000: 72). Jean Altidor, a Haitian immigrant who had been working on banana plantations for about twenty years told his story to *Sept-Magazine*. Altidor argued that: "the Haitian community is not well-integrated into Guadeloupean society. You just need to observe the Guadeloupeans' attitude. They clearly do not wish to socialize with us. I do not think that this is a problem of racism. I believe it is a problem of perception. I think that the population of Guadeloupe does not know us well enough" (quoted in Grugeaux-Etna 2000b: 15). Altidor complained that Guadeloupean television and popular newspapers fed their audience with overwhelmingly negative representations of Haitians. What was Altidor's impression founded upon?

Beginning in 2000, Haitians often made headlines as popular newspapers and magazines began to report an unprecedented number of immigrants arriving in Guadeloupe. Landing on the island's extensive shorelines, often after a costly and dangerous journey on the Caribbean Sea, many Haitians entered the island illegally (Vidal 2005: 2). As horrified Guadeloupeans discovered the lifeless bodies of hopeful immigrants brought upon their beaches by maritime currents, they began to perceive the new immigration trend as a dangerous invasion. *Sept-Magazine* noted, for instance, that in 2003, 130 petitions for asylum were filed at French administration offices on the island. By 2004—only one year later—petitioners reached the astonishing number of 3,335. 1,544 among them were Haitians.[3] French authorities estimated undocumented immigrants to be between 10,000 and 30,000 individuals. This made the presence of undocumented immigrants at least as important as legal foreign residents in Guadeloupe. With 12,443 individuals legally registered in December 2003, Haitians dominated the foreign community of 27,030 persons.[4]

This sharp influx of Haitians was attributed by Guadeloupean popular media to a series of intertwined factors. They included Haiti's continual economic degradation, its political instability, and a stream of natural disasters such as the catastrophic flood of the town of Gonaives in 2004.

For Guadeloupean popular media, uncontrolled illegal immigration was responsible for rising violence and insecurity, among other social ills. This tendency is exemplified by left-wing *Le Progrès Social*. The newspaper published twenty articles about Haiti and Haitians during the years 2003 and 2004. A majority (70 percent) of these articles featured Haitian immigrants as prostitutes, gangsters, rapists, and drug dealers responsible for rising violence in Guadeloupe (n. a. 2003).

Widespread concerns over uncontrolled immigration from Haiti and its consequences made Ibo's violent anti-Haitian discourse more pervasive than ever. While Ibo was silenced after the closing of his television show, his message was taken up by another controversial figure. Beginning in 2005, every evening between 8:30 P.M. and midnight, Radio Contact host and owner Henri Yoyotte launched violent attacks against Haitians and gave license to all those who wished to express their disgust at the Haitian presence in Guadeloupe (Louis 2006). Following Ibo's lead, Yoyotte skillfully exploited public fears of an invasion of Guadeloupe by foreigners. Ignoring official immigration numbers, he dismissed "political disguises" and denounced the presence of "eighty thousand foreigners on Guadeloupean soil, who insult us, who look down upon us, who pretend being our masters. They tell nonsense and hope to humiliate Guadeloupeans" (Journal Officiel de la République Française 2005). He ominously predicted "the extinction of the people of Guadeloupe" in the next ten to fifteen years.

A self-proclaimed painter and sculptor who also makes a living as a health practitioner, Yoyotte often borrows his most powerful arguments from the medical imaginary. For him, Haitians pose a particularly deadly threat to Guadeloupeans in a world "in which diseases are expanding, AIDS is still synonymous to death." In like manner, one auditor of Yoyotte's radio show expressed concern at the unchecked arrival of potentially disease-ridden Haitians: "thus we are not safe from infectious diseases, viruses, endemic germs, whooping cough, contagious illnesses, meningitis, rabies, scabies, cholera, leprosy, tuberculosis, etc . . ." (quoted in Journal Officiel 2005) In presenting Haitians as diseased, Yoyotte and his listeners symbolically re-affirmed the imagined Guadeloupean cleanliness and purity. They hoped to prevent any contamination of the allegedly authentic "Guadeloupean space."

On the other hand, movements of solidarity were simultaneously active in Guadeloupe as noted in the conclusion of Hurbon's 1983 article: "a large network of medical doctors, nurses, social workers, nationalist militant, militants of catholic movements and of the Christian community . . . have repeatedly attempted to stand in the way of pogroms and barbaric hunts for 'foreigners.' They invoked the very necessity of a Caribbean solidarity" (Hurbon 1983: 2002). For Hurbon, a powerful line of fracture came to divide the people of Guadeloupe into two camps.

Hurbon's observation was corroborated nearly two decades later. Ibo's virulent anti-Haitian discourse has engendered compelling expressions of solidarity toward Haitian immigrants. In the spring of 2001, a few months before his trial, the creation of the Collectif contre la Barbarie [Collective against Barbarism] brought together a number of Guadeloupean men and women from diverse professional backgrounds, such as painter Michel Rovélas and environmental activist Edouard Bénito-Espinal. In April of 2001, they circulated a petition throughout the island. Entitled "Appel contre la barbarie" [Call against Barbarism], the petition aimed at bringing Guadeloupeans together against Ibo and his imitators (Fleming 2001a: 8–9). Expressing himself in Creole in an interview with *Sept-Magazine*, the mayor of the commune of Trois-Rivière Albert Dorville communicated the reasons of his commitment in favor of Haitians: "I am the first politician who signed this petition against Ibo Ibo. I defend a strategy of ethnic solidarity with all our Caribbean neighbors. We must consider all Caribbean peoples as our friends. They speak Creole like us and we are all black people. That makes sense" (Quoted in Fleming 2001a: 8).

By stressing the fact that Guadeloupeans and Haitians share a common language and ethnic identity, Dorville validates Hurbon's contention that the people of the French Caribbean were unlikely to "escape from the conundrum of inter-ethnicity and inter-regionalism" (Hurbon 1983: 2002–2003). Dorville's statement signals a repudiation of the vision of Guadeloupe as a homogeneous pure ensemble. As Kachig Tölölyan puts it in his introduction to the journal *Diaspora* in 1991, "the vision of a homogeneous nation [was] now being replaced by a vision of the world as a 'space' continually reshaped by forces—cultural, political, technological, demographic, and above all economic . . ." (Tölölyan 1991: 6). This reimagined Guadeloupean space is also well illustrated by Benito-Espinal's declaration for *Sept-Magazine*: "Everyone of us has a parent from Haiti, from the Dominican Republic, from Saint Lucia, from Dominica, etc . . ." For the same reason, honorary university professor Bertène Juminer called upon Guadeloupeans to look back upon their past: "Ibo's discourse stems from the ignorance of the history of the Caribbean. Haitians deserve our respect. They were the first who fought to win our freedom back . . . If Guadeloupeans knew their history, they would have a better attitude toward Haitians." (quoted in Fleming 2001a: 8)

Looking back to the past is precisely what popular media also invited their readers and listeners to do (Dodart-Nankin 2001: 11–13; Fleming 2001b: 16). *Les Nouvelles Étincelles* argued that negative representations of Haitians in the Guadeloupean imagination are linked to the historical conditions of their arrival. For *Les Nouvelles Étincelles*, wealthy French landowners with the active support of French political authorities encouraged the immigration of Haitian workers so that they would break strikes of Guadeloupean workers in the sugar cane and banana industries. As a result, many ordinary Guadeloupeans saw Haitians as undesirable, foreign strike breakers and unbeatable rivals for unskilled jobs. Banana planters and a number of other Guadeloupeans did not hesitate to shamelessly exploit the newcomers. Haitian immigrants were forced to accept miserable wages and pay high rent for shacks. Like slaves, Haitian immigrants were denied their family name in everyday conversations. When a Guadeloupean native introduced a Haitian worker to another Guadeloupean native, he/she would say "this is my Haitian" (Alvarez 2001: 7). For *Les Nouvelles Étincelles*, Ibo only served the interests of the same powerful planters and industrialists who had encouraged Haitian immigration in the first place.

In 2004, popular media focused extensively on Haitian history. The bicentennial of Haitian independence led to the publication of a number of articles on the history of the Revolution.[5] Undoubtedly, this was a reflection of the many intimate historical and cultural links existing between Haiti and the French Caribbean. Haitians, Guadeloupeans, Martiniquans, and French Guianese share a comparable colonial history marked by French colonization and African slavery. Haitian independence in 1804 set these territories on radically distinct historical trajectories. Guadeloupe, Martinique, and French Guiana remained French colonies until their official assimilation as French overseas *départements* in 1946. Haitian revolutionary heroes, however, have figured prominently in the thoughts and writings of French Caribbean thinkers such as Aimé Césaire and Édouard Glissant (Salien 2004: 1166–1180).

Building upon such literary and philosophical traditions, *Les Nouvelles Étincelles* extolled the achievement of the slaves in former Saint-Domingue: " . . . these men, who had been relegated to a sub-human condition, who had suffered treatments of rare inhumanity, accomplished the first triumphant Revolution of black slaves in the world. They inflicted a political and military defeat to the most powerful army of their time, the army of Napoleon Bonaparte" (Bangou 2003a: 12–13). For *Les Nouvelles Étincelles*, there was no doubt that the Haitian revolution had a strong impact on slave societies in the Americas. The newspaper saw the Haitian achievement as a prelude to a century of abolitionist laws in Latin America, the United States, and the French, Dutch, and British colonies in the Caribbean. Free Haiti played "a critical role, as a model, but also as a direct provider of men, money and weapons to the revolutions of the region" (Bangou 2003b. 8–9). For *Les Nouvelles Étincelles*, the example of Haitian president Alexandre Pétion extending much needed support to Ibo Bolívar showed that the Republic of Haiti unquestionably stood as a symbol of liberty and resistance against oppression in the region.

This favorable view of Haiti was not contradicted in any way by pro-French periodicals. *Sept-Magazine*, for instance, opened its pages to Jacques Adélaïde-Merlande. The well-known Guadeloupean historian argued that it was the slave revolt in Saint-Domingue that forced the French revolutionaries to apply the principles of the Declaration of the Rights of Men in their slaveholding Caribbean colonies. In 1794, five years after these principles were proclaimed, revolutionary France took steps to abolish African slavery. For Adélaïde-Merlande, Guadeloupeans owed much to their Haitian brothers in servitude (Adélaïde-Merlande 2004: 9). For *Le Progrès Social*, the commemoration of the Haitian revolution was the opportunity to inform its readers about examples of solidarity between Haitians and other French Caribbeans. Indeed, when Guadeloupeans waged war against Napoleonic troops that had come to restore slavery in 1802, men from Saint-Domingue fought alongside them at Baimbridge, one of Guadeloupe's most well-known sites of resistance. Similarly, Guadeloupean resistance leader Palène—one of the few who escaped from French repression—fled to Saint-Domingue, met with Dessalines, and joined with revolutionary forces (Rodes 2003: 4).

Beyond history, popular media presented other examples of the impact of Haiti on French Caribbean culture. Publishing an article by Hurbon, *Sept Magazine* revealed that Haitian Vodou "has become an essential ingredient of Guadeloupean culture" (Hurbon 2001: 18–20) In another article of August 2001, the same magazine discussed the case of *Bolèt*, a type of lottery once exclusively played by Haitian immigrants residing in Guadeloupe. The author of the article stated that "*Bolèt* has penetrated Guadeloupean cultural habits. Haitians are no longer alone playing the game . . . Every day, more Guadeloupean natives, without distinction of age, gender or social background, try their luck" (Méphon 2001: 5). Guadeloupeans' rising passion for *Bolèt* has been particularly remarkable since the game has not yet been officially approved by French law. Playing *Bolèt* is illegal, but it has become apparent that Guadeloupean police are turning a blind eye on this practice.

Other examples of French Caribbeans' passion for Haitian culture included the arrival in Guadeloupe for the 2004 Book Fair of several Haitian writers (Martial 2004: 18–19). Gary Victor, Evelyne Trouillot, and Jean-Robert Cadet among others were the highlights of this cultural event centered on Haiti. The well-attended book fair provided Guadeloupeans with an excellent opportunity to remember that they had a lot in common with Haitians. Finally, popular media pointed out that music has helped tie Haitians and Guadeloupeans together culturally for the last forty years. *Konpa direct*, Haiti's most well-known musical genre, largely dominated the French Caribbean musical scene until the end of the 1980s and helped transform French Caribbean popular music. More than ever, radio stations must feature Haitian artists and *Konpa* music to attract a Guadeloupean audience.

In sum, profound contradictions have divided Guadeloupeans vis-à-vis Haiti and the growing Haitian diaspora living in their midst. Violent anti-Haitian discourse and attitudes have thrived along with acknowledgements and appraisal of Haitian history and culture as essential elements of the Guadeloupean makeup. Popular media played an essential role in both spreading anti-Haitian discourse and popularizing Haitian history and cultural forms in Guadeloupe.

Recent developments show that such contradictions remain pervasive in Guadeloupean society. Ibo's subsequent political fortune and the story of a little Haitian boy by the name of Jephté constitute very telling examples. Ibo's party made a remarkable showing in the 2007 local and French national elections. Ibo rejoiced that his discourse continued to be anchored in the Guadeloupean imaginary, and his television show was far from forgotten. On the other hand, only a few months later, Guadeloupeans were particularly moved by the story of Jephté. Jephté was born on Guadeloupean soil, the son of undocumented Haitian immigrants. He was four years old when on a September morning in 2008, nearly seven years after the beginning of Ibo's trial, he went along with his father on a few errands in the commune of Sainte Rose. A new school year was fast approaching and like all ordinary Guadeloupean families, they knew that the time had come to buy new shoes and other school supplies. Things did not turn out the way they expected, however. The father was arrested by the border police. Later in the afternoon, they were both put on a plane back to Haiti, a country where the young boy had never set foot. Jephté discovered the country of his parents in the worst of circumstances. Devastating hurricanes had left behind a trail of death and destruction, adding to the misfortunes of the people of Haiti and undoubtedly throwing more of them on the route to exile (Joint 2008: 9–11).

Guadeloupean popular media played a decisive role in telling the story of Jephté and his father and in provoking widespread public outcry. As they had already been profoundly moved by a relentless flow of bad news and pictures of hurricane destruction in Haiti, many Guadeloupeans denounced the blatant inhumanity and lack of compassion of the state authorities that carried out the hasty deportation of Jephté and his father. Many demanded a moratorium on the deportation of undocumented Haitians and loudly voiced their desire to see Jephté and his father returned to Guadeloupe.

Notes

1. The term "pirate television" was used to make reference to channels that broadcasted without legal authorization. For more information on television channels in the French Caribbean, see Conseil Supérieur de l'Audiovisuel, *La Lettre du CSA*, no. 136, 15 jan. 2001, http://prod-csa.integra.fr/actualite.

2. Guadeloupean Creole or *Kréyol* is spoken and understood by most people on the island. However, it has been significantly weakened and altered by decades of denigration by such major colonial institutions as state, church, and school. Speaking Creole has been associated with lack of education and culture. For many Guadeloupeans, banning Creole meant preserving their chance to achieve proper French culture and a higher social and economic status. The Guadeloupean language has gained greater acceptance by official institutions and the media since the 1990s. On the politics of Creole in the French Caribbean, see among many other publications Dany Bébel-Gisler, *La langue créole, force jugulée. Etude socio-linguistique des rapports de force entre le créole et le français aux Antilles*. Paris: L'Harmattan, 1976.

3. An undetermined number of petitioners have been living in Guadeloupe illegally for many years before applying for the refugee status.

4. According to Daveira (1986), there were about 6,000 Haitians on the island in 1981. They comprised approximately half the number of foreigners estimated at that date at 13,550. With respectively 6,805 and 2,397 individuals immigrants from the Commonwealth of Dominica and the Dominican Republic came in distant second and third. See also Grugeaux-Etna 2004.

5. Articles on the Haitian Revolution include, among others, Adélaïde-Merlande 2004a: 14; Adélaïde-Merlande 2004b: 20.

References

Adélaïde-Merlande, Jacques. 2004a. "Haïti, 1804–1843: les premiers pas de la jeune République (I)." *Sept Magazine*, no. 1288: 14.

———. 2004b. "Haïti, 1804–1843: les premiers pas de la jeune République (II)." *Sept Magazine*, no. 1291: 20.

———. 2004c. "Février 1794: la Convention abolit l'esclavage." *Sept Magazine*, no. 1292: 9.

Alvarez, Lucio. 2001. "On ne joue pas avec le racisme et la xénophobie: On les combat!" *Les Nouvelles Étincelles*, no. 182: 6–7.

n. a. 2003. "Quand les passeurs haïtiens se conduisent en Guadeloupe comme des tontons macoutes." *Le Progrès Social*, no. 2422: 1–2.

n. a. 2000. "Rémy Ervilus: un exemple d'intégration." *Sept Magazine*, 1092, 72.

Bangou, Michel. 2003a. "Haïti (1ère partie)." *Les Nouvelles Étincelles*, no. 67: 12–13.

———. 2003b. "Haïti (2ème partie)," *Les Nouvelles Étincelles*, no. 68: 8–9.

Brodwin, Paul. 2003. "Marginality and Subjectivity in the Haitian Diaspora." Anthropological Quarterly, 76 no. 1: 383–410.

C. J. 2001. "Xénophobie: les Haïtiens de Guadeloupe résistent." *Sept Magazine*, no. 1157: 4.

Chanlot, Philippe. 2001. "Faut-il interdire Ibo Ibo d'antenne?" *Sept Magazine*, no. 1153: 8–9.

———.2002a. "Ibo et la contre-attaque judiciaire." *Sept Magazine*, no. 1173: 15.

———.2002b. "La vraie plaie, c'est l'intolérance." *Sept Magazine*, no. 1176: 9.

Conseil Supérieur de l'Audiovisuel. 2001. *La Lettre du CSA*, no. 136, http://prod-csa.integra.fr/actualite.

Daveira, Denise. 1986. "Douze ans d'Immigration Haïtienne en Guadeloupe." *Revue du CERC*, no. 3: 164–180.

Delachet-Guillon, Claude.1996. La Communauté haïtienne en île de France. Paris: L'Harmattan.

Dodart-Nankin, Geneviève. 2001. "Une communauté au tournant de son histoire." *Sept Magazine*, no. 1157: 11–13.

Fanon, Frantz. 1952. *Peau noire masques blancs*. Paris: Éditions du Seuil.

Fleming, Kareen. 2001a. "Pourquoi ils ont signé l'Appel contre la barbarie." *Sept Magazine*, no. 1157: 8–9.

———. 2001b. "BTP: Les Haïtiens ont construit la Guadeloupe." *Sept Magazine*, no. 1157: 16.

Grugeaux-Etna, Marie-France. 2000a "La clandestinité: une fatalité bien plus qu'un choix." *Sept Magazine*, no. 1092: 16.

———. 2000b. "Communauté haïtienne: une image à changer." *Sept Magazine*, no. 1092: 15.

———. 2004. "Enquête sur une population 'fantôme,'" *Sept Magazine*, no. 1328: 11–14.

Hurbon, Laënnec. 1983. "Racisme et sous-produit du racisme: immigrés haïtiens et dominicains en Guadeloupe." *Les Temps Modernes* 39, no. 441–442: 1988–2003.

———. 2001. "Mort et sexualité dans le vodou haïtien: le culte des 'Gédé.'" *Sept* Magazine, no. 1151 : 18–21.

Institut National de la Statistique et des Études Économiques (INSEE), *Atlas des populations immigrées en Guadeloupe*, 2006.

Joint, Louis-Auguste. 2008. "La condition haïtienne en Guadeloupe." *Nouvelles Étincelles*, no. 316: 11.

Journal Officiel de la République Française. 2005. "Décision no. 2005–245 du 17 mai 2005 mettant en demeure l'association Parti libéral modéré, Radio Contact." http://www.admi.net/jp/20050608/CSAX0501245S.html.

L.P. 2001. "Guadeloupe: réactions contre la propagande xénophobe d'un journaliste." *Lutte Ouvrière*, http://www.lutte-ouvriere-journal.org/?act=artl&num=1728&id=10.

Lesueur, Alain. 2001. "Fantasmes et réalités de l'immigration." *Sept Magazine*, no. 1143: 16.

Ligue des Droits de l'Homme, *LDH—GISTI—MRAP et autres contre Canal 10 et Ibo: Jugement du 15 février 2002—Tribunal de Grande Instance de Pointe-à-Pitre*, 15 février 2002, http://www.ldh-france.org/docu_printjur.cfm?idJur=17.

Louis, Cyrille. 2006. "A Pointe-à-Pitre, une radio attise les rivalités communautaires." Le Figaro, http://www.lefigaro.fr/france/20060706.WWW000000292_pointe_a-pitre

Martial, Gladys. 2004. "Salon du livre 2004: Ghislaine Nanga, directrice artistique 'Haïti est notre invitée.'" *Sept-Magazine*, no. 1292: 18–19.

Méphon, Mireille. 2001. "La 'bolèt': illégale mais tolérée." *Sept-Magazine*, no. 1152: 5.

R. E. 2001. "DURBAN Appel au meurtre sur petit écran." *Journal L'Humanité*, http://www.humanite.presse.fr/popup_print.php3?_article=249800.

Réno, Fred. 2008. "L'immigrant haïtien entre persécution et xénophobie." *Hommes et Migration*, no. 1274: 132–142.

Rodes, Félix. 2003. "'Toussaint Louverture, Pétion, Palène, Dessalines." *Le Progrès Social*, no. 2414: 4.

Salien, Jean-Marie. 2004. "Haïti vue de la Martinique." *The French Review* 77 no. 6: 1166–1180.

Tölölyan, Kachig. 1991. "The Nation-State and its Others: In Lieu of a Preface." *Diaspora: a journal of transnational studies* 1 no. 1: 3–7.

Vidal, André-Jean. 2005. "Dans l'enfer des clandestins." *France-Antilles*, no. 10489: 2.

3

"The Mirror That We Don't Want"

Literary Confrontations between Haitians and Guadeloupeans

ODILE FERLY

The Caribbean remains divided by rivalries and prejudices that most particularly affect the Haitians, who have long been considered in the region as "nègres des nègres," or the niggers' niggers.[1] The thorny relationship between Haiti and its neighbor, which culminated in the 1937 slaughter of some 20,000 immigrant cane-cutters by the Dominican government, is by far the most gruesome illustration of this phenomenon (Ferguson 2003: 10; Matibag 2003: 139–155; Rodríguez 2005: 26, 40). With estimates ranging from about 500,000 to 1 million Haitians living across the border today, there are still important tensions between the two peoples. Cultural differences and the successive Haitian invasions of the Dominican Republic, especially the 1822 to 1844 occupation, partly account for this antagonism.[2]

Yet such tensions equally characterize the confrontation—at once encounter and conflict—between Haitians and Guadeloupeans, despite numerous affinities. Haitians share with French Antilleans similar customs, including healing and magical practices, the Creole language—with its proverbs, sayings, oral tradition, and the mindset it carries, notably popular wisdom—as well as a sense of identity derived from a common history of colonialism until 1791. The Haitian Revolution tightened the ties with Guadeloupe, as it effected the abolition of slavery in both countries in 1794; its subsequent restoration in Guadeloupe motivated the 1802 uprisings. Besides greater geographical proximity, the unique resonance of the Haitian Revolution in Guadeloupe may well explain why today Haitians emigrate in larger numbers to this island than to Martinique.[3]

These affinities notwithstanding, anti-Haitian prejudice is found in Guadeloupe as elsewhere in the region. Indeed, Haiti constitutes a paradox in the French Antillean (and wider Caribbean) imaginary. On the one hand, the Revolution with its cohort of heroes has aroused admiration and respect, inspiring a series of poetry, plays, and essays that most often center on the iconic figure of Toussaint Louverture. On the other hand, contemporary Haiti and Haitian immigrants commonly face contempt and hostility. Women writers from the French Caribbean more readily focus on this reality than their male counterparts such as Aimé Césaire, Édouard Glissant, and others.[4] The depiction of Haitians in Maryse Condé's novel *Traversée de la mangrove* and in *Ton Beau capitaine*, a play by fellow Guadeloupean Simone Schwarz-Bart, will be read against the representation of Guadeloupeans in "Seeing Things Simply," a short story by Haitian diaspora writer Edwidge Danticat.

Examined together, these three texts reveal the patterns of demarcation and demonization at work in the elaboration of Guadeloupean and Haitian collective identities, as well as the ambivalence that underlies the mutual perceptions of the two communities and conditions their interactions. This ambivalence largely stems from the widely divergent sociopolitical predicaments of the French Antillean territory and the first Caribbean nation to shake the colonial yoke. At the same time, this reading of Caribbean literature validates Stuart Hall's contention that identity, particularly when it is diasporic, is "a production . . . always in process, and always constituted within, not outside representation" (Hall 2003 [1990]: 234) and that "cultural identities are . . . not an essence, but a *positioning*. Hence, there is always a politics of identity" (237, emphasis his). As will be shown in relation to both communities, the Haitian or Guadeloupean intruder generates a specific response, a positioning that aims to reinforce a sense of collective selfhood.

As noted by Philippe Zacaïr, Haiti and its diaspora have had a cultural impact on French Antillean fine arts, crafts, and notably music; thus *konpa*, which gained popularity in the 1970s and 1980s, largely conditioned the emergence of zouk. Furthermore, Guadeloupean culture has now integrated elements such as Vodou and *bolèt*, an illegal lottery once played exclusively by the Haitian community.[5] Similarly, solidarity wall slogans appeared throughout Guadeloupe following the fall of dictator Duvalier in 1986.

Despite such cultural proximity, today many Guadeloupeans harbor a strong animosity toward the Haitian community. This feeling escalated in 2001 and unleashed verbal as well as physical violence incited by the television show host and local politician Ibo Simon. Although the confrontations rapidly subsided and some Guadeloupeans vehemently demonstrated in protest, the influx of Haitians—accelerated since Jean-Bertrand Aristide's departure in February 2004—is watched with increasing unease, as attested by the live debates on illegal immigration broadcast on Radio Contact in February 2005, in which callers expressed their virulent xenophobia (AC'DOM 2005, Payot 2005, Montchovi 2005).[6]

It is highly ironic yet symptomatic that this anti-Haitian sentiment should be spurred by Ibo Simon, whose stage name and successive looks— rasta back in the 1970s and 1980s, West African dress today—would imply an adherence to pan-Caribbean and pan-African ideals. Such a discrepancy points to the paradoxes embedded in the French Antillean status, which has left its population oscillating between a call for regional unity and a pull toward France and the European Union. Ibo Simon's contradictions could also be viewed more broadly as a symptom of the Guadeloupeans' ambivalent perception of Haitianness, connoting now glory, now abjection in the collective imaginary.

Certainly the image of Haitian immigrants has changed radically over the past two decades: in stark contrast with the immigrant communities from Dominica and the Dominican Republic, in the 1980s and early 1990s Haitians were widely regarded in Guadeloupe as honest, quiet, and hardworking, often considered to be the best-skilled agricultural labor whose docility and willingness to accept miserable wages particularly appealed to landowners. Today, they are most frequently labeled lazy, delinquent—if not criminals or *tontons macoutes*, François Duvalier's infamously ruthless militia—and a threat to public health for allegedly spreading a variety of diseases.[7] As noted by Haitian banana industry worker Jean Altidor, the ignorance resulting from the segregation of immigrants largely breeds such misperceptions: "la population guadeloupéenne nous connaît mal" [Guadeloupean people know very little about us] (Grugeaux-Etna 2000: 15).

Implanted since the 1960s, the Haitian community in Guadeloupe has been growing since the 1980s, with a surge in 2004. Today it is officially estimated at 15,000, 80 percent of which has legal residence, although because of increasing undocumented immigration, numbers can only be approximate.[8] While most initially plan to use the island as a stepping stone to reach the U.S. or Canada, many see their hopes frustrated and end up settling down permanently. Apart from a tiny group of well-integrated professionals fluent in both French (the official language of Guadeloupe) and Creole (the vernacular), the majority are individuals from the rural and urban underclass, often illiterate and speaking virtually no French.

Prior to the early 1980s, Haitian immigrants usually came on contracts as agricultural laborers; their original role as strikebreakers in a sugar cane industry in crisis soured from the start their relationship with native fellow workers (Brodwin 2003: 389). A significant portion of the later arrivants—to borrow Edward Kamau Brathwaite's term—have an illegal residence status, an undeclared occupation (as domestic helpers, gardeners, but also agricultural and construction workers), or earn a living in informal economic sectors (such as unlicensed retailing or cockfighting). The children of these poorer migrants often face obstacles within the school system, and social ascension is very limited, although legal residence helps. These Haitians are often treated with condescension, disdain, or even hostility, especially by authorities such as customs officials. This is the reality depicted in Maryse Condé's and Simone Schwarz-Bart's works, both set in the mid-to late 1980s.

Condé's *Traversée de la mangrove* focuses on a Haitian protagonist in the chapter "Désinor, l'Haïtien." From the outset, the eponymous character is associated with deprivation and social inferiority, readily admitting that he is taking advantage of the central character's wake to eat his full, and concluding his testimony with a loud burp that earns him the unanimous disapproval of the guests. Désinor deliberately plays into the stereotypes of Haitians:

> Il mangeait voracement, y allant de la main, et sentit sur lui le regard de mépris de ses voisins qui eux s'étaient servis avec habileté de leurs cuillers après avoir déposé un rectangle de papier sur leurs genoux. Il s'en réjouit, car il le faisait exprès, d'être si sale. . . . il aurait aimé les insulter, les choquer (Condé 1989: 198).

> [He ate voraciously, using his hands, and he could feel the look of contempt from his neighbors, who had skillfully served themselves with their spoons and placed a paper rectangle on their laps. He behaved so uncouthly on purpose and took delight in it. . . . he wished he could have insulted them, shocked them] (Condé 1995: 163).[9]

The villagers' contempt for Désinor and his fellow countrymen is underlined throughout the novel, for instance when Désinor is handed down an old, shabby suit, which he accepts with feigned gratitude. The title, "Désinor, l'Haïtien," conveys the stigma attached to his nationality within the community of Rivière au Sel. While the central character Francis Sancher, another foreigner mistaken for Cuban, also fails to win acceptance, unlike Désinor he does not become a pariah. As a Haitian, Désinor ends up doing the work despised by Guadeloupeans, specifically in the agricultural sector. Thus, in the cane fields, "la majorité des coupeurs étaient des Haïtiens" (Condé 1989: 199) [Most of the cane cutters were Haitians] (Condé 1995: 165). Later, in Rivière au Sel, he survives on gardening and menial jobs, while the near exclusive labor of Loulou's flower business is comprised of his compatriots, "reconnaissables au noir sans nuances de leur peau et à la manière furtive dont ils se rendaient à leurs cases de boue et de tôle" (Condé 1989: 200) [recognizable by the very blackness of their skin and by the way they stole back furtively to the corrugated iron and mud huts] (Condé 1995: 165–166).

In addition to their darker skin and illegal status, Vodou further sets the Haitians apart from the local population. To Désinor, reaching Guadeloupe on the Day of the Dead is a bad omen that conjures up visions of Baron Samedi greeting him from the shore with a malicious wink.[10] To this somewhat stereotypical portrayal replicating the autochthons' preconceptions, Condé opposes a more complex vision of the Haitian immigrant, who emerges from his own testimony as proud (initially infuriated by the shabby suit) and independent (resolutely distant from the Haitian settlement).

Not surprisingly, Désinor was long set on escaping the economic and political turmoil of the Duvaliers' regime, originally hoping to join his friend Carlos in New York. But he resigns himself: "Je sais bien que je ne la verrai jamais, la Statue de la Liberté. . . . D'ailleurs, on m'a dit qu'elle n'est pas belle et ne fait bon visage qu'aux immigrants d'une autre sorte que la nôtre. Nous n'avons pas la bonne couleur" (Condé 1989: 202) [I know I'll never see the Statue of Liberty. . . . Besides, they say she's nothing to look at and only looks kindly on those immigrants that are not like us. We're not the right color] (Condé 1995: 168). Here the author insinuates that the situation of Haitians in Guadeloupe is by no means unique: they would certainly endure comparable conditions beyond Caribbean waters in the United States. Nevertheless, the U.S. seems to offer working-class Haitians greater opportunities: while Désinor's arrival in Guadeloupe is likened to entering "un royaume de ténèbres et désolation" (Condé 1989: 198) [a realm of darkness and desolation] (Condé 1995: 164), Carlos can afford to send Désinor regular dollar remittances.

Despite the stigma it carries, his Haitianness is not the only decisive factor in Désinor's exclusion. Whereas Francis Sancher's foreignness elicits far less contempt than Désinor's, on the other hand, Xantippe, a native characterized as "un Nègre noir comme le deuil et l'éternité" (Condé 1989: 202) [as black as mourning and infinity] (Condé 1995: 167), is likewise ostracized for his darker color, his poverty, and his mysterious origins. Xantippe holds a special status in the novel. More than a protagonist in his own right, he is a character type representing the suffering black man; the original Afro-Antillean. In the chapter dedicated to his testimony, Xantippe claims to have named the plants and places of the island, to know the secret past of the village, and to have witnessed the social evolution of the country. He is thus an Adamic figure whose lifetime, like that of Alejo Carpentier's Ti Noel in *El reino de este mundo* [The Kingdom of This World], spans over a century. That Xantippe symbolizes the Antillean underdog from slavery times to the present explains the fear he inspires in everybody in the community and even, initially, in Désinor himself. In this respect, his function is similar to that of Haitians, who, as Désinor reflects, have come to signify modern slavery in Guadeloupe and around the Caribbean: "Ah, l'esclavage du Nègre d'Haïti n'est pas fini!" (Condé 1989: 199) [Ah, the enslavement of the Haitian is not over yet!] (Condé 1995: 165).

Their state of near servitude may illuminate the motives behind the treatment that the Haitian underclass receives throughout the region despite its crucial economic role. The contempt they inspire could be meant to cover discomforting truths, as Haitians bring up painful recollections of a history of exploitation that Guadeloupeans and other Caribbean nationals would rather leave behind. In this area, the cane fields are indeed the epitome of slavery. As argued by Paul Brodwin, in Guadeloupe, sugar cane cutting is "the quintessential slave's occupation that is geographically and socially distant from the urban French-oriented worlds of business and administration" (Brodwin 2003: 398–399). At the same time, Brodwin adds that Haitians are a vivid reminder to Guadeloupeans of the Caribbean identity discarded in return for economic prosperity and sociopolitical stability through assimilation to France. Consequently, Haitians "represent to Guadeloupeans a past phase of their own society, and they provoke an anxious self-recognition" (400).[11] They thus compel their hosts to assess the impact of their own Faustian pact with France, the 1946 *départementalisation,* or full integration to the *métropole,* whose material gains entailed a psychic loss.

Indeed, Laënnec Hurbon contends, the sense of vulnerability that Guadeloupeans have developed because of their colonial situation makes them extremely sensitive to the issue of cultural preservation. In response, they have proceeded to view themselves as a homogeneous nation under siege by the foreign presence of the French, as well as Haitians and Dominicans (from Dominica). And, given the power dynamics, aggressiveness is more often directed toward the latter two groups than toward the colonial oppressors (Hurbon 1983: 1998).

This pattern corroborates Stuart Hall's point that since "identities are

constructed within, not outside discourse," they respond to specific strategies and "emerge within the play of specific modalities of power, and thus
are more the product of the marking of difference and exclusion, than they
are the sign of an identical, naturally-constituted unity—an identity in its
traditional meaning" (Hall 1996: 4).

As early as 1791, the Haitian Revolution led to the initially voluntary,
then enforced departure of the French masters and hence to the (partial)
decline of the French cultural influence.[12] As a result, Haitians are commonly deemed the most African people of the Caribbean, and this belief
is reflected in the literature from the region. The work of ethnologist Jean
Price-Mars, who in the 1920s and 1930s sought to revaluate the African legacy to Haiti, may have contributed in substantiating this view.[13] Yet France's
lingering influence is felt across Haitian society, as illustrated in Toussaint's
1801 constitution stipulating the adoption of the language, religion, and social norms of the *métropole*, together with its administrative, judicial, and
economic organization, or in Henri Christophe's reenactment of Versailles
in Sans-Souci, or as most patent in a Francophile elite that has to this day
preserved its French cultural heritage and maintained its primacy in the
country, notably by imposing French—only spoken by a tiny minority—as
the exclusive official language until 1987.[14]

In addition, as Haitian writer Jacques Stephen Alexis argues in his 1956
essay "Du réalisme merveilleux des Haïtiens," Haitian popular culture—no
doubt of predominantly African origin—nevertheless derives from a syncretism between Taino, various African, and several European (mainly French
and Spanish) elements: like any other Caribbean culture, it is therefore considerably creolized (Alexis 1956). In his 1980 essay "Bonjour et adieu à la
négritude," René Depestre likewise comments on the process of creolization
in Haitian culture (what he calls *américanité haïtienne*) in which, as he sees
it, *all three* of its components, including the African, have undergone modi-
fications in the American context (Depestre 1980). Thus, Depestre notes
the absence in the original West African cult of the Haitian Vodou concept
of *zombification*, symbolizing in his opinion the alienating experience of
slavery.[15] The recourse to *marronnage culturel*, or the spiritual and cultural
resistance of the blacks and Amerindians to counter the onslaughts of racist and assimilationist colonial rule, resulted in further syncretism. For instance, Haitian Vodou first merged African with Taino deities, onto which
Christian saints were later superimposed in order to comply (ostensibly)
with the religious demands of the system.

Despite the heterogeneous nature of Haitian culture, its salient African-ness is widely read as a signifier of the Haitians' refusal to collaborate with or assimilate to the colonial power. This partly explains why Haitians have functioned as the "Other" par excellence throughout the Caribbean, including the Bahamas, Cuba, Puerto Rico, Guadeloupe, and above all the Dominican Republic. Hall comments on the role of Otherness in identity formation: "identities actually come from outside, they are the way in which we are recognized and then come to step into the place of recognitions which others give us. Without the others, there is no self, there is no self-recognition" (Hall 1995: 8). Haitianness has therefore become a foil against which several Caribbean peoples elaborate their own sense of identity.[16]

Their common status as outcasts binds Xantippe and Désinor in an emblematic solidarity.[17] Their perceived Africanness, embodied in their dark complexion, is what singles them out from the community of Rivière au Sel, along with their pride, independence, and solitude. These elements clearly point to the symbolic role played by these two characters, that of allegorical maroons, or Antilleans who have refused to compromise with the plantation society and/or French assimilation. In this sense, they can be seen as other representations of the figure of the Negator, the original as well as contemporary maroon in Glissant's fiction. Thus, like Xantippe, Désinor acquires a timeless stature when his flight from an inopportune immigration check is likened to that of runaway slaves: "Fuite éternelle du Nègre devant la misère et le malheur!" (Condé 1989: 200) [The eternal flight of the black man from his misery and misfortune!] (Condé 1995: 165).

Certainly, Xantippe's and Désinor's dark skin may be interpreted as the physical marker of their non-creolized (that is, at once unaltered and foreign) nature, a trait that would be consistent with their absence from the plantation. Their symbolic role would also account for their pride and independence, as well as their isolation and poverty: by and large, assimilation brought the French Antilleans economic benefits. In this regard, the contrast is starkest between Haiti's trajectory since 1804 and that of Guadeloupe and Martinique. Yet except perhaps Haiti, all Caribbean states have in varying degrees negotiated with the neocolonial power well into the mid-twentieth century.[18]

It is therefore fitting that Désinor should function in the novel as a fierce critic of Guadeloupean society, denouncing in particular its excessive political and economic dependence on France: "Non, ce pays-là n'était pas un pays comme tous les pays. Les avions n'effectuaient que des aller-retour [sic] La

Pointe-Paris! Les gens ne voyageaient qu'en métropole!" (Condé 1989: 201) [No, this place was not like any other place. The planes only went to Paris and back. People only traveled to French France!] (Condé 1995: 166–167).

Brodwin points out that "Haitian migrants claim they are the secret sharers of Guadeloupe's deep cultural essence" (Brodwin 2003: 402), and that their presence forces "Guadeloupeans to acknowledge that they acquired French citizenship at a high cultural cost" (401). They believe that their unwilling hosts therefore "both denigrate and overtly envy the (Creole-speaking, politically independent, and culturally autonomous) Haitians in their midst" (402). The subjectivity they construct overemphasizes the cultural link with Africa as a seal of authenticity, notably regarding healing practices and the supernatural (401), thereby "partially recuperat[ing] the imposed representations" on their community (396). Conversely, this subjectivity accentuates the Guadeloupeans' cultural and political assimilation to France, which the latter are the first to acknowledge as debilitating, thus becoming a tool of empowerment. Such dynamics are at work in the short story by Danticat, as will be shown later.

In Condé, Xantippe's alliance with Désinor and his characterization as less creolized than his compatriots somewhat nuances what would have otherwise resulted in a rather simplistic binary opposition between Haitianness as Afro-Caribbean resistance and Guadeloupeanness as assimilation to France, illustrated, for instance, in Désinor's disregard for table manners contrasting with the villagers' strict adherence to French etiquette. In this respect, Xantippe functions as what Trinh T. Minh-ha calls the "inappropriate other," at once insider and outsider, who disrupts the clear cut dualistic oppositions on which communities most often rely to elaborate their subjectivity, thereby questioning conventional conceptions of identity. However, since Xantippe is a timeless character, a ghost from the past, the novel actually echoes Brodwin in envisioning the Haitian Other as a reflection of the Guadeloupean former cultural self, whether actual or imagined. The Guadeloupean Renée Gilles expresses the same view when she claims that Haitians "are the mirror that we don't want" (quoted in Brodwin 2003: 400). That Haitians and Guadeloupeans could be construed as reflections of each other filtered through the mirror of time attests to their actual kinship.[19]

While in Condé's novel the Haitian immigrant is a secondary character, Schwarz-Bart's play *Ton Beau capitaine* focuses exclusively on this figure. The sole protagonist on stage, Wilnor, comes to Guadeloupe to make money, leaving his wife Marie-Ange behind, with the hope to return to Haiti within a few months. Facing unanticipated adversity, he eventually stays for several years. During the play, Wilnor listens to a tape from his wife who reveals to him that she had a brief affair with his friend and fellow Haitian immigrant, by whom she is now pregnant.

The play poignantly recreates the realities of the Haitian exile. Wilnor's story is highly personified, and the stage directions specify that the dramatic use of traditional dances should not express collective moods and feelings, but an individual drama ("elles n'expriment pas des états d'âme collectifs, mais les divers moments d'un drame individuel") (Schwarz-Bart 1987: 8). Despite these recommendations, there is a strong sense that Wilnor's experience reflects that of the Haitian immigrant community in Guadeloupe as a whole. Through his monologue as well as through Marie-Ange's recorded voice, we learn of the discrimination and exploitation of Haitians, of the hardships they undergo, of their loneliness and isolation. The representation of Schwarz-Bart's Wilnor is far more complex than that of Condé's Désinor, partly as a result of the use of the first person. In *Ton Beau capitaine*, for instance, Vodou is not mentioned once, and at no time is Haitian culture depicted as somehow more African and less creolized than Guadeloupean culture.

Like Désinor, Wilnor is extremely lonely, and his isolation stems from his destitution as well as his Haitianness. Indeed Haitian immigrants are not welcome: "Wilnor, mon cher, je t'apprends que rien ne t'appartient ici, pas même l'herbe des chemins, pas même le vent" (12) [My dear Wilnor, let me inform you that nothing belongs to you here, not even the grass on the paths, not even the wind] says Wilnor at the opening of the play, as he enters his shabby dwellings comprising a single room devoid of electricity and proper furniture.[20] Marie-Ange remarks that she heard, "nos frères exilés en Guadeloupe n'habitent pas des demeures à colonnades et portails, mais plutôt, révérence parler, des pots de chambre" (15) [our brothers exiled in Guadeloupe do not live in mansions with columns and gates, but rather, if you excuse the expression, in chamber pots]. Toward the end of the play, Wilnor gives up the pretense of having made it in Guadeloupe, and admits: "Je ne suis qu'un Haïtien. Leur nègre à eux, le nègre des nègres, si tu veux tout savoir, Marie-Ange" (40) [I am just a Haitian. Their own nigger, the niggers' nigger, if you really want to know, Marie-Ange].

Marie-Ange comments on the transformations undergone by Wilnor: "Il m'a dit que tu avais beaucoup changé, maigri, fondu comme une chandelle. Que tu faisais maintenant l'impression d'un nègre tout rétréci. *Rétréci au-dehors et rétréci du dedans. Rétréci rétréci. Rétréci*" (15–16, emphasis added)

[He told me that you had changed a great deal, that you had lost weight, melted like a candle. That you now look like a shrunk up man. *Shrunk up at the outside and shrunk up from within. All shrunk up. Shrunk up. (*emphasis mine)]. While the phrase "rétréci au-dehors" [shrunk up at the outside] conveys the physical deprivations that exile involves for Wilnor, the expression "rétréci du dedans" [shrunk up from within] signals the psychological scars that it brings about. Wilnor's gauntness indicates not only his destitution—pointing to his malnutrition—but his unhappiness too, as a lack of appetite, rather than scarce resources, might account for his weight loss. Traditionally there is great significance attached to growing thinner in the Caribbean: if putting on weight is regarded as a mark of prosperity and self-fulfillment, then losing weight signifies the exact opposite: worries and a low morale. It is therefore no coincidence that it is precisely at this point in the play—just after mentioning Wilnor's physical state—that Marie-Ange should break into tears. Marie-Ange's repetition of the word "rétréci"—six times in five consecutive sentences—highlights how for her this aspect encapsulates the extent of Wilnor's tribulations and unhappiness.

Their tragedy makes Wilnor and his wife very human. Their marriage ultimately fails because of the necessity of remaining apart from each other in order to improve their standard of living. But, the text suggests, it also fails because at some point Wilnor gets caught up in the immigrant's ethics: he cannot go back home until he has saved sufficient money to be able to live there comfortably. Although originally intending to stay abroad for only a few months, he finds himself repeatedly postponing his return, obsessed with earning more money to the point that going back home becomes secondary: "A cause de certains rêves *bizarres plus qu'il n'est permis,* des rêves qui m'entraînent dans des pays de plus en plus éloignés, de plus en plus étranges, étrangers, et j'ai peur un de ces quatre matins de ne plus trouver le chemin du retour" (50, emphasis added) [Because of *some weird, inappropriate dreams,* some dreams that take me to countries further and further away, more and more strange, foreign, and I am afraid one day I will no longer find my way back (emphasis added)]. Eventually, his wife cannot cope with the years of separation.

Marie-Ange's expression "rétréci du dedans" thus emerges in all its ambiguity. Besides referring to the mental and physical hardships entailed by exile, it could also allude to a psychic loss that has affected Wilnor, a transformation in his character that is not altogether positive: as if by living among Guadeloupeans, he had adopted their allegedly fierce materialism, thereby losing his true Haitian self. In his foreword to Karen E. Richman's *Migra-*

tion and Vodou, Kevin A. Yelvington reminds us that the term "dyaspora" can be loaded with pejorative overtones, with many Haitians fearing that those emigrating lose their selves in the process (Yelvington 2005: xv-xvi). The word, as Georges Fouron and Nina Glick Schiller put it, can design "a person who is vain, crass, and a self-centered upstart" (Glick Schiller and Fouron 2001: 125).[21]

However, despite Wilnor's own sense that his dreams of wealth were beyond decency for a Haitian of his condition ("ces rêves bizarres plus qu'il n'est permis"), the actual modesty of his goals—a veranda around his small house back home, a couple of goats as well as a cow, some enamel crockery, a white dress with matching shoes for his wife, and a cassette recorder to play the tapes the couple has been exchanging all these years—only attests to the acuteness of the poverty Wilnor has escaped by emigrating, the poverty from which he wishes to spare Marie-Ange. The text thus appears to justify the presence of Haitians among their relatively wealthy Guadeloupean neighbors.

It is indeed interesting that the author, hitherto an acclaimed novelist, should have chosen the genre of the play to deal with this important issue. A play, by definition, has the potential to reach a wider audience than a novel. This is especially true in the Caribbean, where the popular tradition remains predominantly oral, and where people in general read little. With this play, Schwarz-Bart can therefore sensitize her fellow citizens to the treatment of Haitian immigrants. The play was also timely, as it was initially performed in 1987, just a year after the fall of dictator Jean-Claude Duvalier, when the surge in arrivals of Haitians was beginning to be felt in Guadeloupe.[22]

Through his tragedy, Wilnor takes on universal dimensions, which explains how the play could be transposed to a New York City setting with the story of a Mexican immigrant. The cultural differences with Guadeloupeans are toned down, and the gap appears as chiefly social. The approach is very different in Condé, where instead the sociocultural divergences are inflated almost to the point of caricature by both parties. Although Désinor's portrait at times acquires universalizing overtones, as we have seen, the truly universal character in the novel is Xantippe. As discussed next, the same insistence on difference is found in Danticat's short story.

The implication of Schwarz-Bart's strategy may be that the social integration of the Haitian community would lead to a resolution of conflicts. Given the ambivalence of the interactions between the two communities discussed above, however, one wonders whether the integration of Haitians alone would iron out the disagreements. This would certainly not solve the

French Antillean anxieties stemming from the sociopolitical predicament that is at the root of their response to Haitianness.

The depiction of a Guadeloupean character in a story by Haitian diaspora writer Edwidge Danticat provides an interesting counterpoint to the portrayal of Haitians by the Guadeloupeans Condé and Schwarz-Bart. "Seeing Things Simply" tells of the encounter between Princesse, a Haitian adolescent from a humble background, and Catherine, a Guadeloupean artist. Catherine is an educated, liberated woman whom Princesse sees as French on account of her prolonged residence in Paris. The story therefore repeatedly stresses the divide between the girl and the young woman. The gap is at once economic, social, and cultural. Although Catherine is a bohemian artist, to Princesse she is clearly wealthy, renting a beach house and regularly traveling to Paris and Guadeloupe.

Added to this is the difference in skin color between the two protagonists: "[Catherine] sunbathed endlessly, but her skin stayed the same copper-tinged shade. . . . Of any black person that Princesse knew, Catherine had spent the most time in the sun without changing color" (Danticat 1995: 128). This apparently trivial remark from Princesse acquires significance in the context of Haiti, where the importance attached to skin complexion and the corollary sociocultural divide has led to a rivalry between blacks and mulattoes since independence (Nicholls 1988 [1979], Charles 1992: 108). The divergence in attitudes between Catherine sunbathing and Princesse shunning the direct sun conveys the extent to which Catherine is westernized.

Catherine's "relative whiteness" also recalls the equation of whiteness to foreignness commonly found in Haiti, which further underscores the rift separating the two characters. As Fouron and Glick Schiller explain: "All foreigners, whatever the color of their skin, are by definition white . . . Those Haitians who left their homeland became in a certain sense foreign; that is, they became white and could not be trusted" (Glick Schiller and Fouron 2001: 110). Whether for having left her native island at an early age, or simply because of her foreignness, Catherine is thereby presented as essentially distinct from Haitians. The artist's appearance and behavior lead the girl to class her as a French woman, and this becomes the most salient difference between the two. Yet Fouron and Glick Schiller further note that "among the disempowered [in Haiti], *blan* [white] is used as a form of social commentary about distances in education and resources, rather than nationality" (126), which illuminates how the economic disparity underlies Princesse's perception of Catherine.

Frenchness has retained its prestige in the town, where good students are rewarded "by being introduced to the French-speaking artists and writers who liv[e] in the ginger-bread houses perched on the hills that overloo[k] Ville Rose's white sand beaches" (Danticat 1995: 127–128). This topographical description of Ville Rose, with the foreigners—mostly French-speaking, it seems—living in houses high up with a view on the beach, illustrates the visitors' economic power. However, the esteem in which they are held derives first and foremost from their familiarity with French culture and language, which clearly determines social status in Ville Rose. Thus, one of the villagers believed to have studied at the Sorbonne arouses admiration: "The word was that such a man would only live with a woman who carried a basket on her head because he himself had taken a big fall in the world" (127). The 1990s Haiti described here therefore appears to be rigidly divided between a Francophile elite and the folk that remains closer to its Afro-Haitian roots, embodied in the woman who carries a basket on her head. No longer valued exclusively by the elite, however, French appeals to the wider population, including humble schoolgirls like Princesse.[23]

Consequently, when Princesse meets Catherine, not only does she speak French to her rather than Creole, she also painfully tries to erase what she regards as the first mark of her Haitianness, that is, her accent, "calling upon her phonetics lessons in order to sound less native and more French" (128). Interestingly, in actuality there is little difference between Guadeloupean and Haitian diction, unless the Guadeloupean has lived mostly outside of the island and speaks metropolitan French, as is apparently implied. To Princesse, Catherine is thus the epitome of Frenchness, embodied in the "Petit Écolier" biscuits she offers the girl on her visits. Turned into a French woman by virtue of her place of residence, Catherine stands in Princesse's mind for modernity and independence, while her profession as an artist is evocative of bohemia, knowledge, and a certain freedom regarding social norms, notably concerning sexuality, as discussed shortly.

The story thereby totally obliterates Catherine's Guadeloupean cultural background, equating her to being (metropolitan) French. It is perhaps no coincidence that this single Guadeloupean character in Danticat's fiction should be so closely connected to France. As for Condé's Désinor, Guadeloupeans come to personify assimilation to French values. Beyond a certain gender complicity, nowhere in the story is there a sense of solidarity based on a cultural common ground between Princesse and Catherine. So, while Condé envisages Haitians as culturally more African, Guadeloupeans are viewed by Danticat as virtually French.

Yet as the story shows, the Haitians' own relationship to their colonial past and its ongoing influence is ambivalent. In this respect, Catherine too is for Princesse "a mirror she doesn't want," what literary critic Kathleen Gyssels calls "negated francophilia." Indeed, Catherine's very assimilation is also what ensures her material comfort, a comfort aspired to by most Haitians, such as Princesse herself, that motivates them to emigrate massively. By contrast, Haitians find themselves in the delicate position of having to recognize that they achieved a sovereignty that failed to secure the well-being of the majority.

The friendship—if it can be called such—that develops between Catherine and Princesse is, to say the least, ambiguous. In exchange for modest sums of money, the adolescent acts as a nude model for the painter, which clearly embarrasses her because of the value she attaches to purity and chastity: there are repeated allusions to the immaculate white undershirt from her school uniform, which gradually becomes stained in the story. It is also evident that, although actually a trifle for Catherine, the money she receives means a lot to Princesse. The ease with which the painter departs without warning, leaving the girl to await her return for a week, also reveals little emotional attachment on her part, whereas she obviously represents a lot more than a source of income to Princesse.

The relationship is thus abusive on various levels: "Catherine never displayed any intention of sharing her work with Princesse. After she felt that she had painted enough of them, Catherine would pack up her canvases and bring them to either Paris or to Guadeloupe for safekeeping" (130). Yet apparently Princesse does gain from the encounter. In particular, the artist opens her horizons, first by attempting to free her of the social conventions that impede her self-fulfillment, especially with regard to her sexuality: "One day Catherine hoped to get Princesse to roam naked on the beach attempting to make love to the crest of an ocean wave, but for now it was enough for her to make Princesse comfortable with her nudity" (129). Catherine also becomes Princesse's informal art teacher, and as the story progresses, the girl's aesthetic sensibility awakens and eventually blooms: "Princesse thought that she could paint that [the horizon], giving it light and color, shape and texture, all those things that Catherine spoke of" (137).

Nevertheless, noting how Catherine's paintings reproduce the exoticization and eroticization of Haiti that is so common in the West, Gyssels argues that Catherine is driven by profit, not art. Although I do not fully concur with this interpretation, I agree that Danticat depicts a Guadeloupean artist whose vision remains at the surface of things, producing, like so many Western visitors, simplistic realistic art, while the tormented reality of Haiti would be more adequately captured on abstract canvases, such as those Princesse composes in her head: "Princesse wanted to paint the sound that came out of the shell, a moan like a call to a distant ship, an SOS with a dissonant melody. She wanted to paint the feel of the sand beneath her toes, the crackling of dray empty crab shells as she popped them between her palms" (137).

"Seeing things simply," Catherine fails to grasp the complexity of Haitian reality. Nowhere in the story is there a sense that her double condition as Antillean and artist makes her more sensitive to and understanding of Haiti and Haitians. Her inability to "change color" in the sun could be a metaphor for her incapacity to connect with Princesse, and by extension the Haitian people, in any meaningful way that would make her cease to be an outsider. Unlike Condé's Xantippe, Catherine does not function as an "inappropriate other." Her regular trips to Guadeloupe and Paris to store her works likewise imply her mistrust of the Haitians, suggesting that she is no Caribbean sister.

The ambiguity of the relationship depicted in the text is all the more unsettling when we contrast Catherine to the U.S.-Haitian journalist Emilie in another story, "The Missing Peace," which in the depiction of the encounter between a Haitian teenager (Lamort, the pendant to Princesse) and a young, foreign woman (Emilie in the second story, Catherine in the first) echoes "Seeing Things Simply" on several levels. In "The Missing Peace," which in fact immediately precedes "Seeing Things Simply" in the collection, Emilie is unequivocally a model for Lamort, a catalyst for change as she leads her to inner growth and self-discovery. What her friendship with the painter has in store for Princesse, however, is less tangible. Despite a sharpened awareness of the beauty that surrounds her, she is left with a longing for abroad which will most likely never concretize. Little of what she gains from her friendship with Catherine will help her carry on with her life in Haiti. Why the interaction between a Haitian girl and a Guadeloupean is envisaged as ambivalent is open to questions. The contrast between the two stories may reflect the harsh realities of exile for the Haitian community in Guadeloupe. The story certainly offers a rather pessimistic view of the relationships between Haitians and Guadeloupeans, implying a lack of solidarity despite their cultural affinities.

The divide between Haitians and Guadeloupeans presented in these literary texts is rather disquieting, as it no doubt reflects preconceptions within both communities that then foment confrontations such as those instigated by Ibo Simon in 2001 and the 2005 Radio Contact broadcasts mentioned above. A comparable rift is reflected in literature from across the Caribbean, including the Bahamas, Cuba, the Dominican Republic, and Puerto Rico, illustrating that, together with people and cultural practices, prejudices too—and anti-Haitian sentiment in particular—circulate around the archipelago.

Schwarz-Bart's play is a plea for true pan-Caribbean solidarity in which cultural differences are put aside, arguably somewhat idealistically. On the other hand, besides exposing the naiveté of an intellectual pan-Caribbeanism and Creoleness divorced from Caribbean reality (Moudileno 2006), Condé's novel also points to the social malaise underlying the Guadeloupeans' reception of Haitians, as dark complexion and destitution also become signifiers of resistance to French assimilation. As alter egos, Haitians figure as what the Guadeloupeans could have become; if the reflection is not at all flattering as regards socioeconomics, it is extremely appealing in terms of cultural and national pride.

Likewise, Danticat's story signals the discrepancies between pan-Caribbean theories and region-wide anti-Haitian sentiment. At the same time, this text also reveals preconceptions about Guadeloupeans, who are deemed *blan*, or assimilated, the implication being that this differentiates them from Haitians. This illustrates what Hall calls "positioning," a phenomenon observed by Brodwin among the Haitian community in Guadeloupe. Ironically, the equation of Guadeloupeanness with assimilation in Danticat's story reproduces precisely the Guadeloupeans' perception of Martiniquans, a perception that conveniently overlooks figures such as Louis Delgrès, Aimé Césaire, Frantz Fanon, Édouard Glissant, and Joseph Zobel. Furthermore, the centrality of Frenchness in the story as well as the evident patterns of dependency on France and the U.S. in Haiti's trajectory after independence undermines the view of Haitianness as glorious anticolonial resistance commonly found among intellectuals across the region.

Acknowledgments

This article originated in a conference paper presented at the 2006 Meeting of the Latin American Studies Association, San Juan, Puerto Rico, March 2006. I wish to thank Philippe Zacaïr for inviting me to take part in the panel "So Similar and Yet So Foreign: Haiti and Haitians in the Wider Caribbean." I am also indebted to the Higgins School of Humanities at Clark University for funding my trip to the conference.

Notes

1. While trivial, the rivalries between Martiniquans and Guadeloupeans—reported by Frantz Fanon in his 1952 *Peau noire, masques blancs* and expressed more recently in the refusal of both islands to create a common regional assembly despite the increased autonomy toward France this would have meant—remain crippling. It is likewise widely held that unresolved intestine quarrels—notably between Jamaica and Trinidad—largely accounted for the failure of the Federation of the West Indies in 1962. Nevis's desire to secede from St. Kitts, or French St. Martin's request to be directly attached to France rather than being administered by Guadeloupe further attest to the fact that these divisions do not affect exclusively the larger territories. The tensions between Haiti and the Dominican Republic are of a more serious nature. For a discussion of anti-Haitian prejudice as reflected in literature from across the region, see N'Zengou-Tayo 2001.

2. James Ferguson (2003: 8) notes the near impossibility of obtaining reliable statistics on Haitians who reside in the Dominican Republic. He also remarks that estimates are often politically motivated, so that in his opinion the higher numbers of one to one and a half million sometimes quoted are likely to be inflated. As a result of the 1822 Haitian invasion that effectively thwarted their newly acquired independence, the Dominican people have largely forged their identity in opposition to Haitianness in terms of race, language, religion, and culture. This aspect has been examined by many scholars. Among recent discussions, see Ferguson 2003: 19–22, Matibag 2003, and Rodríguez 2005: 18–24, 38–57, and 60–84.

3. In 1802 the Martiniquan mulatto officer Louis Delgrès deserted the French Revolutionary army and organized his own troops in Guadeloupe in order to fight Napoleon's forces aiming to reestablish slavery after the first abolition of 1794. Delgrès's 300 troops and followers, including a few women, were finally besieged in what has lately been renamed Fort Delgrès in Basse-Terre. They escaped to the heights of Matouba, where they chose to blow themselves up rather than surrender. Meanwhile, Jean Ignace fought the French troops in Baimbridge. None of the upheaval that shook Saint Domingue and Guadeloupe reached Martinique, occupied by the British from the early days of the Haitian independence war, which means that the first abolition of slavery was never implemented there. After a 1792 decree granted equal political and social rights to whites and mulattoes, and even more so in the wake of the 1794 abolition of slavery, Haitian plantation owners often opted to relocate with their slaves to Martinique (or Santo Domingo or Trinidad) rather than Guadeloupe, as the latter was also affected by the revolutionary turmoil. The trend is reversed in contemporary times, however: Ferguson (2003: 23) cites estimates of 15,000 Haitians in Guadeloupe—that is, threefold the community in Martinique (5,000)—30,000 to 40,000 in French Guiana, and 15,000 in French Saint Martin.

4. Women writers have also focused on other immigrant communities. Thus Sylviane Telchid's *Throvia de la Dominique* (Paris: L'Harmattan, 1996) looks at the Dominican community in Guadeloupe, while Nicole Cage-Florentini's *L'Espagnole* (Paris: Hâtier International, 2002) deals with the Dominicans (from the Dominican Republic) and Haitians in Martinique. They have been joined by some male writers such as Max Jeanne, whose novel *Brisants* (Montréal: Mémoire d'encrier, 2007) chronicles the anti-Haitian events in Guadeloupe between 2001 and 2005, including the trial of Ibo Simon.

5. In Haiti as well as Puerto Rico, the *bolita*, an illegal lottery from the Dominican Republic, is very popular. The *bolèt* played by the Haitian community in Guadeloupe is quite likely the exact same game—as the name suggests—only translated and transplanted. The Bahamian Haitians also play an illegal lottery, which again could be the same game.

6. Ibo Simon was later banned from broadcasting until June 2005, and *Association Parti Libéral Modéré*, the political arm of Radio Contact, was subsequently tried for the broadcasts (*Conseil supérieur de l'audiovisuel* 2005). In April 2005 the Congress of Guadeloupe met to discuss Haitian illegal immigration and the climate of xenophobia and violence (Anonymous 2005).

7. Unlike Haitians in the 1980s and 1990s, Dominicans (from Dominica) were often seen as drug dealers. As for immigrants from the Dominican Republic, typically female, they were envisaged as hairdressers or prostitutes, both stereotypes that originate in the Caribbean-wide myth of the *mulata*, deemed particularly apt at hairdressing because of her long, straight hair and extremely attractive because of her phenotype. For an account of the portrayal of the Haitians in the Guadeloupean press today, see Zacaïr's contribution to this volume.

8. The Préfecture of Guadeloupe recorded 12,433 Haitians residing legally in Guadeloupe in 2005, and estimated another 3,000 undocumented immigrants, which would make the Haitian community amount to approximately 3.5 percent of the total population (Montchovi 2005). However, despite citing similar figures from the INSEE (*Institut National de la Statistique et des Études Économiques*) 1999 data, Paul Brodwin (2000: 7, footnote 4) estimates the actual number of Haitians in Guadeloupe to 25,000, based on unofficial figures provided by Guadeloupean and Haitian social workers, lawyers, and pastors.

9. Translation by Richard Philcox, from *Crossing the Mangrove*, 1995. All subsequent translations are from this edition.

10. Baron Samedi is the Spirit of Cemeteries in Haitian Vodou. Catching a glimpse of him on arrival to Guadeloupe would be all the more frightful for Désinor, as dictator François Duvalier consolidated his power by deliberately cultivating a resemblance with the spirit, exploiting the population's supernatural beliefs and fear. By the time of the action in 1980, the terror of "Papa Doc" Duvalier's regime was somewhat subdued, succeeded by that of "Baby Doc." Désinor's vision thereby turns his hopes for freedom and a brighter future into a descent in Hell and a return to a nightmarish past. In addition, the vision shatters Désinor's expectations of leaving malevolent forces behind him in Haiti, since Caribbean people commonly hold the traditional belief that spirits cannot cross water.

11. A clear parallel can be drawn with the relationship between Dominicans and Puerto Ricans. Thus Yolanda Martínez-San Miguel states in *Caribe Two Ways*: "El puertorriqueño utiliza al dominicano para exteriorizar sus prejuicios contra las personas de raza negra, mientras cuestiona la similitud racial de estas dos poblaciones caribeñas que comparten las mismas zonas del mapa urbano en el municipio de San Juan [Santurce]" [156–157: The Puerto Rican uses the Dominican to exteriorize his/her prejudices against blacks, as s/he questions the racial similarity of these two Caribbean populations sharing the same urban areas of the city of San Juan (translation mine)]. An obvious difference with the Guadeloupean-Haitian relation, however, is that of race: Puerto Ricans often view themselves as white, despite the existence of an important Afro-Puerto Rican population to refute this view, and therefore find it easier to see Afro-Caribbean people— whether Dominicans or Afro-Puerto Ricans—as foreign. Guadeloupeans, however, are in vast majority black, and therefore cannot base solely on race the distinction they draw between themselves and Haitians.

12. On the voluntary or enforced departure of the French colonists, see Matibag 2003: 63–65, 78, 79.

13. See Jean Price-Mars, *Ainsi parla l'oncle* (1928). The representation of Haitian culture as essentially African abounds in texts from Cuba and Puerto Rico, and even more so from the Dominican Republic. In fact, most Caribbean writers who deal with Haitian characters emphasize—certainly beyond reality—what they perceive as the Africanness of Haitian culture, as illustrated by the works of Cubans Alejo Carpentier (*El reino de este mundo*, 1949) and Marta Rojas (*El columpio de Rey Spencer*, 1993), or Dominican Julia Álvarez (*How the García Girls Lost Their Accents*, 1991); other examples are found in Anglophone Caribbean writing, for instance C.L.R. James's essays, or George Lamming's *The Pleasures of Exile* (1960). In his essay "Negotiating Caribbean Identities," Jamaican cultural critic Stuart Hall likewise refers to Haiti as "the symbolic island of black culture, where one feels closer to the African inheritance than anywhere else [in the Caribbean]" (Hall 1995: 6). Similarly, Craton and Saunders state that unlike their hosts, the Haitian community in the Bahamas "retained African-based beliefs and customs that Bahamians had come to regard as outlandish, or superstitious, or which they were outgrowing" (Craton and Saunders 1998: 461).

14. Carolle Charles notes that while in Haiti blackness is "the basis for a cultural nationalism," the francophone nation "also disaffiliates itself from Africa and praises its ties to Western culture" (Charles 1992: 108).

15. In Haitian Vodou, a zombie is a person whose soul has been removed through supernatural means (in punishment for a crime, or as the work of evil spirits) and therefore under the will of the living. In Frankétienne's novel *Dézafi* (Port-au-Prince: Editions Fardin, 1975), the connection between *zombification* and slavery is explicit: one character *zombifies* a whole village in order to secure himself gratis, forced labor.

16. The contiguity of Haiti and the Dominican Republic and the historical upheavals played out along their border, together with their confinement on one exiguous island certainly exacerbates the antagonism between the two nations, so that the process of dissociation from Haitianness is most extreme in the Dominican case. Yet such a dissociation pattern is repeated throughout the Caribbean. Thus Michael Craton and Gail

Saunders note how Haitians, who make up 20 percent of the total population, and whose presence in the Bahamas dates back to pre-Columbian times, constitute the ultimate Other for the Bahamians, despite the existence of other Caribbean immigrant communities: "No people . . . has served more effectively as the defining other for the Bahamian self than have the Haitian migrants to and through the Bahamas, particularly since the 1950s" (Craton and Saunders 1998: 450). On the Bahamians' views on Haitians, see Craton and Saunders (1998: 450–466), and Treco (2002). See also Hall (1996: 4–5).

17. Condé establishes a similar alliance between Haitians and social outcasts in a later novel also set in Guadeloupe, *La Belle Créole* (2001), in which the young protagonist, ironically named Dieudonné, finds himself rejected by all except for Dorisca, a Haitian teenager who befriends him.

18. The former British territories did not reach independence until the 1960s. While Haiti, the Dominican Republic, and Cuba achieved nominal independence in the nineteenth century, this was in reality seriously compromised by the U.S. imperialist policy within the Monroe doctrine, which led the U.S. to control these states at various points during the twentieth century, notably through financial supervision and the occupations of Haiti (1915–1934) and the Dominican Republic (1916–1924, and then again 1965–1966), as well as the more indirect intervention in Cuban internal politics until 1959.

19. Arguably, in the case of Haitians and Dominicans these mutual reflections would be distorted not so much by the mirror of time as by that of race and language. Yet to Matibag, Haitian characters in some Dominican texts also embody "a forgotten otherness within the Dominican psyche" (Matibag 2003: 173), which would imply that to Dominicans as to Guadeloupeans, Haitians represent a past phase of their society best forgotten.

20. All translations from *Ton Beau capitaine* are my own.

21. For a more detailed discussion of the different meanings of the term "diaspora" among Haitians at home and worldwide and of the various Haitian communities that claim or reject the term, see Dimitri Béchacq's 2003 article "La diaspora haïtienne à Paris: significations, appartenances et sociabilités," on the *Gens de la Caraïbe* website, posted June 2003.

22. The play enjoyed immense success when inaugurated in Guadeloupe in 1987 under the direction of Haitian Syto Cavé (Bérard 2004). Since then, it was produced again in Guadeloupe and in various locations in France (including Paris in 1988, 1999, and 2005, with a reading at the *Comédie Française* in April 2005, as well as the Avignon Drama Festival, Limoges, and Bordeaux) and Europe (notably in Switzerland). The play was staged in the U.S. at Hunter College and Ohio State University, the latter directed by Adrian Brown in October-November 2004 in commemoration of the bicentennial of Haiti (Conteh-Morgan 2004). "Manhatitlán," an adaptation of the play focusing on a Mexican immigrant was featured at the New York Fringe Festival in 2003 (Brooke 2003 and Anonymous 2003). Most importantly perhaps, there were several productions of the play in Guadeloupe and its dependencies: it was directed by Michèle Montantin in 1998, and staged at the Artchipel in Basse-Terre in 2004, the Saint Barthelemy Drama Festival in May 2005, and the Centre des Arts in Pointe-à-Pitre in May 2005. Both the Artchipel and the Centre des Arts have school matinees.

23. On the continuing prestige of French in Haiti and its diaspora, see Zéphir 1997: 396–97.

References

AC'DOM (Association des Communes d'Outre Mer). 2005. "La Problématique de l'immigration en Guadeloupe." Contribution de l'Association des Communes d'Outre Mer—AC'DOM—au Congrès des élus départementaux et régionaux de Guadeloupe, Réunion du 15 avril, http://www.france-acdom.net/acdom/contribution_congres_guadeloupe.htm

Alexis, Jacques Stephen. 1956. "Du réalisme merveilleux des Haïtiens." *Présence Africaine*, no. 8–10: 245–271.

Anonymous. 2005. "Guadeloupe—Réunion du Congrès sur l'immigration clandestine. Impuissance et calculs des politiciens." *Combat Ouvrier*, no. 923.

Anonymous [Lipfert]. 2003. "Manhatitlán." Online document, http://www.curtainup.com/fringe2003.html

Béchacq, Dimitri. 2003. "La diaspora haïtienne à Paris: significations, appartenances et sociabilités." *Recherche sur la Caraïbe*, http://www.gensdelacaraibe.org/recherche/articles.php?id_story=28

Bérard, Stéphanie. 2004. "Entretien avec Noël Jovignot, metteur en scène de *Ton beau capitaine* de Simone Schwarz-Bart." http://www.africultures.com//popup_article.asp

Brodwin, Paul. 2000. "Pentecostalism and the Production of Community in the Haitian Diaspora." University of Wisconsin-Milwaukee: Discussion Paper, 90, http://www.uwm.edu/Dept/CLACS/resources/pdf/brodwin90.pdf

———. 2003. "Marginality and Subjectivity in the Haitian Diaspora." *Anthropological Quarterly* 76, no. 3: 383–410.

Charles, Carolle. 1992. "Transnationalism in the Construct of Haitian Migrants' Racial Categories of Identity in New York City." In *Towards a Transnational Perspective on Migration: Race, Class, Ethnicity, and Nationalism Reconsidered*, eds. Nina Glick Schiller, Linda Basch, and Cristina Blanc-Szanton, 101–123. New York: The New York Academy of Sciences.

Condé, Maryse. 1989. *Traversée de la mangrove*. Paris: Mercure de France. Translated by Richard Philcox as *Crossing the Mangrove*, New York: Anchor Books/ Doubleday, 1995.

Conseil supérieur de l'audiovisuel. 2005. "Décision no. 2005–245 du 17 mai 2005 mettant en demeure l'association Parti Libéral Modéré, Radio Contact (NOR: CSAX0501245S)." http://www.admi.net/jo/20050608/CSAX0501245S.html

Conteh-Morgan, John. 2004. "Your Handsome Captain." *Four Plays, Two Characters, Alternate Days*, The Ohio State University Theatre, October 27 to November 13 2004. http://theatre.osu.edu/2_productions/level_3_productions/productions/2004_05/assests/4x2%20PGR.pdf

Craton, Michael and Gail Saunders. 1998. *Islanders in the Stream: A History of the Bahamian People, Volume 2: From the Ending of Slavery to the Twenty-First Century*. Athens and London: University of Georgia Press.

Danticat, Edwidge. 1995. "Seeing Things Simply." *Krik? Krak!*, New York: Vintage Books, Random House, originally published by Soho Press.

Depestre, René. 1980. "Bonjour et adieu à la négritude." *Bonjour et adieu à la négritude.* 82–160. Paris: Robert Laffont.

Fanon, Frantz. 1952. *Peau noire, masques blancs.* Paris: Le Seuil.

Ferguson, James. 2003. "Migration in the Caribbean: Haiti, the Dominican Republic and Beyond." London: Minority Rights Groups International. http://www.minorityrights. org/admin/Download/pdf/MRGCaribbeanReport.pdf

Glick Schiller, Nina and Georges Eugene Fouron. 2001. *Georges Woke Up Laughing: Long-Distance Nationalism and the Search for Home.* Durham/London: Duke University Press.

Grugeaux-Etna, Marie-France. 2000. "Communauté haïtienne: une image à changer." *Sept Magazine*, no. 1092: 15.

Gyssels, Kathleen. 2005. "Simplement voir les choses: *la francophilie dérivée dans l'écriture d'Edwidge Danticat.*" *Tanbou*, no. 23, http://www.tanbou.com/2005/FrancophonieDanticat.htm

Hall, Stuart. 1995. "Negotiating Caribbean Identities." *New Left Review* no. 209: 3–14.

———. 1996. "Introduction: Who Needs Identity?" In *Questions of Cultural Identity*, eds. Stuart Hall and Paul Du Gay, 1–17. London: Sage Publications.

———. 2003 [1990]. "Cultural Identity and Diaspora." In *Theorizing Diaspora. A Reader*, eds. Jana Evans Braziel and Anita Mannur, 233–246. Oxford: Blackwell. First published in *Identity, Community, Culture, Difference*, ed. Jonathan Rutherford. London: Lawrence and Wishart.

Hurbon, Laënnec. 1983. "Racisme et sous-produit du racisme: immigrés haïtiens et dominicains en Guadeloupe." *Les Temps Modernes* 39, no. 441–442: 1988–2003.

Martínez-San Miguel, Yolanda. 2003. *Caribe Two Ways. Cultura de la migración en el Caribe insular hispánico.* Río Piedras: Ediciones Callejón.

Matibag, Eugenio. 2003. *Haitian-Dominican Counterpoint: Nation, State, and Race on Hispaniola.* New York/Basingstoke: Palgrave Macmillan.

Montchovi, Lucie. 2005. "Non à la xénophobie envers les Haïtiens." *L'actualité des Caraïbes au 10 mars.* Grioo.com, 11 mars 2005, http://www.grioo.com/inf04274.html

Moudileno, Lydie. 2006. "Stéréotypes et préjugés dans l'espace créole: Maryse Condé et les 'voisins haïtiens.'" *Journal of Caribbean Literatures* 4, no. 1: 147–158.

Nicholls, David. 1988 [1979]. *From Dessalines to Duvalier: Race, Colour, and National Independence in Haiti.* London and Basingstoke: Macmillan. First published by Cambridge University Press.

N'Zengou-Tayo, Marie-José. 2001. "Unwelcome Neighbors: The Haitian Popular Migration in the Writings of Some Caribbean Writers." *Journal of Caribbean Literatures* 3, no. 1: 129–142.

Payot, Marianne. 2005. "Le problème haïtien." *L'Express*, section "Antilles." http://www. lexpress.fr/info/france/dossier/domtom/dossier.asp?ida=434937

Pierce, Brooke. 2003. "Manhatitlán." *Fringe NYC Roundup #4*, http://www.theatermania. com/content/news.cfm?int_news_id=3820

Price-Mars, Jean. 1928. *Ainsi parla l'oncle.* Compiègne: Imprimerie de Compiègne.

Reinhardt, Catherine. 2006. "Unified Prejudice: Anti-Haitian Sentiment in Ana Lydia Vega's 'Encancaranublado,' Edwidge Danticat's *The Farming of Bones*, and Ian Strachan's *God's Angry Babies*." Unpublished paper presented at the 2006 Meeting of the Latin American Studies Association, San Juan, Puerto Rico.

Rodríguez, Néstor E. 2005. *Escrituras de desencuentro en la República Dominicana*. D. F., México: Siglo Veintiuno Editores/Estado Libre y Soberano de Quintana Roo.

Schwarz-Bart, Simone. 1987. *Ton Beau capitaine*. Paris: Le Seuil.

Treco, Ria N. M. 2002. "The Haitian Diaspora in the Bahamas." Florida International University, http://lacc.fiu.edu/research_publications/working_papers/working_paper_04.pdf

Trinh, T. Minh-ha. 1988. "Not You/Like You. PostColonial Women and the Interlocking Questions of Identity and Difference." In *Inscriptions* 3–4, ed. Deborah Gordon. Reprinted in 1997 in *Dangerous Liaisons: Gender, Nation, and Postcolonial Perspectives*, eds. A. McClintock, A. Mufti, and E. Shohat, 415–419. Minneapolis: University of Minnesota Press.

Yelvington, Kevin A. 2005. "Foreword." In *Migration and Vodou*, by Karen E. Richman, xiii-xvi. Gainesville: University Press of Florida.

Zéphir, Flore. 1997. "The Social Value of French for Bilingual Haitian Immigrants." *The French Review* 70, no. 3: 395–406.

4

Identifications and Kinships among Haitians in French Guiana

Observations on a Diaspora

MAUD LAËTHIER

In her pioneer work on French Guiana, *La question créole*, Marie-José Jolivet maintained, more than twenty years ago, "that there are as many Creole cultures as there are places where they have been able to take form and develop in accordance with, on the one hand, the diversity of cultures imposed during servitude and the bits of the African past masters allowed to filter through, and on the other hand, the regional variations in the conditions of pre- and post-slavery formations" (Jolivet 1982: 88).

These lines remind us of the logic of creation from which Creole societies and cultures were formed.[1] From this viewpoint, the processes of creolization that gave rise to these social formations unveil their unity as much as their diversity. To return to the cases of Guiana and Haiti, upon which the following reflection is based, the diversity of Creole unity can be read as dissimilarity within proximity. Both stemming from French colonization, Guianese and Haitian societies have been formed by several colonizing sequences followed by very different "liberations." In these two contexts, the processes of social structuring, and correlatively "the Creole identity," as well as the relationships of domination transposed in relationship to "the civilization of whites," have led to the organization of singular social and cultural models. Today, Haitian migration to Guiana brings into contact these two contexts. Although it is little known, this migration adds new perspectives to the study of Haitian emigration.[2] It reveals and thereby illustrates the contemporary diversity of Creole unity.

In Guiana, Haitians constitute one of the most numerous migrant groups. In 2006, they officially number more than 15,000 and represent approximately 30 percent of the immigrant population (INSEE, 2006). Although these numbers signal the important sociological weight of this migration, locally, Haitians remain surrounded by a certain misappreciation. Despite their proximity with elements of Guianese culture, Haitians are socially labeled. The national origin is transformed into an "ethnic origin" and the process of ethnicization functions with the help of cultural traits set down as characteristic: differences that are allegedly unchanging fix "Haitian identity" as a monolithic image.

These findings provide grounds for reflecting upon the specificity of the Haitians' migratory situation in Guiana according to two complementary reasonings. The first reasoning reflects upon the Haitian question in Guiana by associating the French framework, the singularity of the Guianese social space, and the migrants whose sense of identity is part of this dynamic situation. The second reasoning originates in a reflection on the dissimilarities and proximity of Creole cultural systems. It examines the notion of "black diaspora" used to account for the singularity of the black Americas.

I will successively pursue three main lines of research. It is initially important to understand the situation of Haitian migration in regard to the process of cultural and political affirmation in Guiana that specifically addresses the question of immigration within the social structure since the 1980s. Secondly, I will present the migratory networks, the living situations of the migrants, and the sense of identity claimed. Finally, this evidence will lead to a broader reflection on the theoretical notion of "diaspora" and, more precisely, the "black diaspora." Is this category of analysis—retracing the first migratory experience to the slave trade—applicable to the study of contemporary migrations since it brings out a unity of the black Americas, valid in different places and times?

The Guianese Context and the Haitian Presence

French Guiana, a former French colony of the Americas that has become an overseas *département*,[3] has been historically characterized by the presence of Amerindian, *Bushinenge*,[4] and Creole populations.[5] Since the end of the nineteenth century, Guianese society has been constituted by numerous migratory movements. While population movements are an integral part of the Guianese sociocultural fabric, the sheer magnitude and diversity of migrations during the past thirty years have brought out the specificity of Guiana. Since the 1970s, migrations have generated demographic shifts and have contributed to the threefold increase of the population. The number of "strangers" is now estimated at 50,000, or nearly one third of the total population (29.7 percent, INSEE 2006).[6] From a sociodemographic perspective, migratory movements have led the Creole group—for a long time the majority—to lose its numerical preeminence to the point that it has become a minority among others, even though it remains politically dominant (Jolivet 1997). This transformation of the sociological context, which continues to be modified by the constant arrival of migrants, has changed the way Creoles construct their sense of identity. Their relationship to "others" has progressively become modified. Leading to controversy and speculation, the issue of migration continues to cause concern as far as a possible calling into question of "Guianese identity." While the politicization of ethno-cultural pluralism acutely poses the question of the "Other," sociodemographic transformations place the processes of creolization at the heart of Guiana's destiny. The dynamic of these processes no longer allows for the absorption of different migrants as was previously the case. The phenomenon of "ethnic" belonging and the notion of "community" now dominate individual and collective relationships. Despite the widespread representation of Guiana as a multicultural society, the migrant population is rejected. Economic dependency, rising unemployment, an upsurge in immigration, increasing academic failure, and the spread of delinquency have become important arguments to denounce the migrants' presence.

In this context, as previously mentioned, Haitians constitute the most numerous migrant group. In the opinion of the local population, in particular of Creoles, the Haitian presence is perceived as an invasion. The relative social marginalization of migrants within society reinforces their negative cultural representation.

Haitian Immigration in Guiana: From Past to Present

The first Haitians arrive in Guiana during the early 1960s. Between 1963 and 1967, a French landowner by the name of Lily Ganot, previously established in the Haitian region of Fond-des-Nègres (*Département de la Grande Anse*, south of Haiti) organizes an initial migration. He decides to develop a farm in Guiana and recruits workers in his Haitian home region. Jean-Jacques Chalifoux (1988) holds that this first migratory movement may be considered to have initiated the others. This explains the overrepresentation of individuals originally from the south of Haiti. In fact, on the island of Cayenne, most migrants are originally from those rural communities and are former agricultural workers.[7] They cultivated the land, sold their crops, and bred livestock. The relative familiarity among migrants in Guiana can often be explained by this common regional origin. People frequently know each other before migrating, then meet up in Guiana and discover, often with surprise, that the other also managed to travel. Similarly, two individuals who were not necessarily acquainted in Haiti often know from which village the other person is from. The other, the compatriot (*konpatryot*), is situated in terms of his/her home village.

While Haitian migration in Guiana begins in the 1960s, it is from the beginning of the 1980s that their arrivals become numerically significant. The need for a large workforce at building sites (notably the spatial base of Kourou) encourages these arrivals. Furthermore, the relative closure of the American and Canadian borders contributes to the migrants' orientation toward Guiana. According to the 1978 census, there are 1,600 annual arrivals and in 1979 there are 1,800 (Calmont 1988a). In 1980, the added requirement of a visa momentarily makes the number of arrivals drop to 1,000 per year (Gorgeon 1985a, 1985c; Calmont 1988b). Crossings through neighboring Suriname are organized and this network progressively ensures the majority of entries into Guianese territory (migrants pass through Paramaribo before reaching Saint-Laurent-du-Maroni and then Cayenne). From this period onward, family networks start to play an important role and allow migration to acquire autonomy. It must be noted that the memory of the "first migration" mediated by L. Ganot, "a white" person, no longer exists for most migrants. This episode provides a framework for a genealogy that traces the contours of a "mythical" narration of the "origins of Haitians in Guiana" as a construction of memory, defined temporally, spatially, and in terms of identity. It is, however, most present among educated people who, at the head of associations, want to be representative of a "Haitian community in Guiana."

Although during the 1980s, the need for workers allows for their relative integration in the labor market, the increase in the migratory influx is nonetheless cause for concern and leads municipalities to take measures. Joined together in an association, the mayors systematize the problems posed by Haitian immigration on the island of Cayenne. The rural origins of the migrants, their lack of formal schooling and professional qualifications, their participation in the informal economy, and their spatial marginalization are pointed out in the media and in local political discourse. "Characterized" in this way, Haitians are in no way considered beneficial for Guiana.[8] And, to the social and cultural boundaries are soon added those of political discrimination which reinforce the sense of separation. Haitian migrants become the emblematic symbol of the "clandestine." The relationship to otherness is no longer solely dependent upon the "Haitian subject," in relation to whom foreignness is determined, but also to the judicial status defined by the state. Within a context that becomes more and more culturally hetero-geneous, local politicians begin a general reflection in 1984 on the ways in which the different migrations affect the *département*. This reflection leads to the drafting of a document entitled *Trente mesures pour une politique de l'immigration en Guyane* [*Thirty measures for a policy on immigration in Guiana*]. Globally speaking, the immigration policy hoped for is the es-tablishment of legislation specific to Guiana and justified by a concern for the protection of "Guianese identity."[9] It is revealing that a policy control-ling the migratory influx is still current at the local level.[10] Similarly, one finds the same arguments that stigmatized Haitians during the 1980s still expressed today by popular media and in ordinary political discussions. On the island of Cayenne, where Haitians represent one of the most numerous migrant groups, the same terms are used to denounce their presence. Today, within a supposedly multicultural context, this representation has remained unchanged: "the Haitian" represents "the stranger." This relegation, linked to the process of ethnicization and rooted in its hierarchical organization, turns Haitian migrants into distinctive units at the heart of Guianese soci-ety.

Identity and "Origin" in Multicultural Circumstances:
"Tell Me Where You are From, and I Will Tell You What You Are"

The idea of "origin," which combines culture and nationality, sets Haitians apart. They become stereotypical social figures because of the national and cultural exteriority they embody. Viewed through elements that position them outside of modernity, they appear endowed with a cultural substratum that prevents them from attaining modernity. Their clandestine existence further impedes this process. People often evoke their poverty, analpha-betism, ignorance, violence, and involvement with magic when speaking about Haitians. The color of their skin is considered darker than that of Guianese Creoles. They are believed to be capable of sacrificing their energy for money, living in housing that is unfit for habitation, and fall prey to the magic of Vodou. According to a logic that subordinates the individual to the group in a metonymic way, each migrant is identified with stereotypi-cal actions according to the behavioral model known and founded by the idea of "community." Embodying an image that is ethnologically centered on a *postulated nature*, "the Haitian" plays a primordial role in the imagi-nary construction of "the Other." Because the role of migrants in the local economy and in the process of cultural exchange is too often neglected, interactions are either minimized or occulted and often marginalized. This process of designation, through which power is enacted, erases the realities of the Haitians' living conditions while immediately impacting their daily life. It simultaneously falls within a taxonomic operation and that of a subjective identification of the members. In the process of identity construction, the notion of "origin" is a relevant category that "explains" individual and collective actions. This same notion is also an integral part of the migrants' self-construction. The idea that "identities" are elaborated through the notion of "origins" corresponds with the concept of "cultural existence" incorporated into the migrants' perception of identity. Haitians have sometimes internalized (as are internalized the power relations in which they are caught) this conception which can play an important role in the way they present themselves to others. The migrants' identity constructions thus appear as elaborations marked by the imposition and reappropriation of an "*exo-identification.*"

The sense of identification is tied to the notion of nationality and the feeling of representing a singular entity at the heart of Guiana ("we, the Haitians") is a central aspect of identity constructions. Without being elaborated into a dominant ideology, this "origin" constitutes an axis around which discourses and practices find their meaning. It is through the "origin" that individuals recognize their common belonging. In contrast to Guianese Creoles, Haitians are not very sensitive to defining the Creole aspect of their identity. The belonging to a national collectivity is based on common references to the past, history, and tradition—to which is added a shared "migratory destiny." However, in Guiana, it is interesting to note that the emergence of this "ethnic subjectivity" (Wieviorka 1993) is articulated within the migratory context of the *département*. The organization of "foreigners" into a hierarchy is determined by the specificities characterizing each group and adopted by migrants against other migrants. Hence, Haitians, whose arrival was posterior to that of Brazilians, replaced the latter at the bottom rung of society. The more recent and massive arrival of Surinamese has modified this hierarchy and Haitians have sometimes appropriated cultural clichés against highly stigmatized maroons who make up the majority of Surinamese migrants. For instance, "taki-taki," thought to be the language of maroons, has become the target of constant mockery from Haitians (Laëthier 2007b)[11] In other words, the Haitians' identity formation inscribes itself in a context where each individual belongs first to a "community." This is one possible path to constructing the intercultural in a context of extreme "community protectionism." Nonetheless, the identity process which leads Haitians to share one and the same definition of themselves and to elaborate a "sense of togetherness" must be considered in light of another organizing principle: networks of fellowship. In fact, Haitian migration in Guiana is structured by networks of family and friends as primary systems of available resources and belonging.

Migratory Networks and Processes of Territorialization: Behind the Scenes Identity Formation

Even though Guiana acts as an interface with metropolitan France, it is far from corresponding to the representation of the United States, Canada, or France in the Haitians' migratory imaginary. Nonetheless, since the 1980s, the demographic weight of Haitians in Guiana has continually grown.[12] According to the most recent census, they represent 30 percent of the immigrant population in the *département*. This figure, which only takes into consideration those individuals who have legalized their status and agreed to be included in the census, is probably inaccurate. There are, in fact, a number of illegal immigrants. Among this group, some entered illegally while others arrived legally but did not renew their visas;[13] they are not accounted for in the official census. In order to understand the evolution and maintenance of emigration to Guiana, one must investigate the networks of family relations and friends within which each individual trajectory inscribes itself, rather than focusing on clandestinity—an aspect of emigration that is not characteristic of Haitians. These networks influence the cost of migration, allow migrants to maintain links, and determine who can migrate. A migratory resource, these valuable support networks provide recent arrivals with emotional, material, and legal support in the framework of family reunifications. While this migratory movement is characterized by an expansion that is not the result of a specific Guianese labor demand, the networks allow migrants to have access to certain socioeconomic spheres, and sometimes even to determine those spheres. The presence of compatriots already implanted in a specific market constitutes an important nexus for economic insertion, even though this insertion tends to perpetuate the ethnicization of certain professional openings. In light of the economic saturation of Guiana, these networks have become independent. However, the networks do not prevent the clash of realities: rural and urban, linguistic and cultural, social and political. In the hierarchy of migratory spaces, Guiana is situated at the bottom. If migrants have this image of Guiana, and if the idea of reemigration or of repeated migration exists, it is primarily because this idea is reinforced by the living conditions in the *département*. The hostility from the local population and the economic marginalization make the stay in Guiana sometimes difficult and increases the desire to leave or sometimes even to return to Haiti. Some of those who live clandestinely, whose work is unstable, and who are subjected to xenophobic comments do not want to stay and say that they would not repeat their migration to Guiana. Some even regret having left Haiti to come to Guiana, imagining that it would "be like France." Dozens of testimonies show that illegality, social precariousness, and racism generate dissatisfaction. In general, "traveling to Guiana" is connected with exclusion. However, despite these difficulties, few return permanently to Haiti. Migration continues to be a way of acquiring monetary and symbolic capital, and from this point of view Guiana continues to be attractive.

The confrontation with a new universe of norms reinforces the networks organized by family, friends, and regional belonging. These ties tend to intensify the sense of belonging to the same "community" and a shared "identity." To illustrate this point, I will discuss the organization of living quarters and the process of territorialization.

Kinship and Neighborhood: From the Space of Regulation . . .

It is on the island of Cayenne that the majority of migrants are concentrated.[14] The principal city of the *département*, Cayenne is Guiana's urban space par excellence. It is in this city and its periphery that the majority of the population resides and that most of the political and economic activities take place. In an urban setting that is characterized by socioeconomically differentiated living conditions, many migrants live in peripheral zones of the city, sometimes unfit for habitation.[15] There are no specifically Haitian living quarters, although there are areas of greater concentration. Despite their marginalization, these neighborhoods engender a sense of appropriation among the inhabitants. Reproducing the functioning of migratory currents, living quarters are organized by family ties, friends, village origins, and relationships.

The physical organization of living quarters is often similar. Certain aspects of the *lakou*—found in rural and urban Haiti—make their appearance: groups of contiguous dwellings with an open space in the middle.[16] This organization is significantly different from residences in urban centers in New York, Montreal, or Paris. From the point of view of social organization, the comparison with dwellings in Haiti should be nuanced. In Guiana, *lakous* are not exclusively composed of relatives. Their foundation is also tied to migration: the date of arrival, the village origin, and interpersonal affinities structure these groupings. At the heart of these spaces, daily life is organized by parents, neighbors, symbolic parents, and other individuals constituting the networks. The social units, relatively reduced in size, are organized around certain principles of life that could justify applying the term *lakou* to the Guianese context: the behavior of individual actors defines the social context where mutual aid and assistance produce solidarity. Daily cooperation, loans, and the exchange of work organize the socialization and "functioning" of living quarters around the social utility of respect, sharing the same codes, complicity, and familial and affective links. By superposing themselves to compose a common inhabited space, these elements express a common belonging to a place and a group. These sociospatial, self-perpetuating forms of organization are characterized by a strong feeling of attachment founded upon definitions of identity and otherness. The ensuing processes of territorialization show that these spaces take advantage of the borders they establish. For the inhabitants, the borders exist and they like to repeat that "strangers" (those who do not live there) cannot enter. While the creation of a sociospatial "us" is linked to the awareness that local acknowledgement does not come without stigmatization, the relationship to space mixes spatial sharing with the spatialization of relationships.[17] This creates a specific mode of sociality that works on the principle of inclusion and exclusion. Transformed into useable resources which are integrated into daily conversations and practices, these living spaces make identity affirmations conceivable. In the migratory context, territorial reconstruction becomes an instrument defining belonging. Social construction through territorialization appears then like a game between a stigmatized, imposed identity and, in the private sphere, a mobilized heritage, in order to build a sense of belonging within this gap. One must nonetheless keep in mind that these processes of territorialization do not necessarily bring about inward-looking communities; the point is not to take up the idea of rootedness. While the living space becomes an identity anchor, the concrete and daily experience of the habitat does not embody a fixed identity. In the last part of this paper, I will further discuss the questions posed by this approach in light of analyses that develop the notion of "black diaspora." For the moment, I want to insist that the sense of belonging to a group—which repeats itself in multiple residential units—is first envisioned spatially before supporting ethnical community logic. Certainly, the recourse to nationality in the process of self-definition and definition of others influences the construction of a collective entity in which each one recognizes him/herself. However, the sharing of a collective reference does not engender discourse around a community-centered identity.

. . . to Differentiated Identity Constructions

In Guiana, collective "self comprehension" (R. Brubaker, 2001)[18], implied by the Creole word *nasyon*, exists, but takes on a different meaning at an individual level. From there, the migrants' identity constructions reveal different individual associations. The differentiated perceptions and reappropriations of unified and homogenous self-identification impel going beyond the paradigm identifying migrants as a coherent and stable whole.

Let's take, for instance, the example of individuals born in Guiana (between ages fifteen and twenty-five) to illustrate the way in which association inscribes itself in the networks. In general, the youth born in Guiana do not found the construction of their identity upon a claimed "Haitian origin." The interviews reveal a relative lack of comprehension of Haiti and a set of negative representations of life in Haiti. Not very interested in Haiti—which often appears removed from the horizon of possibilities—youth born in Guiana tend to stigmatize poverty, material destitution, and political life in Haiti. Their relationships with "the country of origin" differ from those of the elders. The identity claims are more motivated by the will to find an "anchorage" locally or an imagined investment in other places such as France or the United States. The depreciatory look at Haiti, which affects a whole combination of practices and values attributed to the "culture" of the elders, marks a distance and allows the claiming of a different belonging. The latter is often self-defined in terms of "Guianese" and/or "Haitian born in Guiana." Individuals who define themselves in these terms accentuate the fact that they relate primarily to the "Guianese." From their point of view, even if Guiana is far less desirable than French or American models, the image of successful westernization is embodied by the Creoles. In the context of the territory of origin, the use of the term "Guianese" continually oscillates between definitions: if the speakers include themselves, "Guianese" signifies "being born in Guiana," while if they put forward their friendly relations with non-Haitians, "Guianese" refers to Creoles. Practically speaking, the declarations regarding friendly relations are invalidated by observations: relations are principally—and often exclusively—developed with individuals whose parents are Haitians and with persons born in Haiti. As with their elders, the networks inscribe themselves primarily at the heart of the living quarters. Young people are very conscious of the differences between the groups. And, while they are not very interested in Haiti and do not empha-size their "Haitian origin," some admit that this search for identity is linked to the "racist" attitudes encountered because they are Haitian. For instance, the term "haïchien" [Haitian dog] is often used instead of "Haïtien" [Hai-tian]. While some believe these to be isolated verbal manifestations from racist individuals rather than the reflection of Guianese society as a whole, others feel restricted when labeled as Haitian and deplore the distance and suspicion they perceive from the "Guianese." It is interesting to note that these individuals may in turn use certain aspects of Haitian culture as signs of a modern "Haitian identity." This is the case, for instance, with the music *konpa*, which is unanimously appreciated.

Generally speaking, the data recorded among individuals born in Gui-ana lead one to wonder if the creolization process has not already begun. An in-depth study would need to be conducted. Clearly, the next few years will provide important elements to answer this question. For the moment, Haitians have reappropriated and internalized a sociocultural hierarchy in which they do not appear at the top. One can furthermore observe the con-science of a stigmatized "Haitian community" produced from the exterior. This production originates in a type of power that spreads into categories of identification. The production of groups is intricately linked to social rela-tions of domination that shape and reproduce "ethnic" inequalities. This leads to another question: are we witness to networks staging a "Haitian community from Guiana" that could be qualified as voluntary diasporic networks?

The notion of "Haitian community" does not exist among all migrants, but is used by associations. This reappropriation takes on considerable sig-nificance. While I do not wish to enter into a detailed analysis here, I would like to point out that the leaders of associations represent an identifiable group among migrants. They constitute an active minority around a small founding group that has ensured the continuity of associations and/or the birth of new ones. These individuals—all born in Haiti—belong to a modest but not underprivileged socioeconomic section of the population. The per-sons in charge of these associations have all benefited from more than ten years of schooling and are Francophone even if they consistently speak Cre-ole with their kin and with the members of their association. Nonetheless, the manipulation of the notion of "Haitian community from Guiana" by these individuals sheds light on contradictory interests and a double mean-ing. Vis-à-vis other Haitians, on one hand, one can observe how social links are forged through the recollection of a collective belonging and a shared migratory trajectory. On the other hand, in their search for legitimacy in the Guianese context, these individuals aspire to go beyond the symbolic violence and assignation inherent to this Haitian belonging.[19] This second logic shows that they are more or less at a remove in their relationships with the rest of the migrants.

These different logics of identity—sometimes entangled, sometimes antagonistic—and the diverse relationships of domination, contradict the readings which postulate homogeneity among the migrant group. Presupposing a singular organization of identifications, the experience of migration allows identity configurations that empower multiple referents. The migratory situation implies a selection of the modes of belonging. The maintenance, reinforcement, or, on the contrary, negation of otherness ("self-otherness"), form overlapping patterns which influence and modify each other. Despite a context in which representations immemorialize "identity," identity processes retain their interactive dynamism. This dynamism testifies to the fact that the social existence of a group is developed over time and results from a historicity that is linked to "a group's capacity to transform itself by re-employing the means at its disposition to other ends and for new uses" (De Certeau 1985: 161).

Even though there is no "fundamental or permanent similarity" between the migrants, a similarity is nonetheless experienced and perceived subjectively. While these identity constructions cannot be summarized by community representation, all nonetheless work around the borders they create. In this case, the consciousness of a common belonging is transformed into a "category of practice" to use Pierre Bourdieu's expression, used in certain daily situations to tell what is shared and what differentiates. Going back to the twofold question of territorialization and the elaboration of belonging, networks of family and neighbor relations shape a sense of identity that possesses a symbolic effectiveness in the foundation of a relationship and the resettlement of a place. While this internal reference is not yet used as support for communal representation in the Guianese context, it nonetheless progresses through recompositions of "micro-territories." This territorial logic unveils the elaboration of an identification marked by the imposition of an "exo-identification" and the appropriation of a place to which meaning has been attributed. From this perspective, the problematic of territorialization remains a privileged tool to analyze enunciations of identity which the notions of "community" and "diaspora" have rendered difficult to understand.

Diaspora and the Black Americas

The theoretical orientations of recent analyses of the Caribbean, and more generally, of what one may call the black Americas, shed light on enunciations about territorial relationships. In fact, the analyses of sociohistorical contexts generally referred to as "Afro-American" tend to no longer define the latter negatively as has been previously done. Instead, they consider the diversity of social, cultural, and territorial patterns of organization from the perspective of "transversality" and "hybridity." Postmodern spheres of social apprehension tend to consider the pair memory/territory somewhat outdated. The paradigm of "everything mobile" seems more innovative to apprehend references of identity in regard to "the diaspora of the black Americas" (Chivallon 2002, 2004).

From Diasporic Communities to Diasporic Identities

The history of the "black Americas" specifically questions the notion of diaspora. According to the classic definition of diaspora, dispersion linked to the enslavement of Africans in the Americas would seem appropriate.[20] Characterized by the Jewish experience, the interpretations that have led to the generalizing of the term "diaspora" have nonetheless allowed groups that left their territories while maintaining a collective memory and myths linked to their past as part of a shared sense of ethnicity, to be qualified as "diaspora."[21] It is this iconoclastic vision of diaspora that applies to Caribbean migrations of the twentieth century. An Anglo-Saxon trend of postmodern sociology sees in the experience of Caribbean migrants a paradigmatic example of "hybridity" and "postmodernity."[22] The populations descendant from slaves who migrate today to former colonial metropolis constitute a "naturally hybrid diaspora" (Cohen 2002b) while the Caribbean is a place of "double diasporization" (ibid.).

The work of Paul Gilroy, *Black Atlantic* (1993), is significant in this regard. His notion of a transatlantic culture, made up of connections between continents, envisions a political and cultural formation where national and ethnic boundaries are transcended. Identity is no longer conceived as a stable form, but as continually modified moments of belonging. In order to capture the range of Caribbean identity references, the sociologist Stuart Hall also takes up the term diaspora (Hall 1993). According to his work, diaspora studies show that identity affirmation can do without spatialized and state controlled normative systems characterized by stability and permanence. Diasporas contradict the notion of inward-looking cultures that are rooted in a place. Instead—allowing the maintenance of ethnicity (Médam 1993; Sheffer 1993)—unity defines itself in relation to the paradox of the preservation of unitary identity within dispersion.

These approaches, which define social formations of the black Americas through the notion of "black diaspora," favor an analysis of evolving hybrid identities. This analytic framework liberates the groups from all territorial reference and rootedness that found social relations and collective symbols. In the same perspective, the geographer Christine Chivallon (1995, 1996, 1997, 2004) questions the use of the term diaspora to describe the experience of peoples descendent from the African slave trade. Chivallon (2004) interrogates the methodology of analysis that emphasizes a certain unity of the black Americas. The violence of the conditions characterizing the implantation of slaves in the New World is essential to comprehending the social, political, and cultural universe of Afro-Americans. The black diaspora corresponds to two time periods: an initial dispersion which constitutes the first stratum of the diaspora formed by the slave trade, and a second stratum constituted by the migratory movements of the twentieth century. By defining the black diaspora from these two sources, Chivallon argues that in both dispersions, social formations formulate similar "cultural responses" that are characterized by a multiplicity of identity orientations. This plurality, which differs from the stabilized configuration of registers of identity (of all cultural norms erected into a system), exists in direct relationship to the particularly violent foundation of these societies. These social constructions "against politics" can be referred to as "de-centered communities" originating in long-lasting schemas (related to the constraints of the slave regime). Their common expression is the prolongation of oppression by the other beyond the initial traumatic event. The same dynamic can be found among Afro-Americans stemming from current migratory movements. Applied to the analysis of contemporary migrations, this approach challenges the view which considers migrant groups—spread throughout diverse and multiple political spaces—to be reliant on the existence of "micro-territories." It also challenges the definition of "black diaspora" as fulfillment of a unity that escapes "the collective structuring dependent upon a unifying ideology of identity" (Chivallon 2004: 229).

Towards Diasporic Dynamics

Without calling into question the pertinence of these theoretical orientations, it seems to me that a series of questions remains unanswered. Do plural and diversified identity constructions signify the end of demarcated territorial forms that play on the borders they establish? Does recognizing the emergence of identity references—upon which are superimposed a dynamic of transnational networks of relations—imply notions of stability, cohesion, or "ethnic" unity? Does the apprehension of migratory movement with the help of the notion of diaspora—in its classical sense or according to the vision outlined by the studies presented in this paper—provide information on a specific mode of "being in migration?" To what extent is the differential value of diverse diasporas built upon this notion? In the case studied here, what connects Haitians living in Canada, the United States, France, Venezuela, and Guiana? Does the term "black diaspora" offer a perspective allowing one to analyze with the same effectiveness in all places and times the presupposed cohesion of groups? These are important questions that can only be answered by specific case studies.

I would like to recapitulate the examples provided in the framework of this article. One can, without hesitation, adhere to an analysis encompassing the multiplication of identity orientations. However, one must be cautious not to adopt a vision that puts all forms of identity production in the same category of refusal of limits and envisions groups that organize themselves through the activation of "structuring schemas" (Chivallon 2004: 108). According to the approach presented here, "the Caribbean diaspora, similarly to Caribbean cultures in general—intimately aware of the constraint the Other can impose—may formulate an identity project that diverts the direction of dual constructions and of the borders that fashion them" (Chivallon 1996: 54). In the case of Haitian migration in the Guianese context, despite the noted polyphony, social constructions do not renounce modes of difference, separation, or the hierarchy that structures them.

The data presented here have raised questions about the relationship between sociocultural groups, the territory, and migratory phenomena. The apprehension of identity registers built on spatially mapped out social links does not preclude thinking their diversity. In addition, the absence of a collective unitary narration does not prevent the expression of territorial forms. Considered an elaboration of space permitting the visibility of a group through an identifying "we," territorialization is also a moment of negotiation between self-definition and identity assignation. From this perspective, it becomes possible to consider the networks in terms of their links with territories by scrutinizing their territorial foundation. A juxtaposition of space becomes a part of the migrants' identity constructions. In this regard, the migratory networks correspond to "social terrains" where practices are deterritorialized, reterritorialized, and integrated into the construction of various belongings.

Finally, as Sidney Mintz (1998) has shown by questioning the applicability of the term "transnational" based on the Caribbean model, "multi-local communities" are no more removed from the historical backdrop than the relationship between dispersed individuals implies that "uni-local communities" cease to exist. Identity constructions do not go beyond a reference to the nation any more than the autonomy of individuals appears in relationship to national consciousness.[23] National identification, even if it does not give rise to a unitary experience, is no less experienced and claimed. This is true whether the established link is ambivalent, complex, temporary, or paradoxical. The national territory no longer limits the space of identification but remains a major referent (Fibbi and Meyer 2002; Jolivet and Léna, 2000).

Similarly, one must dismantle the notion of homogenous immigration whose actors are subjected to the same situations in the same way. Parallel to collective identification, which affirms itself and is conserved in the historic memory of a group, it is important to envisage the subjects' processes of identification—coexisting within the same group—by analyzing individual experiences. The social processes giving rise to "self-identifications" pass through variable networks of categories and relationships. At the risk of seeming banal, the data remind us that cultural productions do not produce a stable "culture," a permanent "mysterious totality." They indicate, on the contrary, the necessity of problematizing evolving situations and contexts. It is at this level that the social existence of a group is constructed and that its historicity participates in a transformation one cannot alienate by identifying it as an origin.

Overall, the reflections in this article lead to a reading of migration from the open-ended perspective of a "dynamic diaspora"[24] by privileging an analysis of identity elaborations. The application of the category "black diaspora" to the study of different social worlds descendent from slavery is intriguing. Does the definition of this category based on the superposition of dispersion (the slave trade and contemporary migrations) and of socioidentity organization, contravening against a centralized community due to its rapport with an initial constraint, account for an open and unfinished reality?

Translated from the French by Catherine Reinhardt

Notes

1. In the fields of French sociology and anthropology we owe the introduction and development of Afro-American research to R. Bastide. Bastide demonstrated that cultures born in servitude can only be understood in terms of creation, as constructions of models that are different from those produced by the original cultures. Bastide developed the notion of "negro culture" to render the new sociocultural forms born of a process of creolization that he defined as "a spontaneous movement, internal to Afro-American culture, by adaptation to the environment and assimilation of European elements" ([1967] 1996: 184).

2. There are more than 3 million Haitians living outside of Haiti and 8 million living in Haiti (IHSI, 2003). The importance of economic, political, and cultural relations between Haiti and its emigrants, called *moun dyaspora*, has led the first government of former President Jean-Bertrand Aristide to consider all the territories inhabited by persons claiming to belong to the "Haitian nation" as a new *département*. It has been called the "Tenth *Département*," to which has been assigned the Ministry of *Haïtiens Vivant à l'Étranger* [Haitians Living Abroad], institutionalized as a legitimized territorial extension by the claims of national belonging (the Tenth *Département* has become the "Eleventh *Département*" since the creation of a Tenth *Département* within the national boundaries in 2005).

3. The law of March 19, 1946 transformed the "old colonies" into overseas *départements* by pursuing the process of political and juridical assimilation. This law is also called "loi d'assimilation" [law of assimilation].

4. The different groups of slave descendants who fled Surinamese plantations since the seventeenth century are called Bushinenge and black maroons. Many have migrated to Guiana. The political unrest that broke out in Suriname beginning in 1986 contributed to the recent migrations to Guiana. Today, Ndjuka, Aluku, Saramaka, and Paramaka are present on Guianese territory, notably in the west.

5. In Guiana, the group of white Creoles was not able to "survive" after the abolition of slavery: the "non-emergence" of a plantation economy contributed to its disappearance as an economically dominant group. The term "Creole" remained to refer to former slaves and freedmen as well as their descendants. While for more than one century, the descendants of migrants could also "become" Creoles, currently this is a precise group which designates itself that way (Jolivet 1982, 1997, 2006).

6. According to the 1999 census there were 46,576 inhabitants including 46,576 "foreigners." In 1954, the 3,449 "foreigners" represented 12.38 percent of the population. In 1982, the 16,868 "foreigners" constituted 23.1 percent of the total population (INSEE, 2006).

7. The majority of migrants come from the *département de la Grande Anse* and the *département du Sud* and more precisely from the cities of Aquin, Vieux-Bourg d'Aquin, l'Asile, Fonds-des-Nègres, Bouzi, Morisseau, Fonds-des-Blancs, La Colline, and Saint-Louis du Sud. A lesser number come from the *arrondissement de la villes des Cayes*. Others come from the communes of Miragoâne and Petite-Rivière de Nippes. Still others are from the *département de l'ouest*: from the *arrondissement de Port-au-Prince* and the

peripheral communes of Carrefour and Delmas, the *arrondissement de Léogane* and its communes (Petit-Goâve and Grand-Goâve), the *arrondissement de l'Arcahaie*, and the commune of Cabaret. A few come from the *arrondissement de Bainet* in the *département du Sud Est* (Laëthier 2007a).

8. In 1976, during the meeting of the Association des Maires de Guyane [Association of the Mayors of Guiana]—Eighteenth Congress—the rise in unemployment, the migrants' lack of skills, their impact on the ecosystem, the cost of their presence, and the upsurge in the malaria epidemic were arguments used to make a case against the presence of migrant workers.

9. These measures were based on two ideas: stopping immigration and integrating the foreigners already settled in Guiana. In 1985, a regularization program was organized for those whose papers could be put in order (individuals who did not compete with the "Guianese," whose children were born in Guiana, or whose spouse was "Guianese"): 2,500 visas and work permits were issued.

10. This is shown by the article published in "Le Monde" on September 19, 2005, in which the politicians denounce "the genocide by substitution of the Guianese people" (remarks made by the senator Georges Othily, February 2004) or "the rupture of the equilibrium of the Guianese population" (remarks made by Antoine Karam, president of the Conseil Régional and secretary of the Parti Socialiste Guyanais [Guianese Socialist Party]. Along the same lines, the recent proposition of the Ministre de l'Outre-mer (French Minister of Overseas Territories) limiting the jus soli in the overseas territories was favorably received even though it was only a "partial solution" (Karam).

11. Surinamese migrants are principally maroons, locally referred to as bushinengue, and belong to the groups aluku, ndjuka, paramaka, and saramaka. The bushinengue Creole languages combine several linguistic variants some of which are present in Guiana. Sranan tongo, the most common language in Suriname, is also common in the region of Saint-Laurent du Maroni. This language is used in exchanges between different groups present in the region and Haitians have been in contact with it. Its common appellation, "taki-taki," is generally depreciatory.

12. During my fieldwork, I was constantly in contact with migrants who had recently arrived to join members of their family. Among these migrants were men, women (an increase in women migrants increased the birthrate in Guiana), children, and young adults.

13. It must be pointed out that illegality does not only characterize recent migrants; it also concerns the "old timers" who arrived in the *département* in the 1980s.

14. The island of Cayenne consolidates three communes: Cayenne, Rémire-Montjoly, and Matoury.

15. The urban inequalities in Guiana, especially in Cayenne, give rise to discourses on the theme of "ghettoization." Substantialist thought about space and the theme of the "ghetto," nourished by clichés, plays a role in the debates on city policy.

16. The Creole term *lakou* comes from the French *la cour* [the courtyard]. For a detailed analysis of *lakou* in Haiti, principally in rural settings, see: Bastien ([1951] 1985); d'Ans (1987); Moral ([1961] 2002).

17. The analysis of socioterritorial identities must take into account the constraints

imposed by local discriminatory processes and by sociocultural norms which originate in a repertory with multiple entries.

18. Brubaker speaks of "self-comprehension," understood as a "dispositional" term to designate "the conception one has of who one is, one's localization in social space and the way (in terms of the first two) one is prepared for action" (2001: 77).

19. See Laëthier 2007a.

20. A Greek word, the term "diaspora" was first used to signify the destiny of the Jewish people, its geographic dispersion, and the maintenance of an "identity" regardless of the places of settlement (Lacoste 1989; Fossaert 1989; Scheffer 1986, 1993; Safran 1991; Tölölyan 1996; Cohen 1997; Cohen 2002a, 2002b).

21. Many authors propose typologies combining different criteria according to which migrant groups can be defined as being more or less diasporic. From this perspective, the term "diaspora" taken as a "metaphoric designation" can, in fact, qualify dissimilar populations such as expatriates, expulsed people, political refugees, and minorities . . . (Safran 1991). Other authors (Médam 1991; Clifford 1994) highlight the fact that identity movements of diasporic groups are a constitutive characteristic of the contemporary world.

22. On the subject, Chivallon writes: "Where post-modernism has flourished—the anglophone world, the Black world has been endowed with new qualities and truly consecrated as a diasporic people. In the francophone world, with its more conventional sociology, the use of the term diaspora does not work as well for this same world which one expects to perfectly adapt to the contours of a classical diaspora with the production of a strong community consciousness" (1997b: 67).

23. Cohen's words are interesting in this regard: "The postmodern vision is sometimes overly hasty when declaring the death of national sovereignty and the nation state, considered products of a bygone modernity. One does not need to entirely adhere to this vision to recognize that among Caribbean migrants exists an exceptional historical predisposition to the construction of hybrid identities and to the transnationalization of their horizon" (Cohen 2002b: 88).

24. On this subject see Hovenessian (1998).

References

Badie, Bertrand. 1994. "Du territoire à l'espace." In *La France au-delà du siècle*, 7–14. Paris: l'Aube-Datar.

Bastide, Roger. 1995 [1967] *Les Amériques Noires, les civilisations africaines dans le nouveau monde*. Paris: L'Harmattan.

———. 1995. *La fin des territoires. Essai sur le désordre international et sur l'utilité sociale du respect*. Paris: Fayard.

Bastien, Rémi. 1985 [1951]. *Le paysan haïtien et sa famille. Vallée de Marbial*. Paris: Karthala.

Brubaker, Rogers. 2001. "Au-delà de l'identité." *Actes de la Recherche en Sciences Sociales*, no. 139: 66–85.

Calmont, Régine. 1988a. "L'impact de l'immigration haïtienne." *Equinoxe*, no. 26: 1–48.

———. 1988b. *Migrations et migrants en Guyane française, l'exemple de la communauté haïtienne*. Doctoral Dissertation. Bordeaux III.

Chalifoux, Jean-Jacques. 1988. *Chercher "lavi" en Guyane française. Témoignages d'Haïtiens et d'Haïtiennes émigrés. Anthropologie*. Québec: Université Laval.

Chivallon, Christine. 1995. "Les espaces de la diaspora antillaise au Royaume-Uni. Limites des concepts socio-anthropologiques." *Les Annales de la recherche urbaine*, no. 68–69: 198–210.

———. 1996. "Repenser le territoire, à propos de l'expérience antillaise." *Géographie et Cultures*, no. 20: 45–55.

———. 1997a "Du territoire au réseau: comment penser l'identité antillaise." *Cahiers d'Études Africaines* 37, no. 4: 767–94.

———. 1997b. "De quelques préconstruits de la notion de diaspora à partir de l'exemple antillais." *Revue Européenne des Migrations Internationales* 13, no. 1: 149–60.

———. 2002. "La Diaspora noire des Amériques. Réflexions sur le modèle de l'hybridité de Paul Gilroy." *L'Homme*, no. 161: 51–74.

———. 2004. *La diaspora noire des Amériques. Expériences et théories à partir de la Caraïbe*. Paris: CNRS Éditions.

Clifford, James. 1994. "Diasporas." *Cultural Anthropology* 9, no. 3: 302–38.

Cohen, James. 2002a. "Diaspora et incorporation, présences publiques des Caribéens aux États-Unis." *Hommes et Migrations*, no. 1237: 82–90.

———. 2002b. "Entre Caraïbes et métropoles: parcours diasporiques et citoyenneté." *Hommes et Migrations* no. 1237: 6–12.

Cohen, Robin. 1997. *Global Diasporas. An Introduction*. London: UCL Press.

D'Ans, André-Marcel. 1987. *Haïti. Paysage et société*. Paris: Karthala.

De Certeau, Michel. 1985. "L'actif et le passif des appartenances." *Esprit*, no. 6: 155–71.

De Rudder, Véronique. 1998. "Identité, origine et étiquetage. De l'ethnique au racial, savamment cultivés . . ." *Journal des Anthropologues*, no. 72–73: 31–47.

Fibbi, Rosita and Jean-Baptiste Meyer. 2002. "Introduction: le lien plus que l'essence." *Autrepart, "Diasporas: développements et mondialisations,"* no. 22: 5–21.

Gilroy, Paul. 1993. *The Black Atlantic. Modernity and Double Consciousness*. London: Verso.

Gorgeon, Catherine. 1985a. "Immigration clandestine et bidonvilles en Guyane, les Haïtiens à Cayenne." *Revue Européenne des Migrations Internationales* 1, no. 1: 143–57.

———. 1985b. *Gestion urbanistique d'une immigration: le cas de l'île de Cayenne*. Doctoral Dissertation, Aix Marseille III, Centre d'Études et de Recherches sur l'Amérique Centrale et les Caraïbes, Institut d'études politiques d'Aix en Provence.

Hall, Stuart. 1993. "Cultural Identity and Diaspora." In *Colonial Discourse and Post-Colonial Theory. A Reader*, eds. Patrick Williams and Laura Chrisman, 392–403. London: Harvester-Wheatsheaf.

Hovanessian, Martine. 1998. "La notion de diaspora; usages et champ sémantique." *Journal des Anthropologues*, no. 72–73: 11–29.

Institut Haïtien de Statistique et d'Informatique. 2003. *Résultats préliminaires du 4ème Recensement Général de Population et d'Habitat*, Port-au-Prince: Haïti.

Institut National de la Statistique et des Études Économiques (INSEE). 1999. *Recensement de la population.*

———. 2006. *Atlas des populations immigrées en Guyane,* INSEE Guyane, ACSE (Agence Nationale pour la Cohésion Sociale et l'Égalité des Chances).

Jolivet, Marie-José. 1982. *La question créole. Éssai de sociologie sur la Guyane française.* Paris: ORSTOM. Coll. Mémoires, no. 96.

———. 1997. "La créolisation en Guyane. Un paradigme pour une anthropologie de la modernité." *Cahiers d'Études Africaines, 'La Caraïbe. Des îles au continent'* 37 no. 148, fasc. 4: 813–38.

———. 2006. "Créoles et Marrons en Guyane: d'une créolisation à l'autre." In *Situations créoles. Pratiques et représentations,* ed. Carlo A. Célius, 107–23. CELAT, Université de Québec, Éditions Nota bene, Coll. Société.

Jolivet, Marie-José and Philippe Léna. 2000. "Des territoires aux identités." *Autrepart,* no. 14: 5–16.

Lacoste, Yves. 1989. "Géopolitique des diasporas." *Hérodote,* no. 53.

Laëthier, Maud. 2006. "Mémoires, historicité et créolisation, le cas des Haïtiens en Guyane française." In *Situations créoles. Pratiques et représentations,* ed. Carlo A. Célius, 125–139. CELAT, Université de Québec, Éditions Nota bene. Coll. Société.

———. 2007a. *Être haïtien et migrant en Guyane française.* Doctoral Dissertation, EHESS.

———. 2007b. "Yo nan peyi laguyan tou. Pratiques et représentations langagières des Haïtiens dans l'île de Cayenne." In *Pratiques et attitudes linguistiques en Guyane : regards croisés,* ed. Isabelle Léglise, 193–201, Paris: PUF.

Médam, Alain. 1993. "Diaspora/Diasporas. Archétype et typologie." *Revue Européenne des Migrations Internationales.* 9, no. 1: 59–65.

Moral, Paul. 2002 [1961]. *Le paysan haïtien: étude sur la vie rurale.* Port-au-Prince: Les Éditions Fardin.

Safran, William. 1991. "Diasporas in Modern Societies, Myths of Homeland and Return." *Diaspora* no. 1: 83–99.

Scheffer, Gabriel. 1986. *Modern Diasporas in International Politics.* Saint-Martin Press.

———. 1993. "Ethnic Diasporas: a Threat to their hosts?" In *International Migration and Security,* ed. Myron Weiner, 264–85. Boulder: Westview Press.

Tölölyan, Khachig. 1996. "Rethinking Diaspora(s), Stateless Power in the Transnational moment." *Diaspora* 5 no. 1: 3–36.

Wieviorka, Michel. 1993. *La Démocratie à l'épreuve. Nationalisme, populisme et ethnicité.* Paris: La Découverte.

5

Medical Humanitarianism and Health as a Human Right on the Haitian-Dominican Border

PIERRE MINN

In December of 2001, the Dominican Republic's Ministry of Public Health and Social Assistance published a 116-page report entitled "Incidence of Demand of Health Services by Foreigners," which tracked the frequency and cost (down to fractions of pesos) of visits to government hospitals and clinics by foreigners during a three-month period in the same year. The document reported that over 98 percent of these foreigners were Haitians (SESPAS 2001: 14). The report was widely disseminated and frequently referenced by Dominican media in the months that followed. Many Dominicans consider the presence of Haitians in their country to be a major social problem, and the report confirmed suspicions that Haitians were using up scarce resources in the form of public health care services.

This paper examines the discourses and practices that accompany the provision of medical services to Haitians in the Dominican Republic. My analysis draws from research I conducted during the summer of 2003 in a Dominican government hospital adjacent to the Haitian-Dominican border, which Haitian patients regularly cross in search of health care.[1] While individuals traveling outside of Haiti for brief periods are not generally considered to be part of the Haitian diaspora, an examination of their encounters and interactions with foreign governments and populations helps to illustrate the diversity of transnational processes that shape life for Haitians in Haiti and abroad.

Over the course of my research, I identified two coexisting but contrasting rhetorics, that of health as a human right, and that of medical humanitarianism.[2] While I examine these rhetorics in a specific geographic and temporal setting, they have gained prominence on a global scale in recent decades. Anthropologists have called for grounded and contextualized studies of human rights in recent years (Wilson 1997) and the subject now appears prominently in a variety of the discipline's subfields. In contrast, anthropological studies directly addressing humanitarianism have emerged only recently. Although humanitarianism and human rights stem from distinct philosophical traditions and can at times be contradictory in nature, they have converged significantly in recent years, a phenomenon which I witnessed frequently over the course of my research. This convergence has important consequences for international medical projects, shaping their form, substance, and the subjective and interpersonal dynamics involved in their implementation.

Methodology

The research for this thesis was conducted in the Dominican town of Dajabón (capital of the province of Dajabón), the neighboring Haitian town of Ouanaminthe, and their surrounding areas. I carried out participant observation research and interviews in a variety of settings on both sides of the border, including hospitals, rural health clinics, marketplaces, private homes, and the offices of non-governmental organizations (NGOs). The majority of my research was carried out at the border hospital in Dajabón, where I observed the interactions between Dominican hospital staff and Haitian patients seeking health services. When necessary, I acted as an interpreter between hospital staff and patients, whose level of proficiency in each other's languages varied considerably. I was careful to inform patients that I was not a member of the hospital staff, and that I was not a medical professional. My ability to communicate with patients in Creole as well as prior experiences working and conducting research in Haiti contributed significantly to establishing rapport with Haitian patients.

I carried out eleven formal, tape-recorded interviews and held many more informal interviews and conversations in settings not conducive to taped conversations. Of the formal interviews, three were with hospital staff, one with a foreign aid worker, and the rest with Haitian patients, former patients, and their family members. I also benefited from significant contact with hospital employees, members of local human rights and humanitarian organizations, and religious leaders from churches in both countries. In addition to the time spent in the border hospital, I traveled to rural health clinics, consulted archival material at government offices and research centers, and met with social scientists in Santo Domingo and Port-au-Prince.

The Setting

The two nations that share the island of Hispaniola have had a strained but close-knit relationship since their inception as Spanish and French colonies in the sixteenth and seventeenth centuries. The Haitian-Dominican border has been the site of battles, commerce, massacres, and partnerships. For the majority of Dominicans, the border area represents an arid no man's land, and while it is sparsely populated, its proximity to crowded, impoverished Haiti makes it the part of the nation most vulnerable to invasion and contamination. Collective memories of a twenty-year Haitian occupation in the early nineteenth century exacerbate these fears, although contemporary concerns are voiced primarily in terms of race, disease, and economics (Boisseron 2000; Howard 2001; Simmons 2003). Haitians' memories of border conflicts center on the 1937 massacre of an estimated 20,000 Haitians in the area, as part of Dominican dictator Rafael Trujillo's campaign to "Dominicanize" the border region. While many Haitians also consider the border region to be harsh and remote, passage to the Dominican Republic for short term trade or long-term work represents possible (albeit risky) economic opportunities.

Statistics from both countries indicate that Haitians suffer from significantly higher rates of infant and maternal mortality, infectious diseases, and malnutrition than their Dominican counterparts (ENDESA 2003; EM-MUS-IV 2006). In 2002, the World Health Organization estimated Healthy Life Expectancy in the Dominican Republic to be fifty-seven years on average, as opposed to forty-three years in Haiti (WHO 2002). However, as a result of low standards of living and the paucity of medical services and infrastructure in the Dominican border area, health conditions there are quite poor compared to other parts of the country. While care is available in private clinics to those who can afford to pay for better care and services, the border hospital is the most important public health care institution in the region. Doctors and nurses there reported that respiratory infections, malaria, parasites, malnutrition, and injuries from accidents (particularly motorcycle accidents) were frequent.

Who Gets Treated?

When I asked hospital staff, "Under what conditions do you treat Haitian patients?" the answer was invariably "emergencias" [emergencies]. This category did not consist of a specific set of illnesses or ailments, but was instead

determined on a case-by-case basis, usually by the attending nurse or physician. Hospital staff generally agreed that Haitians presenting minor ailments
or wounds would not receive treatment. Most of the care I saw given to
Haitians in the hospital relied on straightforward technical interventions:
disinfecting or suturing wounds, providing injections, or casting fractured
limbs. Patients were treated for a short period of time and released.[3] The
majority of Haitians I saw at the hospital were accompanied by at least one
relative who, in addition to providing companionship, could also run errands, gather information, translate, and come to the patient's defense in
cases of abuse or poor treatment. Finally, others came to the hospital to
purchase X-rays or medications unavailable in Haiti, but did so at the labo-
ratory or pharmacy without a clinical consultation.

One kind of emergency that consistently received medical attention at
the border hospital was childbirth. While the hospital does not ordinarily
keep track of Haitian patients through patient files or other documents, the
hospital statistician was able to show me a precise record of which births in
the hospital had been to Haitian women. In his record book, a large "H" appeared next to each Haitian mother's name. Nurses informed me that pregnant Haitian women "liked" to give birth in Dajabón because they received
care immediately and recuperated well. They also told me that expectant
mothers waited until the last possible moment until coming to the hospital
because, "if they come earlier, they don't get treated, they get sent back [to
Haiti]." Finally, they emphasized that the Haitian women who come to give
birth at the hospital are generally older women with very few financial resources, and that unlike other Haitian patients, they often come to the hospital alone—"as if they had no family"—in order to minimize the chances
of being refused treatment.[4]

While hospital staff bemoaned the high volume of Haitian patients they
treated, a much larger number remained without medical care. Many of
these never even attempted to access services at the government hospital,
and those who did had no guarantee that they would receive treatment.
Like the hospital staff, Haitian informants told me that "minor" conditions
would not receive care, and they named fevers, pains, weakness, and minor
or chronic infections as conditions for which they could not expect treatment. I encountered a malnourished Haitian woman who had been carried
out of the hospital and dumped in the street, despite the fact that she was
partially paralyzed and unable to walk. I was told that such cases were not
infrequent. Being refused treatment at a Dominican hospital is often the
final blow in an unsuccessful search for healing. The extremely limited avail-

ability of health services in Haiti is the primary factor motivating the quest for care in Dajabón. Usually, patients first attempt to treat conditions with leaf-based home remedies, and may subsequently seek care at dispensaries, clinics, or hospitals in Haiti, but often fail to obtain relief. Crossing the border to the hospital in Dajabón is often a last resort, one that draws patients from northern and central Haiti, and occasionally from more remote parts of the country as well.

While health services in Haiti are extremely limited, their Dominican counterparts are far from adequate. Much of the tension regarding the treatment of Haitians in Dajabón lies in the fact that Dominican hospitals and clinics are understaffed, lacking in both material and medical resources, and generally run-down. In this context of scarcity, it becomes difficult to accuse the Dominican hospital staff of simply "withholding" medical services from Haitians. While the ill-treatment of and discrimination against Haitians in all spheres of daily life in the Dominican border area occurs within a larger context of racism and xenophobia, I do not interpret the refusal to treat Haitian patients in Dominican hospitals as being based solely on anti-Haitian sentiment. Dominican health institutions do not have access to the means or resources to treat even the Dominican population. I frequently heard doctors and nurses state that they were sympathetic to the Haitians' plight, but that there were just not enough resources to go around. In this context of scarce resources, racial tensions, and suffering, providers and patients must negotiate their way through tense social interactions and competing values.

While the Dominican state bemoans the demands that Haitian patients impose on its health care system, it is not the only body providing them with health care. Numerous national and international NGOs provide services for Haitians in the Dominican Republic, including health care, education, and political advocacy. Two groups are particularly active in the border hospital, and exemplify the prevalence of human rights and humanitarian rhetoric in regards to health services.

Health as a Human Right and Manos Unidas

The right to health, made prominent in the World Health Organization's 1978 Declaration of Alma Ata, is often included among what Messer refers to as "socioeconomic and cultural rights," either explicitly or as the result of a decent standard of living (Messer 1993: 222). Described as "one of the most globalised political values of our time" (Wilson 1997: 1) the language of human rights has a strong presence in various settings in both Haiti and the Dominican Republic. A major promoter of human rights rhetoric in the border area is the NGO Manos Unidas [Hands Together], a group founded in the late 1990s that aims to "strengthen the bond of solidarity" between Dominicans and Haitians.[5] In addition to its office in Dajabón, Manos Unidas also operates an office staffed by Haitian priests and community activists in Ouanaminthe. The group works on a variety of economic, political, and social justice issues in the border area. They operate an informal program through which nuns associated with Manos Unidas who live in Haiti "accompany" Haitians to the border hospital.[6] This service is intended for individuals who are unable to cross the border alone, often because they cannot convince the guards to let them pass, or do not have money to pay for bribes. As one nun explained to me, "When we accompany people, [the guards] say 'Sisters, we know that when you cross, you will come back, you're not going to stay over there.'" For the most part, the nuns accompany patients for X-rays, sonograms, or emergencies that cannot be treated in Ouanaminthe. They also serve as interpreters for patients who do not speak Spanish.

The accompaniment offered by the nuns working with Manos Unidas situates the quest for therapy within the context of a potential human rights violation. This violation could take place at the border itself, if the guards were to refuse permission to cross or demand bribes of the victim. It could also take place at the hospital, in the form of neglect or abuse on the part of the hospital staff. Manos Unidas maintains a very high profile in the community and throughout the country. In response to human rights violations by police, military, and other local authorities, the group has organized press conferences, held demonstrations, and published eyewitness accounts of abuses. The hospital employees are undoubtedly aware that inappropriate or questionable activities on their part could invite scrutiny by the organization, the community, and possibly national and international forces. The presence of an accompanying nun at a medical encounter acts as a kind of surveillance or monitoring to see to it that human rights are respected in the first place. While the group provides workshops, resources, and support to communities on both sides of the border, this particular service was designed specifically for Haitian patients seeking medical care in Dajabón.

As a general rule, the Haitians I spoke with near the border area did not use the explicit human rights vocabulary and rhetoric promoted by groups such as Manos Unidas. Rather, they expressed a range of ideas and emotions related to rights and justice. Some spoke bitterly of Dominicans' ill will toward Haitians, often using the word *rayi* (hate) to describe how they perceived Dominicans' feelings toward Haitians. They claimed that Dominicans were intent on exploiting and abusing Haitians and would not assist them in times of need. Individuals spoke of arbitrary arrest, forced and unpaid labor, and the mechanisms that impeded their social and economic advancement. Access to health care in these accounts is not singled out as a particular domain of discrimination or abuse, but appears simply as one of many resources Dominicans deny Haitians, along with decent jobs, fair wages, adequate living conditions, and the freedom to circulate throughout the country. Haitians' commentary on these wrongs described them as ill will on the part of Dominicans rather than as human rights violations, although informants clearly expressed that Dominicans' treatment of Haitians is inherently unjust.

Individuals also spoke of being *rezinyé* (resigned) to their fates. Years of poverty and oppression in Haiti have created a climate in which people do not readily expect positive changes. People spoke of small, short-term measures to help alleviate their misery, such as planting a new patch of land or putting their child through another year of school. However, talk of perseverance and of not giving up was tempered with words of pessimism and discouragement. Haitians' loftiest hopes are often expressed in religious terms, with people describing heaven as a reward for the suffering they have experienced on earth. In this context, being denied health services in a Dominican hospital becomes once again part of a much larger discourse—this time, it is one of everyday and unexceptional trials: the struggle to feed oneself and one's family, the constant efforts to maintain one's health in squalid conditions, and the difficulty of knowing that the immediate future holds more threats than promises.

These realities underscore that the concept of the right to health cannot be considered without a discussion of economic terms, particularly when health care is practiced in a capitalist system. Like other socioeconomic rights such as education and decent housing, the right to health is dependent on the availability of resources to implement it. The Haitians I spoke with were acutely aware of this fact, and frequently drew conversations out of the sphere of health and medicine to describe economic realities on a broader scale:

PM: If a Haitian is sick but has no money and goes to a [Dominican] hospital, what happens?
Informant: I don't think that person would even go, because she knows she'd have to have money. For example, to go to the hospital, you need

to pay for transportation in a car, or by motorcycle, if someone can bring you there.

In terms of medical care, some items or procedures such as X-rays and medications had fixed costs, while others, such as disinfecting a wound or hospitalization, appeared to vary according to the situation. Biomedicine's reliance on technological treatments and formally-trained practitioners makes it an expensive form of health care when compared to other forms of healing.[7] Even the low prices that result from government subsidies represent an important expense in the budgets of most families.

Applying the human rights framework to field settings has meant broadening its scope of analysis, as social scientists struggle to deal with topics and issues not covered in conventional human rights theorizing. Lack of economic and social rights, described by Amartya Sen as "unfreedoms" have received an increasing amount of attention in recent years (Sen 1999: 15–17). In a compelling article on representations of Haitian braceros in the Dominican Republic, Samuel Martinez argues that by depicting the braceros' plight in terms of coercion and "neo-slavery," human rights activists have not addressed the economic factors that make Haitian migration to the Dominican Republic largely a consensual phenomenon. He argues, "When human rights activists do not regard dire poverty as a form of unfreedom but ignore it or consider it merely a value-free migration 'push factor,' they participate in sustaining public ignorance of and indifference to the wider issue of poverty and its role in undermining individual liberties worldwide" (Martinez 1996: 17). The author calls into question human rights activists' assumptions that laborers are "free" before their work in deplorable conditions in the Dominican Republic, and hopes to use political economy to straddle Marxist and liberal theories on rights and freedoms (Martinez 1996: 18–21).

This perspective is highly relevant at the border hospital, where one must consider the health care options (or relative lack thereof) that Haitians have access to before seeking treatment in Dajabón. Categorizing the refusal of treatment as a human rights violation directs attention away from both the abysmal economic conditions in Haiti as well as the scarcity of resources in Dominican hospitals and clinics. Nevertheless, the language of human rights has become an international language used by activists, NGOs of all kinds, governments, and other agents to denounce suffering and mobilize action. When one aims to garner international support and funds, the term "human rights violation" is particularly effective. It gains, rather than loses, intensity when exported and decontextualized, whether in the form of a published report, news broadcast, or appeal for political or financial support. Scholars have asked, "Human rights claims carry with them an enormous legitimacy . . . Why do they achieve this, and why are they expressed in such a form?" (Dembour 1996: 35) A related question would ask why extreme poverty and the tedium of "ordinary" suffering do not carry a similar legitimacy.

Medical Humanitarianism and the Sisters of Perpetual Mercy

I use the term "medical humanitarianism" here to describe the provision of health care (in the form of services, treatments, or products) by a biomedical practitioner to a sick or injured person whose capacity to pay for the care is restricted or nonexistent. Practitioners and patients understand the provision of health care in this context to be an altruistic gesture on the part of the practitioner, who has been moved to action by the patient's condition. The practitioner is not obliged to treat the patient, but does so out of compassion and benevolence.

Although medical humanitarianism on the Haitian-Dominican border takes place on a wide scale and involves major institutions, those involved often interpret it in individual and humanized terms. This may be due to several factors. Although the hospital staff has a uniform classification for cases that are worthy of receiving services (*emergencias*), this category is not well defined, and treatment ultimately depends on individual judgment. In addition, there are no visible clues that indicate to Haitians that official policies or regulations permit their presence in the hospital. Without a designated waiting area, special hours of service, or documentation such as files or forms, Haitians' medical encounters at the border hospital are indeed highly individualized. Finally, even if the services and resources are ultimately traceable to the Dominican government, it may be easier to conceive of this distant, abstract entity in concrete, human terms. For example, a woman waiting with her friend in the emergency room told me that if Haitians received care in Dominican hospitals, it was because the Dominican state had a "good heart" and described the medical services as "favors." Another informant, when asked if the Dominican government had an obligation to treat Haitian patients, replied: "According to me, I would say yes, but it depends on the state [*léta*], what it knows, and what reasons it has. I can't say that it must give services, but as for me, I would have to give them if I had them."

Patients were not the only ones to describe medical care to Haitians in such terms. Some of the Dominican hospital staff also used similar language. One nurse, when asked about Haitian patients, replied, "We attend them with a thousand loves (*con mil amores*)." Doctors and nurses frequently used the term *humanitario* [humanitarian]. They also used the term *humano*, which can be translated as either "human" or "humane."[8] Some referred to the care provided to Haitians as *asistencia* [assistance], but they also used the standard medical term *atender* [to attend to]. For the most part, Dominican practitioners spoke to me quite matter-of-factly about caring for Haitian patients: it was simply something that made up part of their workday. Given my position as an outside observer and as someone who spoke openly about his experiences in and connections to Haiti, informants may have concealed anti-Haitian sentiments, which are commonplace among Dominicans of all social backgrounds (Howard 2001: 182). Some hospital employees, however, took pains to clarify that if Dominican health care providers treated Haitian patients, it was because of "razones humanas" [humane reasons] rather than obligation. One health outreach worker explained, "The Dominican State does not have . . . should not have any responsibility to give health services to Haiti because we are an independent nation. But for humane reasons and because we share the same island . . . But we are two independent countries." Social processes on the island of Hispaniola are regularly described in such nationalistic terms, despite the common origins of the two countries as former European slave-based colonies, the migration between the countries, and the extensive economic, social, and cultural ties which bind people on both sides of the island.

Since 1997, a U.S.-based Catholic foundation has sponsored low-cost surgeries, sonograms, and other health services to the Dominican border area. The foundation is run by a community of nuns (The Sisters of Perpetual Mercy, or SPM) who offer a variety of health and social services throughout the Dominican Republic. By all accounts, their project—referred to as the *convenio,* or agreement—has had a major impact on the hospital, both in terms of physical structures, staffing, and health services. It pays the salary of two physicians who work at the hospital full-time, and of several physicians and technicians who come to the hospital on a weekly basis, including a gynecologist, a urologist, and a sonographer.

The *convenio* began in response to a perceived absence of government services in the area. During my time in Dajabón, I was repeatedly told that Dominican national leaders and politicians neglected the border area, mainly because of its distance from the capital and its low population. When describing the origins of the *convenio*, informants focused as much, if not more, on structural and bureaucratic inefficiencies as on patients' needs. A doctor and administrator told me his thoughts at the onset of the project: "I'm a surgeon—let's operate!" Improving the hospital's buildings and physical resources was an early priority, followed by the development of human resources. These endeavors generated a certain amount of conflict. My perspectives on these conflicts are limited, as both hospital staff and program representatives were reluctant to discuss them. I was informed, however, that some "enemies of the program" still existed in the hospital, and that the program's staff continues to experience some difficulties when working with the hospital's staff. One informant stated that "there are people who have more to gain from disorder." Overall, however, the consensus seemed to be that the program is a success. The foundation has achieved its goal of making low-cost surgeries (USD 10–50) available for the border population. Basic surgeries, such as hysterectomies, cataract removal, and the removal of tumors take place on a regular basis. Several thousand patients have been treated since the *convenio* was established, including poor patients from other provinces.

It was initially unclear to me whether or not Haitians were eligible for the services offered through the *convenio*. When I asked project administrators about their target population, they told me that they work with "the poorest, most forgotten, most dispossessed of all." I asked if this included Haitians, and was informed that yes, since the beginning of the *convenio*, treating Haitians had been part of the program's "nature." In a telling statement, the program's director said, "There are no differences between Haitians and Dominicans—we see pathology, sick people." While the group's work in the border hospital involves agreements and cooperation with the Dominican government (including use of space, collaborative work on health programs, and meetings with government ministers), no such ties exist with Haitian authorities or Dominican border guards. There are no specific agreements with the guards that permit Haitians to cross the border to obtain services through the *convenio*, and the program's administrators were unsure if the guards even knew of the program. Less than a mile away, at the Haitian government hospital in Ouanaminthe, administrators knew that patients cross to Dajabón for medical services, but were unaware of the SPM's program, and had no official policy or program for referring patients to Dajabón. Like many other NGOs working with Haitians, either in Haiti or from abroad, the *convenio* sidesteps the Haitian government altogether.

Although both humanitarian and human rights rhetorics shaped the discourse and practices of my informants, they remained distinct and at times contradictory in nature. If health is conceived of as a human right, a sick or injured individual has the right to receive health services. Therefore, practitioners have an obligation to treat patients: refusal to do so constitutes a human rights violation. According to humanitarian rhetoric, the indigent patient becomes the object of the practitioner's good will and compassion. The practitioner does not expect to be compensated monetarily for medical services rendered, but rather offers them as a gift to someone less fortunate. Refusal to treat in this context does not constitute a violation of another's right, but rather the personal choice of a free agent.

Compassion: A Moral Emotion

Reflections on the place of compassion in both human rights and humanitarian rhetoric offer insights into the links and distinctions between the two. At the root of the concept of compassion is the notion of "suffering with." The theologian Oliver Davies describes it in the following terms: " . . . the recognition of another's condition, entailing a degree of participation in the suffering of the other, an embrace of that fellow-suffering and a preparedness to act on their behalf" (Davies 2001: 235). Compassion is often included among the moral emotions, which have been described as emotions that "*are linked to the interests or welfare either of society as a whole or at least of persons other than the judge or agent* [italics in original]" (Haidt 2003: 853). Haidt classifies compassion as a member of the "other-suffering" family of emotions, and favors the term over "empathy" or "sympathy," which describe the "ability to feel what another person is feeling, including happiness, anger or boredom" (862) rather than a particular emotion in and of itself.

The philosopher Martha Nussbaum has called compassion the "basic social emotion," and argues that it is "a central bridge between the individual and the community; it is conceived of as our species' way of hooking the interests of others to our own personal goods" (Nussbaum 1996: 28). She makes the following arguments about compassion and justice:

[Compassion] is not sufficient for justice, since it focuses on need and offers no account of liberty, rights, or respect for human dignity. . . . Although compassion does presuppose that the person does not deserve the (full measure) of the hardship he or she endures, it does not entail that the person has a *right* or a just claim to relief. Further argument would be required to get to that conclusion. On the other hand, compassion at least makes us see the importance of the person's lack, and consider with keen interest the claim that such a person might have. In that sense it provides an essential bridge to justice. (37)

The relationship Nussbaum identifies between compassion and justice (and, by extension, to humanitarianism and human rights), however, does not eliminate the difference between the two rhetorics. While compassion may be a motivating factor for human rights activists and institutions, it is not as central therein as it is in humanitarian rhetoric. Compassion implies a shared suffering, whereas human rights rhetoric, with its individualizing focus, creates separations between victims, perpetrators, and advocates. Some activists are working to eliminate these distinctions: when human rights activists claim that the violation of a person's rights threatens the rights of all people, they are promoting notions of collectivity and mutual suffering. The need to verbalize and promote this argument suggests that it is not inherent to individualizing human rights discourses. A sense of collectivity and social obligation is not only central to humanitarian conceptions of human relations, it is also the impetus for action. Another distinction is that human rights are deployed in a preemptive fashion: even in the absence of rights violations, human rights activists can operate for the promotion, dissemination, and protection of rights. Humanitarian activity, on the other hand, is restricted to *responses* to suffering and misery. In the absence of these, humanitarian activities are moot. Anthropologists have argued for new conceptions of human rights that would move from individualized to collective conceptions of human rights and bodily suffering (Adams 1998). Such conceptions would be instrumental for clearer understandings of the lived experiences of human rights and humanitarianism, of justice and compassion.

Conclusion

It should be emphasized that human rights and humanitarian operations, despite their distinctions, are increasingly converging and borrowing each other's language and tactics. Minear (2002) explains that this rapprochement intensified during the 1990s, when human rights organizations began to include the promotion of economic, social, and cultural rights within their mandates. At the same time, humanitarian groups became increasingly concerned with addressing the structural and political dimensions of humanitarian catastrophes. Minear claims that "from each side, the perceived convergence of relief and rights represents a major conceptual breakthrough" (41). Recent promotion of the "right to receive humanitarian aid" illustrates to what extent these movements have become intertwined (Echavé and Chommienne-Abboud 2002). In considering the convergence of humanitarianism and human rights, it is pertinent to mention the career of Paul Farmer, who has worked extensively in Haiti for over twenty years. Best known for his work in the area of health and social justice, Farmer's clinical practice, activism, and numerous publications have attracted attention worldwide. He frequently uses the cases of patients in Haiti to make a convincing point: virtually any case of suffering or illness in impoverished settings can be understood as a consequence of poverty, the legacies of slavery and/or colonialism, and continued exploitation by international forces. Farmer has drawn from and contributed to diverse intellectual traditions, including world systems theories, political economy of health, liberation theology, and theories of structural violence (Farmer 1992; 2003).

Farmer's work is an example of the increasing overlap and intensified relationship between humanitarianism and human rights. Both rhetorics are prominent in Farmer's work, which promotes human rights in what can be interpreted as a classic humanitarian project: the provision of assistance to the poor and suffering. In Farmer's case, the form of assistance (medical services) is particularly salient. He draws frequently on his role as a physician to reinforce his claims and justify his perspectives. Farmer's success has not gone unnoticed—the health and social justice approach has become a model for international health workers who recognize its efficacy both in treating patients and garnering support.

Future research in this area should pay particular attention to the social processes that accompany and result from health and social justice projects, and international health interventions more broadly. When carried out among impoverished populations, these interventions are likely to have a wide range of marked and far-reaching impacts on individuals and communities. International organizations—particularly those with substantial funding and resources—can and do establish themselves as major players in the local political economies of the societies in which they work. Few analyses have considered the complications that emerge from international efforts to treat patients in impoverished settings: triage of patients, implementation of care, dealing with staff turnover and burnout, and confronting local politics and bureaucracies. Health care encounters in settings such as

Haiti are fraught with tensions, as patients and providers negotiate class animosity, scarce resources, and conflicting priorities (Maternowska 2006; Brodwin 1996). The presence of international groups further complicates the picture.

The case of international organizations treating Haitian patients in Dominican hospitals raises complex questions about governance and power. Pandolfi, writing on humanitarian organizations in the Balkans, has identified new forms of "supra-colonial" powers that are deployed in an increasing number of settings around the world (Pandolfi 2002). The directors of the *convenio*, in their elaborate and precise descriptions of the Dominican state's failure to provide for their citizens, situate their project as an explicitly political one, and yet shy away from such politicization in their claims of seeing pathology rather than nationality. Conflicts between the program administrators and the hospital administrators are examples of the tensions that can emerge out of contests for power under a weak state.

Similar complications are present in the work carried out by innumerable international agencies and organizations in Haiti. Their very presence underlines the complex and conflicted relationship between the Haitian state and the country's population. When present, agents of the Haitian state (including ministers, officials, police, and military personnel) have historically worked against the interest of the people by taxing, exploiting, and terrorizing them (Trouillot, 1990). Oftentimes, however, the state is simply missing or absent, and much of the infrastructure and resources generally considered to be the state's responsibility—roads, schools, health care, environmental regulation, sanitation—are nowhere near adequate. During my research, I frequently heard individuals complain "Léta pa fè anyen pou nou" [The state does nothing for us]. New projects and emerging infrastructure in Haiti often result from the initiatives or support of international organizations, which operate in virtually every sphere of life there. Future work is needed to understand the social relations and forms of governance that emerge out of this aid.

In addition, attention should be paid to the relationships *between* foreign organizations and agencies. In Haiti and the Dominican Republic, international groups and agencies from the United States, Canada, Cuba, Europe, and Asia operate hospitals and clinics, sponsor medical missions, provide human and material resources, and carry out education campaigns. These groups vary in size, strategy, and activity. Working at a public hospital in northern Haiti, I counted over twenty international entities present there, many of which exemplify the convergence of humanitarian and human rights rhetorics. How this convergence affects the design and implementation of health projects in the long term remains to be seen.

The plights of Haitians and other impoverished populations have no simple solutions. Medical personnel have a professional responsibility to treat the sick and injured, but often lack the resources and capacity to do so. Impoverished patients are often unable to pay for their health care in spite of their arduous labor and careful management of limited finances. Understanding and improving the outcomes of health interventions in resource-poor settings will require further investigation of the moral and ethical landscapes through which patients, providers, administrators, and funders must navigate.

Notes

1. This research was funded by the Social Sciences and Humanities Research Council of Canada. I am grateful to the patients and staff at the border hospital as well to members of the organizations and communities that made this research possible. I was fortunate to receive comments on earlier versions of this text from Allan Young, Paul Brodwin, Vinh-Kim Nguyen, Mark Schuller, and James Clark. Finally, I am indebted to Rose-Marie Chierici and Catherine Maternowska for their ongoing mentorship and encouragement.

2. I have chosen the word "rhetoric" to describe health as a human right and medical humanitarianism, but wish to stress that I am using the term in its broadest sense. While rhetoric generally refers to persuasive speech or language, I will also use it to include actions and dynamic processes that emerge from particular ways of understanding social interactions and identities, and in turn, are employed to obtain results from other individuals. The persuasive dimensions of the term "rhetoric" are particularly relevant given that humanitarians and human rights activists actively promote their visions and techniques, and aspire toward a widespread implementation of their values and practices at the local, national, and international levels.

3. To my knowledge, the only Haitian patient who stayed in the hospital overnight during the time I carried out my research was a man who had been arrested and injured by Dominican police. He was under the continual surveillance of an armed guard.

4. The issue of Haitian women delivering babies in Dominican hospitals is of particular importance in light of the controversies surrounding attribution of Dominican citizenship to children of Haitian parents. While Dominican law clearly states that any individual born on Dominican soil has the right to Dominican citizenship, Dominican authorities often do not provide proof of place of birth. There is therefore a large population of Haitian-Dominicans who were born in the Dominican Republic and whose families have lived there for many years, but who have no documentation to protect

them from arrest and deportation. Infants born to Haitian mothers at the border hospital are not granted Dominican citizenship.

5. The names of organizations described in this essay are pseudonyms.

6. The staff of Manos Unidas either hears about these individuals through community networks or is approached by patients directly. Requests for accompaniment occur frequently, but unpredictably.

7. Leaf-based and/or spiritual healings are not free of cost, however. In a growing number of areas, leaves must be purchased rather than gathered. Consultations with Vodou healing specialists generally involve payment, or at least the purchase of ritual paraphernalia such as alcohol and candles.

8. I suspect that the latter translation more accurately conveys the connotations expressed in their comments.

References

Adams, Vincanne. 1998. "Suffering the Winds of Lhasa: Politicized Bodies, Human Rights, Cultural Difference and Humanism in Tibet." *Medical Anthropology Quarterly* 12, no. 1: 74–102.

Boisseron, Monique. 2002. "Haïti dans le regard de la République Dominicaine dans la seconde moitié du XIXème siècle." Doctoral Dissertation. Université des Antilles et de la Guyane.

Brodwin, Paul. 1996. *Medicine and Morality in Haiti: The Contest for Healing Power.* New York: Cambridge University Press.

Davies, Oliver. 2001. *A Theology of Compassion: Metaphysics of Difference and the Renewal of Tradition.* London: SCM Press.

Dembour, Marie Bénédicte. 1996. "Human rights talk and anthropological ambivalence: the particular contexts of universal claims." In *Inside and Outside the Law: Anthropological Studies of Authority and Ambivalence*, edited by Olivia Harris, 19–40. London: Routledge.

Echavé, Vincent and Marie-Hélène Chomienne-Abboud. 2002. "Mutations dans l'aide humanitaire." In *L'action humanitaire du Canada*, edited by Yvan Conoir and Gérard Verna, 100–119. Laval: Université Laval.

EMMUS IV. 2006. *Enquête Mortalité, Morbidité et Utilisation des Services IV, Haïti 2005–6.* Calverton: Ministère de la Santé Publique et de la Population, Institut Haïtien de l'Enfance et ORC Macro.

Farmer, Paul. 1992. *AIDS and Accusation: Haiti and the Geography of Blame.* Berkeley: University of California Press.

———. 2003. *Pathologies of Power: Health, Human Rights, and the New War on the Poor.* Berkeley: University of California Press.

Haidt, Jonathan. 2003. "The Moral Emotions." In *Handbook of Affective Sciences*, edited by Richard J. Davidson et al., 852–870. Oxford: Oxford University Press.

Howard, David. 2001. *Coloring the Nation: Race and Ethnicity in the Dominican Republic.* Oxford: Signal Books Limited.

Martinez, Samuel. 1996. "Indifference Within Indignation: Anthropology, Human Rights and the Haitian Bracero." *American Anthropologist* 98, no. 1: 17–25.

Maternowska, Catherine M. 2006. *Reproducing Inequities: Poverty and the Politics of Population in Haiti.* Piscataway: Rutgers University Press.

Messer, Ellen. 1993. "Anthropology and Human Rights." *Annual Review of Anthropology*, no. 22: 221–249.

Minear, Larry. 2002. *The Humanitarian Enterprise: Dilemmas and Discoveries.* Bloomfield: Kumarian Press.

Nussbaum, Martha. 1996. "Compassion: The Basic Social Emotion." *Social Philosophy and Policy* 13, no. 1: 27–58.

Pandolfi, Mariella. 2002. "'Moral Entrepreneurs': Souverainetés mouvantes et barbelés: Le biopolitique dans les Balkans postcommunistes." *Anthropologie et Société* 26, no. 1: 29–51.

Sen, Amartya. 1999. *Development as Freedom.* New York: Anchor Books.

SESPAS (*Secretaría de Estado, Salud Publica y Asistencia Social*). 2001. "Incidencia de la Demanda de Servicios de Salud de Extranjeros." Santo Domingo: SESPAS.

Simmons, David. Personal communication. July 2003.

Trouillot, Michel-Rolph. 1990. *Haiti, State Against Nation: The Origins and Legacy of Duvalierism.* New York: Monthly Review Press.

WHO: Online document, http://www.who.int/whosis/en/index.html.

Wilson, Richard A. 1997. "Human Rights, Culture and Context: An Introduction." In *Human Rights, Culture And Context: Anthropological Perspectives*, edited by Richard Wilson, 1–27. London: Pluto.

6

Refugee Rights in the Caribbean

A Study of Haitians in Jamaica

SHARON E. CLARKE

> ... portrayed as stateless wanderers with unimpeded reach to coastal waters ... The
> discourse distances their plight from the human rights abuses, from the conflict
> and dysfunctional inequalities in the global economic system . . . and their need
> for humanitarian assistance is usually ignored in presenting the issue.
>
> Mark Pugh, "Drowning Not Waving: Boat People and Humanitarianism at Sea."

Introduction: A Case of Historical Solidarity?

Throughout their history, from colonial times to the present, Haitians fleeing their land have sought and found refuge in Jamaica. At the time of the
Haitian Revolution, many French planters, often bringing along their slaves,
relocated to Jamaica. In the nineteenth and twentieth centuries, exiled politicians or other members of elite families found in Jamaica a place of refuge
from political persecution. However, Haitian presence in Jamaica remained
relatively insignificant for many years. It was not until 1991, when President
Jean-Bertrand Aristide was ousted, that Haitians began to arrive in Jamaica
in noticeably larger numbers. Forty were granted refugee status in 1991, and
another six in 2002.[1] Over time, an estimated 1,000 Haitians settled in Jamaica. Having previously supported the Aristide regime and objecting to his
latest ouster amid controversial circumstances in January 2004, the island
maintained its political solidarity with the former regime. Thus Aristide
found refuge in Jamaica before heading to Africa, much to the chagrin of
the United States' Bush administration and the Haitian interim government
which threatened to " . . . freeze relations with Jamaica and CARICOM."[2] An
article in the Jamaican press in April 2005 entitled "More Security Needed
For Haitians" triggered the enquiry that follows.[3]

This study contributes to forced migration literature within a geographical region not generally associated with "refugee" issues. To that end it con-

cerns itself with international refugee and human rights law, and by virtue of the subject, forced migration in developing societies. By focusing on the most recent Haitian refugees in Jamaica, my research analyzes how policy toward Haitian refugees is determined and how Haitian identities are produced and reproduced in response to those policies.

What became apparent is that " . . . who is a refugee is as much a matter of pragmatic political interpretation as one based on international law or supranational humanitarian imperatives" (Zetter 1999). Stephen Vasciannie (1996), previously argued that following U.S. geopolitical considerations, the Jamaican government, in its dealings with refugees has a " . . . perception that refugee matters are almost exclusively concerned with political concerns" (Vasciannie 1996: 3–4).[4] This study found that while the Jamaican government's initial response appeared favorable to the initial influx of Haitian refugees, the processes for determining refugee status and the ultimate treatment of the Haitian refugees left much to be desired. The processes were based on the assumption that the refugees as a group would remain in Jamaica for as short a time as possible. The issues of real potential risk in individual circumstances were largely ignored.

Methodology: A Multi-Dimensional Strategy

Using an anthropological case study approach and international human rights instruments, this work explores the phenomenon of forced Haitian migration to Jamaica during the political crisis that shook Haiti in 2004–2005 (See Brownlie and Goodwin-Gill 2002). It also discusses the response of the Jamaican government (henceforth "GoJ") to the Haitian refugee influx.[5] This enquiry, carried out over nine months, began with a fundamental question: how had the GoJ used international treaties and conventions to provide protection for Haitian refugees reaching its shores and seeking asylum?

At the initial stages of this research, I determined that I needed a focused group of informants for collecting credible primary sources. I first arranged -a meeting with government officials in advance of my arrival in Jamaica. I was also fortunate enough to be introduced to a prominent Jamaican queen's counsel (henceforth "QC") with direct contact to the Independent Jamaica Council for Human Rights (henceforth IJCHR).[6] This affected the snowball technique of purposive sampling and proved to be highly successful. In addition to my meeting with government officials, I was able to meet and conduct in-depth interviews with the legal officer of the IJCHR who acted as counsel for the Haitian refugees. This gave me access to case files and opportunities to meet with IJCHR's Haitian clients.

The office of the IJCHR facilitated interviews with the local representative of the United Nations High Commission for Refugees (henceforth UNHCR), and the Jesuit Society. In addition, at an earlier stage of this research, I used newspaper articles and other ephemera from the two years prior to 2004 in order to specifically explore whether Vasciannie's observations remained valid today: that refugee matters in Jamaica were political rather than humanitarian concerns. Subsequently, I carried out further reading of Stuart Hall, Henri Lefebvre, and Eric Wolf in an attempt to analyze the Haitian experience in a society where the host government became increasingly hostile toward them. This led me to an unusual conceptual framework where the realms of Haitian identity and notions of self are examined within a context dominated by contradictory forces: international legal instruments designed to protect refugees and a government—initially sympathetic—eventually determined to be rid of them.

The government argued that socioeconomic conditions made the burden of the Haitian refugees unsustainable, and began referring to them as economic migrants. To this end, there seemed to be a concerted effort by the GoJ to affect Jamaican public perception of these Haitians in a negative way. According to Myrtha Désulmé, the only prominent and vocal Haitian in Jamaica, Haitians settle there regardless of their social backgrounds and opt to maintain very low-key profiles " . . . to hide their origins as much as possible."[7] This may suggest that Haitians in Jamaica who have been offered the rare opportunity to remain, reinvent diasporic identities by distancing themselves from their immediate past. Even though historical and cultural links undoubtedly exist between Haitian refugees and their country of origin, there is no visible Haitian diaspora. The notion of a "Haitian Self" has not transitioned from Haiti into Jamaica and speaks to the elusive phenomenon of identity—a primary feature of migration in general. Identity should be understood " . . . as a 'production,' which is never complete, always in process, and always constituted within, not outside, representation" (Hall 1990: 222).

Jamaica's "Goodwill" Response

Like you, I well remember that I grew up in the house of others and in a foreign land. I faced deadly dangers. So that, whoever asks my hospitality, as you do now, I would not know how to turn away

Theseus, King of Athens counseling Oedipus, the King of Thebes (quoted in UNHCR 2004.)

Haitians began to flee their country by the thousands in January and early February 2004. Recognizing the political catastrophe taking place in Haiti, the UNHCR issued " . . . demarches in February and March to all governments in the region," (UNHCR 2004a: 10) requesting them to receive Haitians under temporary protection(UNHCR 2004b: 462). The UNHCR asked that Haitians not wishing to be returned to Haiti not be made to do so. Regional governments were also asked to " . . . provide them with the basic minimum needs, until the situation . . . stabilized and/or a durable solution . . . found" (UNHCR 2004c). During the same period Haitians had begun to arrive in relatively small numbers on the islands of Cuba, Dominica, St. Kitts and Nevis, St. Lucia, Trinidad and Tobago, and across Haiti's land border into the Dominican Republic. (UNHCR 2004d).

A Jamaican ambassador discussed the role of CARICOM with me and expressed the opinion that while CARICOM had offered "moral support," it could not be relied on for further assistance. Customs officers from Grand Bahamas and Anguilla whom I spoke with had more proactive views. Focusing on the lack of leadership and guidance from CARICOM, these officers stated that public opinion toward Haitians was characterized by empathy in Grand Bahamas and Anguilla. The officers expressed their view that CARICOM should have assumed a more central role in assisting Jamaica with burden-sharing in the region, but that American foreign policy had been integral to their lack of action. Ultimately, the view was that fear of reprisal from the United States in the form of reduced aid assistance had "paralyzed most member states."[8]

The Jamaican government, on the other hand, in fierce defiance of American policy, offered Aristide political sanctuary in March 2004. Jamaica's stance was initially much applauded among its southern neighbors, and its credibility within the international community much enhanced. Long before Aristide arrived, Jamaica had made clear that it would not return Haitians who arrived on its shores.

The first refugees landed along Jamaica's southeastern coast on February 1, 2004. The boat contained ten people: eight policemen and two sailors. The policemen were in uniform and carried their duty weapons.[9] The numbers soon swelled to more than 500 by mid-March, arriving in what newspapers described as "rickety boats."[10] In an article entitled "Jamaica will accept refugees," Minister of National Security Peter Philipps stated that, "We certainly don't propose to throw them back into the sea when they present themselves on our shores," and the Haitians were warmly welcomed. Newspaper and media coverage were initially sympathetic to the plight of the Haitians and a similar public mood was reflected in letters to newspaper editors.[11] Declaring from the outset that local resources were scarce, Phillips nevertheless added, " . . . we will keep them in the best condition that we can . . ."[12]

It was soon to become clear that the previous use of municipal jails or local church halls would be insufficient to serve the increasing numbers arriving, and in negotiations with UNHCR, two reception centers were identified and fully refurbished, in addition to " . . . whatever else was necessary," on the government's behalf by UN agencies.[13] The UNHCR emergency operations officer, having left Geneva, was to change his destination from the Dominican Republic to Jamaica. Such were the rapidly occurring events there. In Jamaica, Paul Saunders, the deputy general of the Office of Disasters Preparedness and Emergency Management (ODPEM), was tasked with administrating both centers.

During my meeting with government officials, it was made clear from the outset that Jamaica's obligations began with the 1951 Refugee Convention and the principle of non-refoulement, and I was reminded that, "throughout the years we have been dealing with Haitian refugees."

The 1951 Refugee Convention on the Status of Refugees (henceforth 1951CSR) defines a refugee as one who: " . . . owing to a well-founded fear of being persecuted for reasons of race, religion, nationality, membership of a particular social group or political opinion, is outside the country of his nationality, and is unable or, owing to such fear, is unwilling to avail himself of the protection of that country . . ."[14]

Fundamental to this convention is the non-derogable nature of non-refoulement, which is especially applicable to refugees at sea as the Haitians were. The 1951CSR, Art. 33(1) of non-refoulement states that: " . . . no contracting state shall expel or return (refouler) a refugee in any manner whatsoever to the frontiers or territories where his life or freedom would be threatened on account of race, religion, nationality, membership of a particular social group or political opinion."

No mention was made of any other international legal instruments and Jamaica's involvement in this most recent episode was explained as " . . . an

extended period of political instability, economic instability, social dislocation, which came to a crescendo . . ." with the "forced departure from Haiti"
of Aristide.[15] Throughout the meeting, persistent references were made to
the "not insignificant costs" incurred by the government in meeting its international obligations.

However, I was soon to learn that the government was not alone in its
concern for the Haitian refugees and their plight. There was an overwhelming and genuine outpouring of goodwill from the Jamaican public and civil
society, and the Haitians received gestures of hospitality in abundance. The
Salvation Army, the Jamaica Red Cross, and the Adventist Development
and Relief Agency International (ADRA) were instrumental at the Winnifred Rest Home in providing food for everyone. Food for the Poor donated
at least two dozen two-bedroom board structure units to the other center
in Montpelier, as well as food items. The Jesuit Refugee Society and smaller
church groups such as the Seventh Day Adventists also donated aid assistance. The UNHCR representative recalled how during visits to Montpelier
she had met with individuals who had attended representing church groups
saying, "we have all these clothes, or we have brought these sets of shoes, or
we have these toys for the children." She was " . . . at Winifred when a group
from the U.S. who had a link with the parish of St. Mary said they'd heard
about this and they came and brought medical supplies . . ."

The private sector also contributed. A local building firm donated roof-
ing for the buildings at Montpelier. The Egg Farmers Association donated
eggs for several weeks to the Winifred camp; the Jamaica Broilers Group
contributed a steady supply of chickens, and the Grace Food Company donated soft drinks and other food items, as did the Jamaica Biscuit company.
An earlier government report had thanked the public for its goodwill and
assistance, stating that "there was still a need for toiletries at the . . . cen-
tres and a deep freeze to be used for preserving meats and other items . .
." requiring refrigeration.[16] It seemed certain, by all accounts, that Jamaica
had received a vast amount of assistance and support in facilitating the Haitian refugees, and Ruud Lubbers, the United Nations high commissioner
for refugees " . . . lauded the government and the people of Jamaica for the
'generosity of spirit' with which the country . . . received . . . displaced Haitians."[17]

It is interesting to note that apart from one Désulmé whose input included offering her services as interpreter, the Haitian diaspora in Jamaica
was silent throughout this entire episode, and any goodwill gestures made
were anonymous. In contrast, the Haitian diaspora in south Florida was

Table 6.1. UNHCR Funding for Reception of Haitians in Jamaica, 2004–2005

2004	BUDGET (USD)
Spent	382,179.00
Unspent (returned to headquarters, Geneva)	33,154.48
Total funding	415,327.00
2005	**BUDGET (USD)**
Legal assistance/asylum appeals	6,000.00
Transport	4,000.00
Food	20,000.00
Shelter/maintenance	5,000.00
Water	2,500.00
Domestic needs/household support	1,150.00
Health	10,000.00
Sanitation	1,000.00
Training	3,000.00
Operational support (to agencies)	53,072.00
Total funding—1st qtr. 2005 (GoJ subproject)	105,722.00
TOTAL UNHCR FUNDING TO GoJ 2004—1st qtr. 2005	521,049.00

Source: data from UNHCR, Jamaica local representative.

extremely visible with aid assistance of clothes and food provided through the Eye on Jamaica Project. The project's aid totaled fifteen thousand USD and was distributed at the Winnifred camp.[18] In an article entitled "Help for Haitian Refugees," the government reported that the Winnifred camp also received, "A trailer-load of food, clothing and medical supplies," from the United Caribbean American Network of New Jersey (UCAN-NJ).[19]

With such "goodwill" from the public and civil society, and with UN funding and logistical assistance, perhaps the Jamaican government keeping " . . . them in the best condition that we can," is best explained through the following social drama. In discussions related to cost-effective use of funding in providing a daily diet that included proteins for the refugees, the UNHCR suggested that the GoJ consider supplementing the food intake with beans. To appreciate the response, one must consider the linguistic arrangement of the dialect in Jamaican patois. Clearly, both horrified and bewildered at this suggestion, the Jamaican official's response was:

But wi don' use beans. Wi cyaan gi di people dem dat! We cyaan gi dem dat type a ting. Beans?!?? We don' use beans here. I don' think wi can gi di people dem beans!

UNHCR considered it incomprehensible that the GoJ could take such a position on the matter. When I asked later how this had been resolved, I was told that the refugees had been given "box-lunches." In Jamaica, a box-lunch refers to a take-away meal of either plain rice or rice and peas; usually cooked chicken—curried, jerked or otherwise—with a portion of fresh green salad, and a side-helping of fried plantain or other vegetable. Discussing this issue with someone else and with no mention of the official's response, this female was staggered by the mere suggestion of beans as being able to constitute or supplement a meal, and she too proclaimed:

> Beans! Beans! Yu can gi smaddy beans fi eat? How people fi survive pon beans? Not even di prisoner dem a St Catherine (those on death row) na get beans fi eat! No, no, no!! Dat is wickedness. Yu cyaan gi people beans . . . Dem need yam and dumpling and rice!

It is perhaps then not so incomprehensible that the Jamaican government took the position it did, since although anecdotal, this separate response some two years later would seem to represent Jamaicans' attitude toward food and what is perceived as providing nourishment.[20] However, what seemed not to be considered was how the cost of these "box-lunches" might impinge on the overall budget for the refugees. In addition, the government had promised that the Haitian refugees would receive vocational skills training to prepare them for their return home since, as the minister for land and environment pointed out, "it is important that we consider their development," adding that " . . . when they leave Jamaica they will be empowered."[21]

In the meanwhile, by June 2004—the same month Aristide departed from Jamaica to Africa—many of the refugees had begun expressing their desire to be voluntarily repatriated. However, "due to the continued climate of volatility in Haiti . . ." and with no field presence there "to monitor . . . return and integration," the UNHCR did not endorse or encourage these returns (UNHCR 2004c). In recognition of the Haitians' human rights, the agency facilitated their wish to return, but each returnee was asked to sign a declaration of voluntary return, which clearly highlighted the UNHCR's concerns. By the end of July 2004, in a UNHCR partnership with the International Organization for Migration (IOM) and the United Nation Development Program (UNDP), and at " . . . absolutely no cost to the Jamaican government," 280 Haitians were voluntarily repatriated. These first repatriations proved to be somewhat revelatory to all concerned.

Although the government had made it clear that Haitians were not per-

mitted to work, many of them demonstrated their resourcefulness by finding employment. It was also reported that "workers at a popular car wash,
located on the outskirts of Montego Bay . . ." were earning, " . . . based on
the number of vehicles they washed. 'If the car cost J$300 to wash, the boss
would give them J$100 out of that,' one worker said, adding that the Haitians
were very hard working. In Portland, refugees said many of them earn between J$600 and J$1,000 a day by doing odd jobs that many locals refuse to
do or would demand more compensation to complete."[22].The Jesuit Refugee
Society confirmed to me that the Haitians were described as " . . . an indus-
trious people who will do the jobs Jamaicans won't do."

State authorities did little to prevent this, although a spokesperson in the
National Security Ministry (MNS) insisted that Jamaicans would be pros-
ecuted for illegally hiring refugees. A Jamaican interviewed in the same article who had hired Haitians said " . . . they work to get items that are needed
for the household and personal use—like tissue, soap and toothpaste . . ."
A Haitian who had sought employment elaborated: "Some of us leave the
camp and get jobs to cut down bush, to do masonry work while others work
in the markets. Most of us want to look nice and smell good so we spend
most of the money on clothes and perfume," and many of those at both the
Montpelier and Winnifred camps worked and accumulated both goods and
independent funds.

The goods accumulated were such that, " . . . they appeared to have been
on shopping trips to Miami." UNHCR recalled that " . . . they had all these
boxes . . ." On the first repatriation flight, the aircraft was unable to carry
the weight and goods had to be sent on later. The UNHCR was prompted to
review the situation and change the voluntary declaration to include weight
limitations. Another forty eight voluntary repatriations were organized by
the UNHCR in August 2004, bringing the total to 328. However, over time,
their resourcefulness—which demonstrated the Haitian's ability to integrate
and lessen the socioeconomic burden on Jamaican society—was miscon-
strued and negatively influenced later events.

Contrary to prevailing perceptions, the socioeconomic integration of
refugees into host societies is more likely to alleviate the burden they are
perceived to be, and in many instances this integration is even beneficial.
In determining their own fate, refugees aid host societies in simultaneously
upholding universal freedoms and fundamental rights of moral and physical integrity and liberty (Rogge 1987; Rutinwa 1996; Verdirame and Harrell-
Bond 2005: 16). It was clear that the Haitians were a proud, hardworking,
and resourceful people who sought to show that they need not be a burden

on the state, provided they were given the opportunity. With the "process" taking so long, they had sought ways of using their time meaningfully.

In a discussion of the tensions between Jamaica meeting its international obligations and providing for the refugees, the Jamaican minister for justice wrote that the government had " . . . sought to afford them the kind of comfort and solace that their circumstances warrant, even as we keep in mind competing demands for the resources of the Jamaican state." Going on to cite socioeconomic concerns he said that Jamaica was caught between conflicting policy options: (a) to allow the Haitians to stay, or (b) to return them to Haiti.[23] The GoJ opted to return them to Haiti, and as Haitians continued to arrive, the initial "goodwill" so widely reported and acclaimed changed to an uncompromising stance of deportation by early 2005.

During an interview with government officials, they persistently complained that many of the Haitians who continued to arrive were the same ones previously repatriated or deported. Furthermore, the government argued that Jamaica did not have the resources to operate an open-door policy for Haitian economic migration. The government used the costs it had incurred in excessive health-screening processes and in housing the refugees at the camps as a measure of the financial burden the Haitians had placed upon Jamaicans. The government also disclosed that it had spent 30 million JMD for 2004, and "figures for 2005 [are] still being tabulated, so no exact figure [is] yet available. . . ." The GoJ further stated that it " . . . spent in excess of JMD 21 million and it may come to substantially more"[24] and was adamant that this was in addition to funds of US\$520,000 provided by the UNHCR. This expenditure did not include additional costs incurred for the refugee status determination process (I received a telephone call immediately after our initial interview, and was told that this information had been forgotten). Table 6.1 shows that funds were not recorded by the government, which may have contributed to UNHCR's initial decision to discontinue funding and subsequent withdrawal. Additionally, as with many developing state authorities, there may have been issues of accountability.

It is perhaps pertinent at this point to remind the reader that Aristide left Jamaica for South Africa in June 2004, and that by July 2004, it was reported that, "Jamaica was working feverishly to get consensus as serious cracks appeared . . . in CARICOM unity over claims there was undue haste to re-integrate the interim regime in Haiti . . ."[25] Apparently, there had been a proposal of "full engagement" with the Haiti regime installed by the coup d'état that had ousted Aristide, after a delegation—including Jamaicans—

had been to Haiti to hold talks. There was "strong disagreement" from three other Caribbean government heads who threatened to "boycott any CARICOM meeting at which interim Prime Minister, Gérard Latortue was present."

It seemed that, as a signal of solidarity with the unconstitutionally installed regime in Haiti, its asylum-seekers would ultimately not be recognized as refugees. Aristide had now left; Jamaica's grand gesture on the international stage had been made and recorded. At this point, government officials' comments tended to indicate that Jamaica was determined to deny refugee status, based on the conception that " . . . 99.9 percent of the individuals are, in fact, economic migrants." The UNHCR expressed grave concern at this statement and although requested, the evidence on which the GoJ based this calculation has never been released. Meanwhile, Haitians were kept incarcerated in camps and eventually in prisons. This served the government's political agenda of demonizing Haitians by constantly citing the significant costs which could not be afforded. This, in turn, served to engender public resentment, especially among some members of the elite stratum of Jamaican society who complained that "they only come here to take jobs from our people. They don't have any protection needs. They're economic migrants!"[26] However, to be fair, other prominent members of Jamaican society such as writers and media professionals critiqued the GoJ's negative stance in defense of the Haitian refugees.[27] Similarly, the main opposition party opposed moves being made to repatriate those denied refugee status.[28]

The significant costs incurred by the Jamaican government in dealing with "these people" (as it referred to the Haitians) were persistently reiterated. Significant costs applied to "total health screening . . . far and beyond what a national in Jamaica would get." The UNHCR, however, felt that the high levels of health screening went "far and beyond which was necessary." This information being repeatedly reported added to the eventual turn of public mood against the Haitians as the government intensified the demonizing drip-feed process with comments such as: "It costs the government in excess of J$10 million per month to host Haitians . . . In addition the illegal landings pose a security and health risk."[29] Anecdotal discussions elicited comments from the elite that included: "Those people and us have nothing in common and the government says they're just here to pillage our scarce resources." Newspaper reports of continued Haitian arrivals were run under headlines such as "They're Back," "Halting the refugee flood," and "Spotlight on Clarendon—Illegal Haitians, squatters, guns, drugs take root."[30] It was within this context and climate of opinion that claims for asylum from Haitian refugees were being considered.

A refugee Policy or an Ad Hoc "Process?"

From very early on and starting with the premise that Jamaica was experienced in dealing with refugees, the ambassadors spoke of "rules and procedures" that Jamaica had in place for refugee status determination. It wasn't until I made a formal request for a copy of the refugee policy that I was advised that, in fact, there was none. I was eventually to discover that since 1991, the process occurs on the basis of executive decisions at each juncture requiring them. As partners/observers and legal counsel, both the UNHCR and the IJCHR confirmed that the "rules and procedures" are subject to change on each occasion: that effectively, those seeking asylum "trigger" the (appropriately named) Ad Hoc Eligibility Committee (henceforth the Committee). I was also informed by the government that "those who . . . are economic migrants . . . will be automatically determined to be illegal aliens and are dealt with under our immigration laws."

Although the ambassadors failed to mention it, I learned from both the IJCHR and the UNHCR that the applicants were not legally represented at those hearings, and in some cases were unaware that their hearings had even taken place. There were also no independent observers at the proceedings and requests made by UNHCR to observe were denied.

Under these already unsatisfactory conditions, claimants were additionally impeded in substantiating a well-founded fear of persecution. The GoJ—in an apparent dismissal of all other categories in Art.2 (1) of the Refugee Convention—insisted that claimants could only substantiate their claims of fear based on "political opinion."[31] Clearly, the government's goodwill had been withdrawn as it came to the decision that enough was enough. Having made its grand gesture, it was now time for the Haitians to go home.

Jamaica Says "Enough is Enough!": Refugee Determination or Immigration Control?

At the onset of Haitian arrivals in February 2004, requests made by the IJCHR for legal access to the refugees had been denied. Subsequently, the refugees, with no legal counsel, were subjected to an unmonitored interview process with the Committee. Preconceived as economic migrants, "it was to become nearly impossible to meet the burden of proof required to establish a subjective fear of persecution, objectively" (Clarke 2005: 12), since as early as July 2004, " . . . Information Minister Burchell Whiteman, had stressed that the screening process would examine issues such as whether the requests were based on political or economic pressures . . ."[32]

After examining the Committee reports on asylum claims, I established that 283 applicants were interviewed. The first ten interviews were conducted in Portland. Seven of the ten applications received favorable recommendations. The Committee reports were completed in August, but it was not until September 29, 2004, that government officials—protected by more than thirty heavily armed police officers—arrived at the Montpelier camp to announce "that all the applications had been denied."[33] Apparently, none had managed to establish a well-founded fear of political persecution. Arrangements would now be made for their return to Haiti. Reports indicated that the Haitians " . . . received the news calmly," " . . . with solemn expressions on their faces."[34] The government gave seven days in which to file any appeal. Speaking through an interpreter, initial details of all those wishing to exercise that right were taken by the IJCHR, acting on the appellants' behalf.

Of the 283 initially denied, 154 gave notices to appeal and the government was subsequently informed. However, even after the announcement that not one of the 283 applications had been granted refugee status, Haitians continued to arrive and there were continued arrivals throughout 2005. Reports show that between January 1 and March 11, 2005, an additional 288 Haitian refugees had landed in Jamaica. Toward the end of 2004, recognizing that its UNHCR funding was drawing to a close, the government made a request for continued funding which was refused. However, representations made on its behalf to UNHCR in Washington by the UNHCR local representative for a further six months of funding were considered. The UNHCR made the decision to fund the GoJ for a further three months to March 31, 2005. This seemed to focus the government's attention on speeding up the process.

In January 2005, with the continued arrivals of refugees, the UNHCR suggested an "expedited screening process" to quickly establish genuine protection cases. Ironically, this offer of assistance to provide training for fast-track procedures was rejected by the government.[35] Meanwhile, the GoJ maintained a conflicted relationship with the IJCHR. It became government policy to inform the IJCHR of hearing dates with as little notice as possible.[36] In addition, the Ministry of Foreign Affairs sent a letter dated January 10, 2005 to the IJCHR listing the names of seven applicants who " . . . were, in fact, granted refugee status in Jamaica" almost nine months after the Haitians were asked to leave. In this letter, the GoJ informed the IJCHR that these individuals' names had been " . . . inadvertently included on the list of persons who were denied refugee status." The GoJ concluded the letter with these words: "The inconvenience caused by this error is regrettable." In the interim period, four of those named had already been returned to Haiti. Not only was the government's response to its error particularly disturbing, it also reflected the general perceptions it held about the refugees.

One of the "rules and procedures" established for appeals was that Haitian appellants would be present for their appeals. However, at the first hearing in January 2005, no appellants and no interpreters were present. The explanation given was that the government could not afford to bring them. Offers of assistance in defraying the cost of transportation were refused, and astonishingly the tribunal proceeded without appellants. Objections were ignored and the Ad Hoc Appeals Tribunal began hearings on February 2, 2005—with no appellants and no legal counsel for them. The result was that of the 154 cases appealed, a total of nineteen individuals (including dependants) were eventually granted refugee status in Jamaica. With the seven cases granted on initial application (of which four had been returned to Haiti), Jamaica eventually gave asylum to a total of twenty-six Haitians from the original thousand who had sought to remain there.

When taken together, these events suggest not only an absolute denial of due process but an unfair bias against Haiti and its citizens that supports the impetus with which policy toward Haitian refugees appears to be determined across the Americas and Caribbean.[37]

Since the Refugee Convention granted no specific rights to refugees, the GoJ made little or no provision for the resettlement of those that it did grant asylum. It was the Jesuit Society, with funding from the UNHCR, which became instrumental in the integration process, assisted in its implementation by Social Services in Montego Bay on the north coast. As late as March 2008, some of those recognized as refugees from as far back as June 2005, along with their dependents, were still being accommodated in the Montpelier camp. Their access to identification and work permit documents was consistently delayed.

As constructed spaces of power, the government's use of camps is analyzed here as the demarcation of political space with the constitutive feature of identity and class (Lefebvre 1991) produced to maintain the notion of difference between the Haitian refugees incarcerated there and their Jamaican host community. However, the large numbers of Haitians encamped over such a long period of time consistently made their voices heard, facilitated by press and media interest. They worked outside of the camp in the local community and staged protests and breakouts of the camps for food when necessary.[38] Contrary to expectations, Jamaicans generally empathized and welcomed their presence. The length of the refugee determination and appeal processes meant that many of the Haitian asylum-seekers were in Jamaica for almost two years.[39]

The lengthy process had, not surprisingly, resulted in long-term relationships being established with Jamaicans. Residents of Montpelier had initially been allowed free access to the camps and had forged close friendships with the Haitians there. As previously noted, Jamaicans in the parish gave work to the Haitian migrants at considerable risk to themselves. Parties were held at the camp to which the local Jamaican community was invited, and in February 2005, "the 279 refugees at the Montpelier facility were feted by UNESCO, as part of the continued observance of Haiti's 200 years of freedom from slavery."[40] Jamaicans attended as well as Désulmé, the chairperson for the Haiti-Jamaican Exchange.

The government's attempts at isolating the refugees from the community clearly failed, and Jamaicans themselves became disturbed by the "lockdown" implemented at both Winnifred and Montpelier, which was designed to demarcate territory and prevent interaction. It was particularly interesting to see reported that Jamaicans " . . . who have been denied their customary free access to the camp . . . were generally peeved at the decision to send home the Haitians, with whom they had forged close friendships during the past two years."[41] This clearly demonstrated that the GoJ's policy of segregation did not, as anthropologist Eric Wolf points out, acknowledge the "processes that transcend separable cases, moving through and beyond them and transforming them as they proceed" (Wolf 1982: 17). These transformed identities of both Haitians and Jamaicans resulted in three marriages between Haitian men and Jamaican women. The government responded by forcing the repatriation of one of the husbands and threatening the prosecution of Jamaican citizens who gave housing and shelter to Haitian nationals.[42]

Married and arriving at Immigration Services with his wife to submit his application for Jamaican citizenship, a Haitian known as Judson was arrested, detained, and deported. After the story was revealed in the media under the heading "I Want My Husband Back," the GoJ indicated that Judson could apply for a visa to return to Jamaica, but the Jamaica Council expressed concern at how he would afford to do this.[43] During a visit to the island in February 2007, I discovered that funds were still being sought to enable his return.[44] The other two husbands remained at the prison facility in Kingston. The IJCHR has vehemently fought for their right to apply for Jamaican citizenship under chapter seven of its constitution.

At the prison, one of those husbands—close to tears—was clearly missing his wife. He pleaded, "I don't eat; can't sleep; I want to get out and go home. Everyday my wife sends me bolla—food, but I can't eat. My wife is not working, I need to support her." Another explained, "My father was in politics. He was working at the embassy. He died because of his politics. He was shot. My mother died because of shock after my father died, leaving seven children. I came to Jamaica so I can help my family. I wouldn't like to go back to Haiti because if I go they will kill me. I wouldn't like to die so I can't help my brothers and sisters. My father died because of his politics. They will think I'm coming for revenge and they will kill me." It would appear, however, that the only issue of importance to the Committee was that he wanted to help his siblings. He was labelled an economic migrant and his subjective fear of being returned to Haiti and the cognizant reasons for that fear were dismissed.

It is unfortunate that the Jamaican government paid such little attention to the possibility that putative economic refugees could have become political refugees by the time they applied for asylum in Jamaica. All Haitian refugees had arrived in small, flimsy vessels after having faced the perils of the open sea, and although not acknowledged by the ambassadors, it is known that many perished in their attempts to reach international protection.[45] Suggesting to the ambassadors that economic migration and migration based on political persecution were not mutually exclusive, the response was: "That's a rational perspective." It is undetermined whether the government's approach was irrational.

Conclusion

Stuart Hall's three presences—African, European, and American—together form black Caribbean identities as a dialogical relationship between the axis of "similarity" and "difference." "Similarity" is represented by the continuity between Haiti and Jamaica grounded in a shared past. At the same time, this "similarity" is juxtaposed with "differences" of culture and history between Haiti, a former French colony now independent for two hundred years, and Jamaica, a former British colony now independent for forty-five years (Hall 1990: 227). Mindful of these issues of identity and culture, this paper attempted to address the relationship between Haitian refugees and their Jamaican host community, as well as the government of Jamaica's response to the refugee crisis as a close neighboring country.

The GoJ's initial grand gesture of goodwill seemed to have been enacted purely for the international stage and, notwithstanding the welcome given to Aristide and the initial "wave" of Haitians, the emerging diaspora was treated as a temporary phenomenon. Haitians were eventually confronted with a process designed to deny them recognition as refugees, in clear violation of a raft of international instruments laid down to protect them and give them the opportunity of resettlement in Jamaica. The GoJ's policy of encampment and imprisonment appeared to serve a wider political agenda, casting the Haitians as significant financial burdens and a potential health risk that the state and its people could not afford.

These policies further served to engender public resentment toward Haitian migrants so that the government could lament its inability to sustain their upkeep within constructed facilities and consistently point to the costs incurred. The Jamaican administration's policy toward Haitian refugees did not, however, escape contradictions. The government allowed Haitians to work, which in turn fuelled the perception that they arrived and returned—when deported—for economic reasons. In addition, cross-cultural influences and shared notions of self amongst the Jamaican population enabled the temporal Haitian community to integrate as much as possible within the confines of encampment and attempted isolation.

The GoJ's argument that its socioeconomic capacity was insufficient to provide protection was only partly valid since many of the costs it incurred were unnecessary and furthermore were covered by international assistance. Furthermore, socioeconomic conditions cannot be used to derogate from international obligations. It has now been twelve years since Vasciannie first brought attention to this phenomenon, and it seems clear that little has changed in either the means of determination or the political considerations of the Jamaican government toward Haitian refugees. The presence of Haitians remains a deeply politicized issue in the context of " . . . the role of the U.S in the post-Cold War Caribbean" (Vasciannie 1996: 6), and this paper demonstrates that, although not wholly comparable to western powers, in this marginalized corner of the world, the GoJ's attitude toward Haitian refugees seemed consistent with many of its Caribbean counterparts. However, it is difficult to reconcile this episode as an example of anti-Haitianism, since Jamaica has historically provided protection to refugees fleeing Haiti, while not extending the same facility to Cuban refugees, thereby confirming the political considerations that take precedence in refugee determination.[46]

The socioeconomic arguments, the posing of security and health risks, and even the violations of international instruments of protection seem to demonstrate the newly formed political affiliation with the unconstitutional interim government of Haiti. January 2007 saw the prime minister of Jamaica very publicly sign a pledge of "continued support to Haiti's development," signifying " . . . a critical step in strengthening bilateral relations between Jamaica and Haiti."[47] Désulmé reminds us that "Haiti is Africa in the Caribbean . . ." with "a great contribution to make to Caribbean life . . . and the development of a Caribbean identity"[48]; an identity positioned and repositioned by the central tenets of Caribbean daily life and manifested in our diversity of music, religion, patois, etc. All of these speak to the presence of Africa in Caribbean identity. In the meantime, for Haitians seeking refuge, the chasm appears ever-widening.

During 2004–2005, the government of Jamaica sought to fix this transient Haitian diaspora in time and space, and was unsuccessful. "Similarity" and "Difference" continue to work as interactive and dialogical processes in the Caribbean notion of self, to which Haiti and Haitians are symbolic.

> . . . we are completely immersed in denial if we tell ourselves that the plight of the Republic of Haiti isn't connected to the plight of brown, yellow and red people all over the world
>
> Lewis, "Toussaint's Legacy" 2004.

Notes

1. Data received during interviews with the Catholic Church, Jesuit Refugee Society, who have consistently assisted Haitian refugees with shelter, food, and clothing.

2. Jamaican Information Service (JIS), Statement to Parliament on Aristide Visit by the Most Honorable P.J. Patterson, Monday, March 22, 2004.

3. "More Security Needed for Haitians," *Weekly Gleaner* (UK), March 28-April 3, 2005. It was reported that fifteen Haitians had cut their way through fence and absconded. However, it was also confirmed that they had returned that same day. The Haitians' explanation had been that food rations were insufficient and they had left the Winnifred Shelter to buy food.

4. Stephen Vasciannie is now consultant to the attorney-general's department providing advice on refugee issues.

5. Fieldwork for this study was conducted during January 2006 for a wider research

thesis. Subsequent visits to Jamaica have enabled the gathering of additional data that inform this paper.

6. Founded in 1968, the IJCHR is the oldest human rights organization in Jamaica and all the Caribbean. It has worked with Haitian and Cuban refugees for some ten years. I discovered that the IJCHR had been intimately involved with the current Haitian refugees since their first arrivals in 2004, and that initial offers of assistance had been rejected by the GoJ. It was also soon to become apparent that their relationship with the GoJ was extremely antagonistic, due to its human rights work on a variety of levels.

7. Myrtha Désulmé is the daughter of the late Thomas Désulmé who pioneered the establishment of the thermo-plastic industry in Jamaica. She lived periodically in Jamaica as a child and is now a permanent resident who contributes regularly in the Jamaican press and media.

When asked about the Haitian diaspora community, she informed me that there are "a couple of Haitian ladies married to wealthy Jamaican men, mainly Syrian Lebanese or Mulatto, who blend into Jamaican society, and remain very low key . . ." Désulmé writes regularly on the negative media representations of Haiti and its people which she believes has resulted in the "systematic isolating of Haiti." See for example "Stop Denigrating Haiti," *Jamaica Gleaner*, November 12, 2006. See also "Caricom and Haiti: The raising of the Caribbean 'Iron Curtain,'" *Jamaica Sunday Gleaner*, October 8 2006. She discusses the reveling of the international press " . . . in the opportunity for showcasing squalor, abject poverty and desperate Haitians fighting for food." See "No Rest for the Weary," *Jamaica Gleaner*, October 10, 2004.

8. Informal discussions with customs officers at Pegasus Hotel, Wednesday, January 25, 2006.

9. Information obtained from the UNHCR ambassador for Jamaica.

10. Online document. http://www.ttgapers.com, accessed September 30, 2004.

11. For example, on February 28, 2004, there were eight letters in the *Daily Gleaner* regarding the refugees. Seven of these were in support of offering assistance.

12. Quoted in the *Jamaica Gleaner*, February 28, 2004.

13. Information obtained from the UNHCR ambassador to Jamaica.

14. The government of Jamaica signed this treaty at Geneva in 1951. The treaty was ratified by the independent government of Jamaica in 1964, and the additional protocol to the treaty signed and ratified in 1967.

15. The transcripts with government officials make it retrospectively clearer why, in response to being asked if it was GoJ's position that Aristide had been forcibly removed illegitimately, I was told: " . . . well, I don't dwell on that . . . It's a political judgment that one is making." In the next sentence reference was made to the refugees as economic migrants.

16. JIS, "Outpouring of Goodwill for Haitian Refugees," March 15, 2004.

17. JIS, "UNHCR Commends Jamaica for Treatment of Haitians," March 24, 2004.

18. Reported on the GoJ website: Go-Local Jamaica, June 7, 2005.

19. JIS, "Help for Haitian Refugees," April 29, 2004

20. Anecdotal evidence of Jamaican on the Haitian situation during fieldwork undertaken in January 2006.

21. "Haitian Refugees to get Skills Training," *Jamaica Gleaner*, March 1, 2004.

22. See "Haitians Being Used for Cheap Labour," *Jamaica Observer*, April 24, 2005. According to this article, the GoJ's position was clear in that "it was up to the police to enforce the law by prosecuting those who illegally hire the refugees."

23. JIS, "Haiti: The Refugee Question," Attorney-General and Minister of Justice, The Honorable A. J. Nicholson QC, June 7, 2004.

24. Exchange rate during fieldwork period: £1 = JMD113; US$1 = JMD64.

25. "Explosive Rifts over Haiti: Jamaica Working Feverishly for CARICOM Consensus," *Jamaica Observer*, August 8, 2004.

26. Information obtained from a Jamaican lawyer of Haitian ancestry.

27. They include Peter Espeut, John Maxwell, and radio presenter Dr. Orville Taylor

28. "Jamaica: Opposition Against Moves to Return Haitian Refugees Yet," UNHCR News Archives.

29. "Jamaica Sends Home 86 Haitians," *Jamaica Observer*, December 14, 2005

30. "They're Back: Latest Wave of Haitian Boat People taking its Toll," *Jamaica Observer*, March 13, 2005; "Halting the Refugee flood," *Jamaica Gleaner*, March 9, 2005; "Spotlight on Clarendon," *Jamaica Gleaner*, January 8, 2006. By the time of this last report the GoJ had become successful in persuading some sections of Jamaican society that Haitians were responsible for all criminal activities in Jamaica.

31. This was established by looking at the Eligibility Committee Reports and after discussions with IJCHR.

32. "Haitians to be Sent Home," *ttGapers.com*, September 30, 2004.

33. Ibid.

34. Ibid.

35. An excerpt from the UNHCR's proposal reads: " . . . Such an expedited process is considered necessary on a temporary basis on account of the specific circumstances of significant numbers of arrivals over a short period of time, threatening to overwhelm the system in Jamaica for dealing with asylum seekers."

36. Interview with Nancy Anderson at the IJCHR.

37. This was established both in conversation with the local UNHCR representative and confirmed in a series of letters I was given access to.

38. "More Haitians sent home, others protest," *Jamaica Gleaner Online*, June 23, 2005.

39. "Haitian refugees protest," *Jamaica Observer*, April 16, 2005.

40. "Haitian refugees feted as part of freedom celebrations," *Jamaica Observer*, February 5, 2005.

41. "More Haitians going home today," *Jamaica Gleaner*, August 17, 2005.

42. "Row over Haitians—Repatriation sparks conflict, Boat people bill $10m a month," *Jamaica Gleaner*, December 14, 2005.

43. "I Want My Husband Back," *Jamaica Gleaner*, December 14, 2005. This is an interview given by Judson's Jamaican wife.

44. An additional US$100 was still required and I made the funds available. So far, I have not had any updates on the case.

45. See "Dangerous Voyage—Haitians Brave Choppy Seas for Better Life," *Jamaica Sunday Gleaner*, March 14, 2004. In this article it was reported that ten Haitians had perished at sea the previous week. The article includes testimonies from Haitians such as: "I have watched persons drown," and "There are so many bad things going on in Haiti where people would rather throw themselves to the sea." See also "Twelve Haitian boat migrants dead, dozens more missing," *Associated Press Report*, March 10, 2005. The boat "packed with about 50 Haitian migrants capsized off the country's north coast" apparently trying to reach Turks and Caicos Islands.

46. A 1996 memorandum of understanding between Cuba and Jamaica " . . . implicitly prevents Cubans from seeking refuge in Jamaica." (U.S. Committee for Refugees, 2004).

47. "Jamaica Pledges Continued Support to Haiti's Development," *Jamaica Observer*, January 5, 2007.

48. Myrtha Désulmé, "Caricom and Haiti: The raising of the Caribbean's 'Iron Curtain,'" *Jamaica Sunday Gleaner*, October 8, 2006.

References

Brownlie, Ian, and Guy S. Goodwin-Gill, eds. 2002. Basic Documents on Human Rights. Oxford: Oxford University Press.

Clarke, Sharon. 2005. "The Refugee Convention is outdated and does not adequately address refugee problems in the 21st century. Discuss," May 2005. A 5,000 word paper prepared as course-work requirement for the unit, International Refugee Law, in the MSc Refugee Studies course at London South Bank University.

Hall, Stuart. 1990. "Culture, Identity and Diaspora." In Identity: Community, Culture, Difference, ed. J. Rutherford, 222–237. London: Lawrence and Wishart.

JIS, "Outpouring of Goodwill for Haitian Refugees," 15 March, 2004, http:// jis.gov.jm/ tools/printable.asp?print=/land_environment/html/20040304T080000, accessed September 25, 2005.

———. "Help for Haitian Refugees." 29 April, 2004, http://www.jis.gov.jm/tools/printable.asp?print=/foreign_affairs/html20040428t2100, accessed September 25, 2005.

Lefebvre, Henri. 1991. The Production of Space. Oxford: Wiley, John & Sons, inc.

Lewis, Edmund W, ed. 2004. "Toussaint's Legacy." Louisanna Weekly, 15 March 2004, http://www.louisannaweekly.com, accessed July 29, 2005.

Pugh, Mark. 2004. "Drowning Not Waving: Boat People and Humanitarianism at Sea." Journal of Refugee Studies 17, no. 1: 50–69.

Rogge, John R. 1987. "Africa's displaced population: dependency or self-sufficiency?" In Refugees: a Third World dilemma, ed. John R.Rogge. Totowa: Rowman & Littlefield.

Rutinwa, Bonaventura. 1996. "The Tanzanian Government's Response to the Rwandan Emergency," Journal of Refugee Studies 9, no. 3: 291–302.

United Nations High Commission for Refugees (UNHCR). 2004a. "Update on the Americas," Newsletter, No 7. UNHCR website, accessed June 18, 2005.

————. 2004b. "North America and the Caribbean, Global Report 2004." UNHCR website, accessed June 18, 2005.

————. 2004c. "Update on the Haiti Situation, March 2004." UNHCR website, accessed June 18, 2005.

————. 2004d. "ExCom2004: The Americas, Part A: Major Developments." UNHCR website, accessed July 29, 2005.

U.S. Committee for Refugees World Refugee Survey 2004—Jamaica, May 2004, http://www.unhcr.ch/cgi-bin/texis/vtx/rsd/print.html?CATEGORY=RSDCOI&id=40b, accessed June 28, 2005.

Vasciannie, Stephen. 1996. The 1996 Cuban Asylum-Seekers in Jamaica: A Case Study of International Law in the Post-Cold War Era. Jamaica: publisher unknown.

Verdirame, Guglielmo and Barbara Harrell-Bond. 2005. Rights in Exile:Janus-faced Humanitarianism. Oxford: Berghahn.

Wolf, Eric. 1982. Europe and the People Without History. Berkeley: University of California Press.

Zetter, Roger. 1999. "International Perspectives on Refugee Assistance." In Refugees: Perspectives on the Experience of Forced Migration. London: Continuum.

II

Testimonies

7

Conversation with Myrtha Désulmé, President of the Haiti-Jamaica Society

PHILIPPE ZACAÏR

A remarkable woman of the Haitian diaspora in Jamaica, Myrtha Désulmé has long been speaking and writing for her fellow Jamaicans about Haiti and Haitians in the wider Caribbean. As a media resource person and contributor to many newspapers including the *Jamaica Gleaner*, she has made it her goal to "redeem the image of Haiti in Jamaica, introduce Haitians and Jamaicans to each other's culture, find sustainable solutions for Haiti, facilitate the integration of Haiti into CARICOM, and generally promote Haitian culture." In 2004, Désulmé served on the UNESCO Haiti 2004 committee, organizing the celebrations of the bicentennial of the first "Black Republic" in Jamaica. In 2005, she founded the Haiti-Jamaica Society with University of the West Indies Professor Marie-José N'Zengou-Tayo, journalist John Maxwell, and other Haitians and Jamaicans. The society's objectives include, among other issues, assisting Haitian refugees and stimulating dialogue in Jamaica geared toward supporting the Haitian people in their struggle for justice and democracy.

The daughter of a well-known Haitian politician who opted for exile in protest to the Duvalier dictatorship, and later pioneered industrial development in newly independent Jamaica, Désulmé's privileged status allows us to reflect on the influence of class on the Haitian diasporic experience. In fact, Désulmé appears very conscious that class issues have made her journey outside of Haiti quite different from that of many who have faced terrible hardships, from active discrimination to outright violence. Although at the onset of our conversation Désulmé expressed doubt about the value of her personal story as a Haitian in diaspora, her testimony adds invaluable diversity to the experiences discussed throughout this volume. She presents us with a compelling story of exile, and of personal and professional achievement in both Jamaica and the United States. She also discusses her personal relationship to Haiti and her work as president of the Haiti-Jamaica society.

Zacaïr: Can you tell us the story of your family's migration from Haiti to Jamaica?

Désulmé: I'm afraid that my experience of being Haitian in Jamaica might not be very representative, and therefore not of much interest to you. My father was a senator and a minister of government in Haiti, in Estimé's government in the 1940s, and in Magloire's government in the 1950s. He was one of the many people who supported Duvalier as a member of the black intelligentsia, a black nationalist, and a respected country doctor in 1957. He was also a minister in Duvalier's government before Duvalier revealed his psychopathic tendencies, at which time he chose to distance himself from Duvalier. He went on a diplomatic mission to Venezuela and Paris and did not return to Haiti. Many people who supported Duvalier and helped him to become president suffered greatly as a result of his ascendancy. Many were killed, imprisoned, or exiled. My father chose exile for himself in 1960, but his two eldest sons, who remained in Haiti, were imprisoned and killed by Duvalier merely for being his sons. This is due to the fact that rumors had been spread that he was planning an invasion to topple the government. I was very young then, and have only seen pictures of my two eldest brothers, but this tragedy left an unfathomable streak of unspoken heartache in my family.

My father was also an industrialist, who had pioneered the industrialization of Haiti with a plastics factory. He spent two years between France and Washington D.C. while trying to decide where he wanted to settle. He knew of Jamaica because he had come here in previous years to visit some friends, including President Estimé when they were in exile in Jamaica. Throughout Haiti's turbulent 204-year history, many politicians, including fourteen Haitian presidents, came to Jamaica in exile. In 1962, Jamaica gained independence and was booming economically. My father became enthused about having the opportunity to once more contribute to nation-building. He consequently decided to settle in Jamaica in order to rebuild his plastics factory, which eventually became the biggest plastics factory in the Caribbean.

I left Haiti at the age of three, and came to Jamaica at the age of five. My mother wanted us to be educated in French, so she took my siblings and me to Paris when I was six. I came back to Jamaica at age nine, returning to Paris when I was twelve. I finished high school in Paris, studied languages in Germany and Spain, and returned to Jamaica when I was twenty. I enrolled at the University of the West Indies (UWI), and then transferred to Georgetown University in Washington D.C. After Georgetown, I lived in Miami for seven years, setting up an import-export company for my father's plastics products, and finally returned to Jamaica for good twenty years ago. I worked in my family's businesses, returned to UWI, and worked with different organizations.

In 2004, I was invited to sit on a UNESCO committee, which was organizing the celebration of the Haitian bicentenary in Jamaica. We spent the year organizing conferences, seminars, lectures, and cultural events celebrating Haiti. We also spoke on radio and on TV, and gave lectures on Haiti. There was an influx of refugees after the fall of president Jean-Bertrand Aristide. I went on a radio gift drive and did some fundraising to organize a Christmas treat for them. I also assisted the Independent Jamaica Council For Human Rights with interpreting for the refugees' depositions, for their asylum request court appearances.

I have been a writer for the newspapers for many years. I therefore started to focus my writings on Haiti, becoming an advocate and media resource person on Haiti. I created the Haiti-Jamaica Society, and am now trying to write a book on my father's biography, within the context of the historical relationship between Haiti and Jamaica. I am also exploring the idea of writing it as an autobiography: my story, as a Europeanized Caribbean woman coming home to the Caribbean and recounting my perspective on my father and his world, on finding my roots and my soul buried in the soil of the Caribbean, and on Caribbean society in general. Given that my father was so passionate about nation-building, and about finding political and economic solutions for Haiti, I would incorporate within that story his ideology and his work. He was a visionary who had a dream of uplifting Haiti and breaking its cycle of poverty through industrialization. In exile, he transferred that dream to developing Jamaica. I would also include my present research and writings, which examine the situation on the ground in Haiti and seek to identify the factors which are blocking the development of sustainable solutions for Haiti.

You asked about my father's experience as a Haitian immigrant. I was too young to know what my father's experience was as a Haitian immigrant, but given that he came with funds from the sale of his factory in Haiti to invest, employed a lot of people, revolutionized Jamaican industry, and was awarded the Order of Jamaica for his contribution to industry and commerce, I don't think that it would be very representative either.

What would be representative, however, is that like many Haitians, I bristle at the negative media reporting on Haiti which has poisoned so many people's minds, that people just routinely have a very pejorative image of Haiti involving poverty, squalor, dictatorships, political instability, violence, corruption, Vodou, and just a general image of darkness, misery, and chaos, a metaphor for black people's inability to govern themselves. The media seems to revel in this negative reporting. I have therefore spent my life on my soapbox, constantly trying to fight the unremitting denigration and letting people know that there is another side to the story, and to Haiti. It has, in a way, become my life's mission and purpose. So I guess that in this regard, my experience would be quite a typical Haitian experience. But the irony is that, though I have become the quintessential Haitian in Jamaica, I have never really lived in Haiti. It's just that my father instilled such a great love of Haiti in us, that I always take it personally whenever I hear a derogatory comment on Haiti, which of course is all the time, as the word "Haiti" is hardly ever pronounced in a positive context. I even wrote an article in the *Jamaica Gleaner* entitled: "Stop denigrating Haiti!" I have at least spent time in Haiti, but it's interesting that even my nieces and nephews—my brothers' children—who are Jamaican, whose mothers are Jamaican, and who have never set foot in Haiti, feel hurt when people say negative things about Haiti. I think that the fact that they are my brothers' children, and therefore also carry this famously Haitian name, probably contributes to their identification with Haiti. My sisters' children are equally sensitive on the subject, but they are not as identifiable as my brothers' children, who carry the name.

Zacaïr: What is a typical Haitian immigrant experience in Jamaica? Do you believe your father's status saved you from intolerance and discrimination?

Désulmé: It would be hard for me to tell you what a typical Haitian immigrant experience in Jamaica is. I am sure that my father's status saved me from intolerance and discrimination. My father employed a lot of people, gave scholarships to Jamaican schools, and assisted many people financially.

There are other Haitians in Jamaica who are students and professionals, or Haitian women married to Jamaican men in the higher echelons of society, who also lead fulfilling lives in Jamaica and are totally integrated. There must also be some Haitian migrants, who while leading modest lives, are quite well integrated and don't experience any discrimination. Haitian professionals have mainly migrated to France, Canada, the U.S., and Africa, and have been very successful in those places.

Zacaïr: Why do you think your father wanted his children to maintain a strong identification with Haiti, and how did he encourage this identification?

Désulmé: He loved Haiti, and always told us great stories about Haitian history and society. He also sometimes told jokes about the character flaws of Haitians. But he was such a proud man, and so proud to be Haitian, that I guess that we just absorbed it by osmosis. The Jamaican government, in fact, offered him Jamaican citizenship, but though he loved Jamaica and was grateful for his new homeland, he declined. He often said that it was a great pity that exile had prevented us from growing up in Haiti.

Zacaïr: You said that you are the "quintessential Haitian in Jamaica." Could you elaborate on this?

Désulmé: That is a statement we should probably edit, lest people think I'm "bigging up" myself, as Jamaicans would say. I just meant that, because my father's business was well-known, it gave us a profile as a well-known Haitian family. Now that I am so much in the media, talking about Haiti all the time, people who can't pronounce my name sometimes just know me as "The Haitian," which is ironic because I consider myself a citizen of the world. So while some Haitians are here "in hiding," telling people intrigued about their accents that they are other nationalities because they don't want to even admit that they're Haitian due to the pervasive misconceptions, I'm in the media bellowing about Haiti. That is what I meant by being *perceived* as "the quintessential Haitian."

Zacaïr: Can you summarize and explain the goals and the activities of the Haiti-Jamaica Society?

Désulmé: The Haiti-Jamaica Society aims to facilitate the integration of Haiti into CARICOM; develop sustainable social, political, and economic solutions for Haiti; stimulate dialogue in Jamaica geared toward supporting the Haitian people in their struggle for justice, human rights, and participatory democracy; introduce Haitians and Jamaicans to each other's culture; and create links between Haiti and other Caribbean countries.

The society was born out of the 2004 UNESCO Bicentenary Committee I mentioned before, which was created to implement Jamaica UNESCO's international tribute to the bicentenary of Haiti's independence. UNESCO had declared 2004 "The Year for the Commemoration of the Struggle to End Slavery" to coincide with the Haitian bicentenary, Haiti being the pioneer of the emancipation and decolonization cycle in the hemisphere.

The committee spent the year organizing conferences and colloquiums discussing Haiti, as well as cultural events promoting Haitian culture. We also gave lectures around Jamaica, spoke on radio and on TV, and wrote articles in the papers, educating the general public about the importance and influence of the Haitian Revolution to world and Caribbean revolutionary theory and practice; Haiti's role in the development of black consciousness; and the longstanding links between Jamaica and Haiti. The overall objective was to redeem the image of Haiti in the collective consciousness. The soul of Haiti and of the Haitian people is powerful and magnificent, and deeply rooted in their African past. People need to understand that Haiti holds the key to the cultural identity of the Caribbean.

When the influx of refugees came to Jamaica following the coup against Aristide, the committee visited the 500 refugees who spent a year in a camp in Jamaica. We also went on a gift drive and organized a Christmas treat for them. We fought to be able to visit those in the detention centers, and to obtain their release and humane treatment.

When the UNESCO bicentenary year ended, the Haiti-Jamaica Society was formed in order to continue the above work. It was a great honor and privilege for me to have the opportunity to be of assistance to my countrymen. I got the chance to spend valuable time with them, to listen to their stories, hopes, and aspirations, and to give them moral support. I took my nieces to bring presents for the children. It is imperative that we learn to show more compassion toward people who have endured great suffering and hardship to reach our shores; risking their lives in horrendous circumstances to escape oppression, deprivation, and persecution at home, only to be imprisoned and experience cruelty and mistreatment when they finally collapse on our doorsteps within an inch of their lives. The Haiti-Jamaica Society tries to promulgate this basic humanitarian principle in every way it can, and aims to contribute to the establishment of legal structures that will guarantee adherence to international protocols which protect the rights of refugees.

Furthermore, I feel that it is important to dispel the myths and prejudices which are so prevalent about Haiti. It is a thankless uphill battle, but someone has to do it. I also believe that it is important to let people know what is happening inside Haiti. The public needs to understand that Haiti is not just a chaotic land of mad people who can't seem to get their act together. There are some very powerful internal and external social and political forces who profit from maintaining Haiti destabilized and contained in poverty, then use violent repression to suppress those who would resist this enforced stagnation on the Haitian people. When the rebellions explode sporadically, as they must, the people are then characterized as violent, and the international community just writes it off as another crazy Haitian upheaval. No one tries to deconstruct what is really happening because most people don't really care.

Right now, many people are starving due to the disastrous neoliberal policies which have been forced upon Haiti for the past five decades. Haiti's agriculture and industries have been completely destroyed by the misguided U.S., World Bank, and IMF policies which have tried to reduce Haiti to being a dumping ground for U.S. surplus and a source of cheap labor. This has resulted in overcrowded ghettoes, in an environment where there is no infrastructure or social services. There is also a serious hunger problem which is not being addressed. The recent food riots speak to the fact that the people's suffering has become unbearable. But rather than find solutions, there will be more repression and killings by the police and the UN occupation force. I hope that the Haiti-Jamaica Society can someday get the kind of funding it needs to organize projects which can make a difference inside Haiti.

Zacaïr: A major task of the Haiti-Jamaica Society is to redeem the image of Haiti in the collective consciousness of Jamaicans. What are your biggest hurdles?

Désulmé: Our biggest hurdle is the overwhelming tide of negative media, which bombards the public from all sides about Haiti. Compared to this powerfully destructive juggernaut, we are just a few lone voices in the wilderness.

Zacaïr: Have you seen any positive changes so far? To what extent are you able to reach the general public?

Désulmé: We can get some articles published, and are sometimes invited to speak on the radio and on TV, or to give speeches. So we use those opportunities to try and reach the public. Sometimes people will be enlightened, and express to us that they appreciate our shedding some light on the reality of the situation. Those moments are most gratifying, to know that we might have changed even one person.

8

Congratulations! You Don't *Look* Haitian

How and When Does One *Look* Haitian?

CÉCILE ACCILIEN

This personal testimony is not a traditional scholarly article. Rather it is a description of my own diasporic identity—that is the many facets of my biculturalism and how it is experienced. The article builds upon my act of defiance against the stereotypes associated with Haiti as well as my desire to transgress and question through my own personal and professional experiences what it means to be Haitian in the United States.

A few years ago at the Latin American Studies Association conference, I gave a talk entitled "Congratulations, You Don't *Look* Haitian." That title, which inspired this chapter, comes from my own experience as a Haitian-American woman who has been living in the U.S. for over twenty years, still speaks with an accent, and is often "congratulated" (by students, colleagues, and strangers alike) for not "*looking* Haitian." These people (who are generally trying to be nice) fail to realize that in many ways they are offending me with their "compliment." What this also demonstrates, as scholar Flore Zéphir notes, is that "Haitians regardless of their social class, skin color, level of education, religious beliefs, language preference (French versus Creole), geographical place of origin in the homeland, and mode of transportation to the United States face the same harsh reality in this country: they are all invisible minorities in the same boat, and they experience the same indignities of being considered members of subordinate populations." (Zéphir 1996: 45) The standard vision of Haiti and Haitians is of boat people on the Miami shores, refugees at Krome Detention Center, or women with buckets on their heads and young children barefoot and dirty, starving in the slums of Port-au-Prince, as shown on ABC, CBS, or CNN.

What does it mean to look Haitian?

Before the 2005 elections, Haiti was in the news nonstop. National newspapers like *Newsday*, the *Washington Post*, and the *New York Times* featured Haiti on the front page at least three times during January and February. We read headlines such as "A Look at Haiti's Troubled History," "A Legacy of Neglect," "American Airlines Canceled Flights to and from Port-au-Prince because of Fears of Unrest Related to Upcoming Elections," "Port-au-Prince, the Lawless Capital"—all emphasizing instability, poverty, and misery. Pictures of United Nations forces carrying ballots on the backs of donkeys and horses were all over the internet and in *Time Magazine* and other media sources.

In its two hundred-plus years as the first black republic, Haiti has had a total of thirty-two coups and a series of presidents in office for periods ranging from two months to over fifteen years. This is the image that the American media has of Haiti: political instability, poverty, and insecurity. This view of insecurity in Haiti was evident to me when I went on a trip to Portland, Oregon in February 2006. I was at the Portland International Airport and noted (yet again) the warning to American citizens that the airport in Haiti does not conform to aviation safety regulations. It was not clear to me whether that meant that Haiti was dangerous or ungovernable, or both. However, American Airlines offers flights to and from Haiti on a regular basis. This is an example of how Haiti and Haitians are represented in the U.S. and I often feel compelled to challenge that representation.

As a bicultural Haitian-American who has lived in the United States for all of my adult life, I often vacillate between my Haitian roots and the reality of my exile life in the U.S. (although I am not sure if I would properly be considered one of the exiled, since my parents decided that the U.S. offered better opportunities than our homeland of Haiti and brought me here over two decades ago). When my father and mother migrated to the U.S. in 1981 and 1983 respectively on tourist visas, there were an estimated 40,000 to 50,000 undocumented Haitians living in the U.S. (Stepick 1982). I am sure that my parents benefited from the Refugee Act issued in March 1980. This act made the term "refugee" more inclusive. My parents' visas eventually expired and like many others they remained in the U.S. illegally. They were lucky to be able to work. They eventually obtained legal residency and sent for my three siblings and me in July 1985. Like our parents, we became diaspora (*dyaspora* as we say in Haitian Creole).

I use the term diaspora in the sense of "communities of people dislocated from their native homelands through migration, immigration, or exile as a consequence of colonial experience." (Braziel, Mannur 2003) Like other diasporic children, we struggled to find our place in this new country and take advantage of the educational opportunities that the U.S. offers. In spite of the young age at which we came to the U.S. (our ages ranged from eleven to sixteen), we remain very close to our homeland in terms of food, culture, and language. I am sometimes asked by students, colleagues, and friends if I feel more Haitian than American and I usually answer: "There are days when I feel very American, other days when I feel strongly Haitian, and days in between when I am totally confused." However, in many ways, my Haitian identity is affected by the negative portrayal of Haiti in the media.

On October 29, 2007, I received a message from a friend with an article from the *New York Times* entitled "AIDS Virus Invaded U.S. From Haiti." The article described the work of two researchers: Michael Worobey, a University of Arizona evolutionary biologist, and Arthur Pitchenik from the University of Miami School of Medicine. The researchers claimed that, through an examination of genetic data from 117 early AIDS patients and samples from five Haitian immigrants from 1982 and 1983, the researchers were able to trace the trajectory of the AIDS epidemic from Central Africa to Haiti, and then to Miami or New York via a single infected Haitian immigrant. Their study concluded, therefore, that there was a "99.8 percent probability that Haiti was the steppingstone" for AIDS in the U.S.[1]

My first reaction was "I thought we had settled that question back in the late 1980s and early 1990s." In the early 1980s the medical community in the United States and around the world was trying to understand the disease that would later be called AIDS. Researchers trying to track the disease found that some American homosexual tourists who had visited Haiti had become infected with HIV. Not long thereafter, the mainstream media followed the medical community with the rumor that AIDS came from Haiti, and thus all Haitians were potentially AIDS carriers. This rumor helped to justify the unfair treatment against Haitian immigrants (both legal and undocumented). Haitians were not allowed to give blood and many Haitian employees from all sectors—but particularly those who worked in health care facilities—were fired. In 1990, Haitians in the U.S. held one of the largest demonstrations in New York City history with approximately 70,000 people protesting this discrimination. Haitian citizens, along with other advocates, primarily from nonprofit organizations, petitioned the Centers for Disease Control and the Food and Drug Administration and the claim was refuted. I was in high school in Newark, New Jersey during that period and

I remember how the other students (including African-Americans, Latinos, and other Caribbean immigrants) shunned Haitians and refused to interact with us in gym class because they assumed that if you were Haitian you were automatically an AIDS carrier. Some students would also tease us and try to fight with us solely because we were Haitians. During this period, some of my Haitian classmates would try to pass off as Jamaicans or even Africans so that they would not deal with the stigma and prejudice encountered by Haitians. For me, this new attack on Haiti and Haitians shows that as Haitians we are still marginalized and viewed as the ones responsible for bringing AIDS to the United States.

After the October 2007 article came out, several friends and colleagues sent me information related to this finding on the connection between Haiti and AIDS. As a Haitian-American, I found myself analyzing the articles, trying to make sense of them and feeling as if I needed to answer in order to change this negative image of Haitians. One of the articles I found interesting was French newspaper *Le Monde*'s November 6, 2007: "Polémique autour de l'origine de l'épidémie du sida" [Polemic Surrounding the Origin of the AIDS Epidemic]. While the article presented both sides of the story, it concluded by quoting a specialist from a research institute in Montpellier who stated that the publication where the article first appeared (the National Academic of Sciences) was "rigorous" and used "good methods of analysis."[2] By legitimizing the researchers' methods of analysis, the article implied that it supported their claim. I did not personally respond to any of the articles linking Haiti and Haitians to AIDS because I felt like a scientific response was needed and I was not capable of giving one. However, I was eagerly waiting for a response.

One day after Worobey's article, on October 30, 2007, the Empire State Medical Association—the New York affiliate of the National Medical Association (NMA) whose goals are "to promote the collective interests of physicians and patients of African descent" and "to serve as the collective force of physicians of African descent and a leading force for parity in medicine"— denounced the "incomplete research claims made by Dr. Gilbert and Dr. Worobey on HIV Coming from Haiti."[3]

I believe that Worobey's article is part of what Robert Lawless calls "Haiti's Bad Press." The standard representation of Haiti in the dominant U.S. news network—whether on television or in written news—can be summed up in the following terms: AIDS, boat people, coups (political instability), poverty, violence, and "voodoo."[4] This is how Haiti is constructed and imagined in the U.S. and how the Haitian diaspora is often viewed.[5]

Since the report came out, there have been myriad reactions from Haitians and Haitian-Americans and there is even talk about a class action lawsuit. The head of the Haitian Lawyers Leadership Network, Marguerite Laurent, is attempting to figure out whether or not the author of the study can legally be asked for a retraction or damages.[6] In an interview with news agency *Alter Presse* on October 31, the general director of the Health and Population Ministry of Haiti, Gabriel Thimothé, cautioned: "We should not react in an emotional manner, but in a pragmatic, scientific, and organized manner."[7] He also expressed his belief that the *New York Times* article represented a setback for the credibility of Haiti's successful AIDS prevention program. This public health initiative has contributed to a decline in the prevalence of AIDS in Haiti, significantly reducing the percentage of infected population from 6 percent to 3.1 percent.

The Association of Haitian Physicians Abroad also sent a statement to the press asserting that the study was biased and showed serious flaws. Likewise, Haiti's ambassador to the United States, Raymond Joseph, stated that for a study that claimed almost 100 percent accuracy, it had too many uncertainties; he also challenged the authors to give detailed information about the single Haitian who supposedly brought HIV from Haiti to the U.S. For many people, the media is their main or only source of news. As a result, when the media misrepresents certain groups it is essential that it be challenged.

In *Black Looks: Race and Representation*, Bell Hooks notes that film is the most important medium in "determining how blackness and black people are seen and how other groups will respond . . . based on their relation to constructed and consumed images." She further states that "theorizing black experience in the United States is a difficult task. Socialized within white supremacist educational systems and by a *racist mass media* [my emphasis], many black people are convinced that our lives are not complex, and are therefore unworthy of sophisticated critical analysis and reflection . . . that the field of representation remains a place of struggle is most evident when we critically examine contemporary representations of blackness and black people."(Hooks 1992: 2–3; 5)[8] There is no doubt that the American media's representation of Haiti and Haitians influences how Haitians are viewed in the Caribbean and the rest of the world and hurts Haiti's image.[9]

In 1998, over a decade after Haiti's struggle to clear its name and association with carriers of the AIDS virus, the negative stereotypes were again brought up in an African-American film. This is significant because both Haitians and African-Americans are minorities who have dealt with oppression and racism from white America. One would have expected more sensitivity on the subject. However, this is not particularly surprising because many Haitians, like other black immigrant groups and especially first-generation immigrants, tend to keep to themselves and do not interact much with African-Americans (Zéphir 1996: 69–96).[10] There is often a certain tension between blacks from Africa or the Caribbean and African-Americans resulting from miscommunication, false assumptions, and stereotypes between the two groups.

When I was in high school in Newark, New Jersey, it was very common to hear African-Americans mock us because of our accents, tell us (black immigrants from other countries) that we were not "black," but rather "Haitians" or "Africans," and tell us to "go back where we came from." We were also commonly referred to as "boat people" or told to "return to the banana boat." I was even told by a classmate once that we had no "business" celebrating Martin Luther King Jr.'s birthday because we were not African-Americans. As a result, many of us Haitians kept to ourselves and did not interact much with African-Americans because we felt excluded and unwelcomed. For me personally, these early interactions unconsciously or consciously shaped my rapport with African-Americans. Oftentimes, relationships between African-Americans and other blacks in general are complex. On the one hand, some of us Caribbean-Americans sometimes feel that some African-Americans seem to resent us because they perceive us as being more "successful" in white America and getting along better with whites. As a result, there is a large cultural gap between African-Americans and other blacks. On the other hand, some Caribbeans do not understand the various historical, social, racial, and economic forces that still influence some African-Americans and assume that they do not succeed because they are not motivated. Yet, a large part of our "success" as Caribbeans is related to our status as immigrants.

For instance, as a Haitian-American, my parents constantly drilled into my head that I needed to be better off than they were as immigrants both economically and socially. Therefore, I had to study and pursue my education because that was how I could be "successful." It was not that I was more intelligent than my African-American classmates, but rather that I experienced more pressure to go to college and "succeed." As a Caribbean-American, I may also interact differently with white Americans than do my African-American friends or colleagues. Teaching in Portland, Oregon and in New Orleans, Louisiana, I have had white students tell me how easy it was to discuss issues of race and culture with me compared to some of my African-American colleagues. At times, I would challenge these students and tell them that this was due to the fact that I did not have the same history with the United States as my African-American colleagues. My black identity is intrinsically linked to my Haitian identity first and foremost; therefore, I have a less passionate relationship with whites. However, this is not to say that I do not face issues of racism or that I am immune to them.

When I lived in New Orleans, because of the strong historical and cultural connections between Haiti and Louisiana, some African-Americans who wanted to trace their roots back to Haiti were proud of Haiti being the first black republic and were more welcoming toward Haitians. However, my general experience is that many African-Americans find it difficult to relate to and understand Caribbeans. Thus, the comments linking AIDS to Haiti in the film *How Stella Got her Groove Back* illustrate the stereotypes and complex rapport between the two groups.

How Stella Got her Groove Back, based on a novel by bestselling author Terry McMillan (who also served as the film's executive producer), unapologetically reiterates the connection between Haitians and AIDS. Stella (played by Angela Bassett) is a forty-plus stockbroker in San Francisco who takes a vacation in Jamaica. There she meets a young man named Wynston Shakespeare, and with sea, sex, sun, and rum as the cliché has it, she gets her "groove back" and returns home. Once in San Francisco, one of her sisters asks her if she hadn't been worried about getting AIDS. Another sister answers, "No, that's Haiti, 'Miss Manners,'" implying that AIDS and Haiti are interrelated and connected. This line does not appear in the book.

Haitian-Americans including Edwidge Danticat and Wyclef Jean (whose lyrics *Mastablasta* were used in the film) and others protested the movie, writing letters and marching in front of 20th Century Fox Studios on the Avenue of the Americas in New York shouting, "Until you fix your movie, Stella isn't groovy." Fox finally took the lines out of the movie. Although Haitians demanded an apology, they never got one. A spokesperson at 20th Century Fox stated that the studio had no comment. Terry McMillan was not available to comment either.

It is shocking and disappointing that well-respected African-Americans condoned and perpetuated unfounded stereotypes about Haitians. The AIDS issue does affect Haiti, like so many other countries, but advertising Haiti as a diseased nation hurts efforts to ameliorate its problems. Haiti is directly affected by U.S. policies and it goes without saying that these policies affect healthcare and particularly the fight against AIDS.[11]

Since the October article linking Haiti with AIDS, many Haitian-Americans as well as some Americans have remained concerned about the negative impact of the research and the way it is covered by American mainstream media. In spite of living in the information age, many Americans often do not know how U.S. policies affect and influence Latin American countries such as Haiti. They are uninformed about the long history linking the U.S. to Haiti. Many know little about the American occupation (1915–1934), and support of subsequent dictators such as François and Jean-Claude Duvalier, to cite only a few examples. The way Haiti and Haitians are often represented in and constructed by the media is directly related to political ideologies and goals; the media is too often not concerned with reporting facts accurately and objectively. Transforming current stereotypes as well as negative and false images and representations of Haiti and Haitians requires that people be challenged to look at the situation with fresh eyes, and to acknowledge that Haiti, like other nations and cultures, has a complex set of values and traditions. Haiti's current struggle—its economic, political, and social instability—is very real but should be judged through informed arguments and analysis. The problem is not only the negative reporting and comments about Haiti in and of themselves, but also the fact that they are too often biased and simplistic.

As a black, Haitian-American, female academic, I often struggle with the issue of cultural identity, not so much in how I define myself but in how others want to define me. Luckily, because I have a sense of humor, I constantly challenge my students and colleagues about the ways in which they are influenced by the mainstream media's representations of Haiti by openly discussing my own bicultural identity with them. I try as much as I can to "teach to transgress." (Hooks 1994: 1–12) I bring my unvarnished and complex *Haitianness* into the classroom to challenge my students in their desire to put me into a box as an "exception." Being Haitian in Newark, New Jersey is very different from being Haitian in Portland, Oregon. In New Jersey, there is a large Haitian community and I had constant and easy access to Haitian food and culture (music, films, theatre, festivals, etc.). My Haitian diasporic identity was generally affirmed within that milieu, and even if I did not participate in the various community events, I knew they existed. There were places I could go to buy Haitian food and participate in Haitian events. On the contrary, when I lived in Portland, Oregon, I often had a sense of alienation regarding my Haitian identity in part because I did not have access to those Haitian things.

That sense of alienation was particularly haunting in February 2004 when former President Jean-Bertrand Aristide left Haiti. A friend who lives on the east coast called me at 4 A.M. Pacific time to tell me what was going on. She said: "Turn on your television. It is all over the news. Aristide has left." We stayed on the phone for a while and I eagerly awaited daylight to go and buy a newspaper. I skimmed through the *New York Times* and all the main regional newspapers and there was nothing. On that day— perhaps more than ever—I felt very alienated and disconnected from my Haitian identity. My cultural and social needs were not being met. Also, the vision that I had built in my mind and heart (a vision that is inherent in many diasporic individuals) of returning to my homeland when the political situation improved, seemed even more unrealistic and impossible while living in Portland, in part because of the location (geographic). Now, a few years later, living in Georgia, this dream seems more attainable because I am closer to Haiti geographically and culturally.

About three years ago, at the university where I currently teach, I was invited to lecture on Haiti to a group of people who participate in a program known as "Academy of Lifelong Learning." The colleague who invited me wrote in an e-mail message: "I am excited about your talk. Your country seems to be doing better. I was at a department store not too long ago and saw that the clothes in the rack were assembled in Haiti." I spoke to a friend of mine who suggested that I use the colleague's comment to initiate my talk, which is what I did. The friend gave me a compact disc containing a song by a group known as *Sweet Honey in the Rock*. The song is titled "Are your Hands Clean?" It traces the origins of garments worn by Americans and how they have been touched by "hands all over the world starting in Central America." The song states:

In the cotton fields of El Salvador . . .
In South Carolina
[where] Burlington factories hum with the business of weaving
Oil and cotton into miles of fabric for Sears
Who takes this bounty back into the Caribbean Sea
Headed for Haiti this time
May she be one day soon free
Far from the Port-au-Prince palace
Third world women toil doing piece work to Sears' specifications
For three dollars a day my sisters make my blouse.[12]

I began my talk by asking everyone to listen to the lyrics. I am not sure if either the lifelong learners or my colleague understood the song or how it related to them, but it did open a door for us to talk about U.S. import/ export, globalization, and fair trade as well as the link between Haiti and the United States. I have found that all too often this link is overlooked. As a Haitian-American, I believe that this kind of oversight contributes to the negative images of Haitians in the U.S. It supports the idea that the relationship between the U.S. and Haiti is simply a parasitic one whereby Haiti only wants to take from the U.S. An exception to this is that in some parts of Louisiana, especially in New Orleans, there are people who are aware of the various connections (religious, culinary, architectural, etc.) between Louisiana and Haiti.

Louisiana is a state that has a strong historical and cultural connection to Haiti, especially the city of New Orleans. Having lived in New Orleans for approximately five years, when Hurricane Katrina hit in August 2005, I stayed closely tuned to the hurricane news before, during, and after. Looking at images of Katrina in 2005, I was reminded of Hurricane Jeanne that devastated Haiti in 2004, and for a split second there was no difference between how CNN and other mainstream news channels represented the New Orleans "refugees" and "evacuees"—for the most part people of color—who were "looting and stealing" and how they usually represent Haitian boat people.

An unbiased media might have represented the Katrina disaster by focusing more on issues such as the links between social inequality, global warming, consumerism, poverty, social policy, and social justice and their relation to the hurricane. An alternative model for media coverage would have been for its representatives and the public to have been conscious of the power of language and image when using a term such as "looting" instead of "finding" next to a picture or in a text describing African-Americans. Additionally, using the word "refugee" may have been misleading because it usually refers to a displaced individual not belonging somewhere. Furthermore, if the people affected by Hurricane Katrina were considered a homogeneous group of victims and not categorized into black and white, looters and finders, refugees and victims, perhaps the news could have been more objective.

As I watched those images, I thought how interesting it would have been if Haiti was geographically closer to New Orleans and Haitians were in a position to come and assist New Orleanians. After all, Haiti and the United States have a long history of immigration that dates as far back as 1824.

In 1824, the Haitian government under the leadership of President Jean-Pierre Boyer sent an agent named Jonathan Granville with 50,000 pounds of coffee to facilitate, finance, and arrange the transport of African-Americans who desired to emigrate and settle in Haiti. Loring D. Dewey, the general agent of the Society for African Colonization at New York, engaged in a correspondence with President Boyer to plan the details of this possible emigration including issues related to defraying the costs of the trip, access to land to cultivate, schools, religious tolerance, and laws regarding marriage.

Boyer welcomed the African-Americans who wished to come to Haiti and promised them the same rights under Haiti's constitution as all Haitian citizens. "The Society for Promoting the Emigration of Free Persons of Colour to Hayti" was formed and an estimated 13,000 African-Americans moved to Haiti. (Bethell 1992: 827–841) In 1824, these American "refugees" became Haitian citizens and integrated into all levels of Haitian society. While the American mainstream media represents contemporary Haitians as "boat people," there is never any reference to this *reverse* migration from the United States to Haiti which took place over 180 years ago.[13] Thus, Haitians and African-Americans have a long history of connecting in the search for freedom. For many critics and intellectuals around the world, Haiti's history of revolt is an inspiring one that remains an example for anyone who believes in freedom.

I am often struck by—and feel ambivalent about—the world's fascination with Haiti. Several Caribbean intellectuals including Maryse Condé, Alejo Carpentier, C.L.R. James, Édouard Glissant, and Aimé Césaire, to name a few, have used Haiti as a trope and have been inspired by the fact that Haiti was the first black republic and the second independent country in the western hemisphere. Yet, in spite of this fascination and admiration, Haiti and Haitians remain in the imaginary consciousness of most of their Caribbean and U.S. neighbors as simply boat people and economic refugees who want to steal other people's jobs. Be it in Guadeloupe or Martinique, the Bahamas or the Dominican Republic, Canada, French Guiana, or the United States, Haiti and Haitians are often perceived negatively. Many intellectuals around the world respect and admire Haiti's history and struggle, but somehow that respect, fascination, and admiration is not carried over to the general public.

In the U.S. imaginary, Haiti and Haitians are also synonymous with insecurity, corruption, disease, and helplessness. In defiance of this image, the popular hip-hop singer Wyclef Jean waved the Haitian flag when his group *The Fugees* (from the word refugees) won two 1997 Grammy awards, and momentarily it was cool to be Haitian. I remember feeling elated, excited, and proud that Wyclef Jean, who was my brother's classmate at Vailsburg High School in Newark, New Jersey was showing the whole world that it was positive to be Haitian. Unfortunately, that soon faded. Many young Haitians deny that they have Haitian roots because of stereotypes associated with Haiti and sometimes want to pass as Trinidadian or Jamaican. This was a common occurrence when I was in high school and it is still the case today. While I do not approve of this behavior, I do sympathize with these young Haitians because I know how it feels to be teased, stigmatized, and shown prejudiced from your classmates because you are from Haiti.

Although there are a few prominent Haitians and Haitian-Americans like Wyclef Jean in the Hollywood media, their "Haitianness" is often downplayed. For example, Wyclef Jean is thought by many to be Jamaican. On several occasions, I have been in situations where I felt like I had to set the record straight and proudly tell students and colleagues that Wyclef Jean is Haitian. Another Haitian in Hollywood is actress Garcelle Beauvais, who appeared in the TV series *The Jamie Foxx Show* (1996–2001). Although Beauvais has advocated on behalf of Haitian immigrants by going to Capitol Hill to discuss the disparity in the ways Haitian and Cuban refugees are treated, the fact that she is Haitian is not widely spread in the media. The actor Jimmy Jean-Louis is an exception to this. Jean-Louis has appeared in movies such as *Phat Girlz* and in the NBC TV series *Heroes*, in which he plays "The Haitian." However, "The Haitian" remains a mystery because the character rarely speaks; he is just there. This can be interpreted in a positive or negative light. It can be that "The Haitian" is so powerful that he does not need to express himself verbally and his strength is in his silence. Or, it can be that everyone else is talking on behalf of and for "The Haitian." In spite of the ambiguous nature of his character, I view it as a positive stance that a Haitian is represented in such a popular series. Maybe Haiti's image is slowly changing. After all, there is a tendency for mainstream America to follow Hollywood. Like Wyclef Jean and Garcelle Beauvais, Jean-Louis is proud and stays close to his Haitian roots. For example, he plays in the recent movie, *Life Outside of Pearl* (2007), directed by Haitian-American Johnny Desarmes. The movie depicts a middle-class Haitian family struggling to assimilate in the United States while maintaining its Haitian identity.

For the Haitian diaspora in the U.S., negative representations of Haiti constantly challenge us to define ourselves as "other"—that is, as different from the images that the media uses to describe us. Many of us become more aware and more conscious (especially when we are congratulated!) that we are viewed by others through a certain stereotypical lens; the moment we do not fit within the stereotypes we become problematic, and people are not sure what to do with us.

To deal with this issue, scholars are often called upon to explain Haiti, give a history lesson, or account for why, after so many years of independence, Haiti is still unstable politically, economically, and socially. Often, I feel like explaining that my Haitian identity is, for the most part, arbitrary. It was just a coincidence that the boat in which my ancestors were shackled went to Haiti instead of Cuba, Brazil, Jamaica, or Louisiana. But because of my passion, my awareness of my history, and my love and sometimes love-hate relationship with Haiti, I feel that I have a responsibility to provide this explanation, to show that Haiti can best be understood in light of one of my favorite proverbs "Dèyè mòn, gen mòn" [Behind the mountains are more mountains]. This is to say that Haiti is complex, fragmented, multilayered, and not reducible to keywords like *poverty, boat people,* and *political turmoil.* Thus, my bicultural identity/ies shape me into a political agent. Like many other exiles, my love-hate relationship with my native land is complex. On the one hand, I have some fond memories of my childhood in Haiti and my identity is shaped by my love for my culture (language, food, music, folktales, proverbs etc.). There are still ideas that I can only express in Haitian Creole. On the other hand, I have feelings of disgust (hate) for some of the memories I grew up with. For instance, the 1969 arrests and killing of several members of the Estiverne family (from my mother's side) in a town called Grand-Bois, a farming community on the border of the Dominican Republic. I am also saddened and disgusted by what Haiti has become today with the constant kidnapping and instability. Yet, somewhere between these two feelings of love and hate is the feeling of hope that I maintain toward Haiti. I sometimes feel like I embody not just Haiti's culture but its history as well. As a result, I feel compelled to explain its history.

I sometimes tell people that in 1825, about twenty years after its founding, Charles X of France recognized Haitian independence in exchange for an indemnity of 150,000 francs (it was later reduced to 60,000). This debt imposed on Haiti did not help its economic infrastructure. Debts from the International Monetary Fund and the World Bank continue to cripple Haiti. When I attempt to explain Haiti and present a more complex picture, I feel that many times I fail. Sometimes I tell people about Haiti's impact in the Atlantic world and explain how gaining its independence meant that France lost Haiti, and as a result Napoleon had to sell Louisiana to the United States. With the Louisiana Purchase, the United States gained over 50 million acres in territory. Thus, the United States "benefited" from Haiti's independence. Unfortunately, the powerful images of Haitians as economically destitute boat people and carriers of AIDS are often stronger than my simple explanations. The connections between Haiti and the United States are long and complex. Soldiers from Saint-Domingue, including Henri Christophe, the future king of Haiti, fought in the Battle of Savannah in the summer of 1779. In fact, on October 9, 2007, a monument was erected in the historic Franklin Square in Savannah, Georgia to honor the Haitians who had fought in the American Revolutionary War. Maybe this will bring recognition to Haiti and Haitians and they will no longer only be considered as "boat people."

In an article in the French magazine *L'Express*, French filmmaker Laurent Cantet discusses the challenges of filming his last film, *Vers le Sud* (*Heading South*, 2006), in Port-au-Prince. The story is a banal one that rehearses clichés about Caribbean exoticism. Three white women from the U.S. and Canada are on vacation in Haiti in the 1970s and, using their wealth, class, and color they are determined to have fun and connect erotically with Legba, a very dark-skinned black man who is "beautiful like a god," to experience Haitian sensuality.[14] When asked why he chose to focus on Haiti, Cantet responded: "La répétition du malheur au fil de l'Histoire [d'Haïti] a quelque chose de pathétique" [The constant repetition of bad luck in Haiti's history has something pathetic about it]. He describes the violence in Haiti as "normal." When asked why filmmakers were attracted to Haiti, he suggested that it was because of a mixture of danger, sensuality, revolt, and fatalism. When *Vers le sud* premiered in France, a Haitian viewer commented that the film was interesting for the ways in which it showed Haiti with neither guilt nor compassion, because he was sick and tired of compassion. His feelings represent what has become a common binary in the representation of Haitians—either guilt or compassion.

When you do not fit in either of these two categories—that is, when you do not have a story that elicits guilt (whether in terms of colonization, post-colonization, or current globalization issues), or you do not elicit compassion when one hears your story of survival (or lack of one), you don't *look* Haitian and must *not be* Haitian. Since I am living in a bicultural situation, I sometimes feel torn, estranged, alienated, dispossessed, and lost. Like other exiles (psychological, political, economic, religious, etc.) I undergo a change in identity to a certain extent by constantly negotiating issues of belonging, particularly in terms of language and culture. With the negative stereotypes associated with Haiti and Haitians, I feel like it is much harder for Haitians like me than for many other bicultural immigrants living in the United States to reconcile their bicultural identities.

Recently, I was talking to a Haitian friend living in Florida and mentioned that I missed living in Portland, Oregon; her response was that I had become too American because "there are no Haitians in Portland." When I told her that there are Haitian communities all around the United States even in Arizona, Nevada, Oregon, Washington, and Utah, she replied that "Haitians are like bugs, they are everywhere." I am not sure what to make of this comment. Does that mean that we are survivors? Or that people cannot get rid of us because we have a strong will to remain where we need to even if it's clear that we are neither liked nor wanted? Maybe this means that we have the capacity to adapt to different environments. Haitians like me who are "out of place"—that is living outside of mainstream Haitian communities—are sometimes labeled *non-Haitian* by Haitians and Americans. Yet, often we are not American enough. So what happens when you do not fit into the American idea of Haitianness? Are you then unrecognizable?

In *Haitians in the United States: Pride Against Prejudice*, Alex Stepick (1998) remarks that "For many Haitian immigrants, life in the United States is a conflict between pride in their roots and prejudice against blacks in general and Haitians in particular." As a "refugee/exiled" living in a constantly changing diasporic community, I remain a "liminal citizen, betwixt and between two states, and struggling [even after over two decades] to be incorporated in [the] new country." (Laguerre 1998: 76) To explain why I *look* or *don't look* Haitian remains a constant challenge for me. I am aware of my hybrid identity/ies as well as my belonging to different cultures even if it is sometimes hard to explain to others. Nevertheless, I am conscious that through this enriching and complex process of becoming I am relentlessly shaping and constructing my future while creating my place in this global world.

Notes

1. Article available from http://www.thenewyorktimes.com, October 29, 2007.

2. See "Polémique autour de l'origine de l'épidémie de sida," *Le Monde*, online version of newspaper, http://www.lemonde.fr, accessed May 19, 2008.

3. See http://www.nyesma.org/?html=news_events.php. In particular, the association rejected the claims that the researchers think an "unknown single infected Haitian immigrant arrived in a large city like Miami or New York, and the AIDS virus circulated for years—first in the U.S. population and then to other nations . . . The researchers virtually

ruled out the possibility that HIV came directly to the United States from Africa . . ." accessed November 22, 2007.

4. On December 8, 2007, I was watching CNN Headline News and there was a segment with the caption "Miami Dolphins Fans Turn to Voodoo." The caption showed two Haitian women, presumably "Voodoo" priestesses, performing a ceremony which involved putting a group photo in a bucket of water and walking around the bucket several times. It was not clear whether the picture was that of the Miami Dolphins or of the opposing team.

5. In *AIDS and Accusation: Haiti and the Geography of Blame*, Paul Farmer notes: "In North America, disease-ridden foreigners are identified and blamed for a worldwide pandemic; in Port-au-Prince or New York, conspiracy theories impute to the powerful evil motives, either the desire to weaken the ranks of outcasts (homosexuals, Haitians, intravenous drug users) or to defame black people."(Farmer 1992: 245) While the other groups may have redeemed themselves (at least in some communities), Haitians have still been unable to do so. Perhaps it is because "AIDS in Haiti is about proximity rather than distance. AIDS in Haiti is a tale of ties to the United States, rather than to Africa, it is a story of unemployment rates greater than 70 percent." (Farmer 1992: 264) Likewise, Chief Science and Health correspondent Robert Bazell in his article "Research Rewrites First Chapter of AIDS in U.S.: Don't Blame Patient Zero or Haitians for the epidemic" also observes: "Haitians already have endured one long bout of blame for the AIDS epidemic. They certainly do not deserve another." See "Research Rewrites First Chapter of AIDS in U.S.: Don't Blame Patient Zero or Haitians for the epidemic," http://www.msnbc.msn.com/id/21653369/, accessed May 19, 2008.

6. See "Haitians May Sue Over HIV Research Claim," *Heart Beat News*, New York, November 9, 2007.

7. The original wording is "Nous ne devons pas réagir de façon émotionnelle mais de façon pragmatique, scientifique et coordonnée," http://www.alterpresse.org, accessed May 19, 2008

8. For reasons of consistency, I capitalize bell hook's name in the text but she generally writes her name without capitalization.

9. There is a strong anti-Haitian feeling in places like the Bahamas and Guadeloupe where there is a large Haitian population (both legal and illegal). Many Guadeloupeans and Bahamians view the Haitians there as pariahs who are only there to steal their jobs and take advantage of the opportunities offered in their countries.

10. This is not to say that there are not prominent African-Americans who understand and support Haitians. For instance, Danny Glover is someone who has been supportive of Haitians and has protested for their rights on numerous occasions. He is currently working on a film on Haitian revolutionary leader Toussaint Louverture.

11. In 2002, Haiti received a $66.7 million grant from the Global Fund in order to establish effective treatment and prevention programs and provide resources. Haiti is one of several demonstration sites developing effective practices for AIDS treatment programs in countries that lack resources. (Miles and Charles 2004: 24–40)

12. See *Sweet Honey in the Rock*, Songtalk Publishing. Lyrics are based on John Cavanagh's article "The Journey of the Blouse: A Global Assembly."

13. In a letter dated March 4, 1824, Dewey writes, "I am not ignorant that you have made offers of a favourable kind, and that even late information from an emigrant with you, shows, that you afford them some strong motives to migrate to your Island; yet I am ignorant of many things, which would be necessary to be known before their emigration could be aided by the Colonization Society." Boyer promised the African-Americans "all the guarantees and rights that the constitution of the Republic has established in their favour." He further stated: "I have aided in freeing those from debt who could not quite pay their passage; I have given land to those who wished to cultivate it . . . I have prepared for the children of Africa, coming out of the United States, all that can assure them of an honourable existence in becoming citizens of the Haytian Republic."

14. Legba, of course, is a reference to Haitian Vodou. In the Vodou religion, Legba is a very powerful *lwa* [spirit]. He is master of the crossroads and can guide someone who is lost. In a Vodou ceremony, he is the first and last spirit invoked.

References

Bethel Rauh, Elizabeth. 1992. "Images of Hayti: The Construction of An Afro-American Lieu De Mémoire." *Callaloo* 15, no. 3: 827–841.

Catanese, Anthony V. 1999. *Haitians: migration and diaspora*. Boulder: Westview Press.

Danticat, Edwidge. 1995. *Krik Krak!* New York: Soho Press.

———. 2007. *Brother, I'm Dying*. New York: Alfred A Knopf.

———. Ed. 2000. *The Butterfly's Way: Voices From the Haitian Dyaspora in the United States*. New York: Soho Press.

Evans, Braziel Jana and Anita Mannur. 2003. *Theorizing Diaspora: A Reader*. Oxford: Blackwell Publishing.

Farmer, Paul. 1992. *Aids and Accusation: Haiti and the Geography of Blame*. Los Angeles: University of California Press.

Farmer, Paul and Adam Taylor. 2004. "Liberation Medicine and U.S. Policy Toward Haiti." In *Let Haiti Live: Unjust U.S. Policies Towards Its Oldest Neighbor*, edited by Eugenia Charles and Melinda Miles, 26–40. Coconut Creek: Educa Vision.

Glick Schiller, Nina and Georges Eugène Fouron. 2001. *Georges Woke Up Laughing: Long-Distance Nationalism and the Search for Home*. Durham: Duke University Press.

Hooks, Bell. 1992. *Black Looks: Race and Representations*. Boston: South End Press.

———. 1994. *Teaching to Transgress: Education as the Practice of Freedom*. New York: Routledge.

Laguerre, Michel S. 1998. *Diasporic Citizenship: Haitian Americans in Transnational America*. New York: St. Martin's Press.

Lawless, Robert. 1992. *Haiti's Bad Press*. Rochester, Vermont: Schenkman Books Inc.

McMillan, Terry. 1996. *How Stella Got Her Groove Back*. New York: Penguin.

Miller, Jake. 1984. *The Plight of Haitian Refugees*. New York: Praeger.

n.a. 1824. *Correspondence relative to the Emigration to Hayti, of the People of Colour #* 372, Pearl Street.

Stepick, Alex. 1982. *Haitian Refugees in the U.S.* New York: Minority Rights Group LTD.

———. 1998. *Pride Against Prejudice: Haitians in the United States*. Boston: Allyn and Bacon.

Sullivan, Kevin Rodney. 1998. *How Stella Got Her Groove Back*. Los Angeles: 20th Century Fox. 124 mins.

Zéphir, Flore. 1996. *Haitian Immigrants in Black America: A Sociological and Sociolinguistic Portrait*. Westport, Conn.: Greenwood Publishing.

9

Picking and Unpicking Time

Contextualizing Haitian Immigration in French Guiana

MARC LONY

The main goal of this introduction to the personal accounts of Haitian immigration to Guiana is to explain the phenomenon in terms of the notion
of time rather than merely examining history by going, as Walter Benjamin would say, "against the grain," i.e. by adopting the viewpoint of the
downtrodden, the migrants fated to articulate past and present, to interpret,
manage, and reconstruct time. Weaving and unpicking the threads that run
through and around Haitian immigration in the specific case of Guiana is
not merely a matter of examining a population overflow, and of paying attention to its narrow everyday activities. It is a matter, rather, of focusing (1)
on the overt and occluded relationships between places, events, people, and
things (symptomatic migrations between the visible and the latent, between
what surfaces and what survives); (2) on the ambivalence of the notions of
liberty and progress with regard to various circumstances of the country's
development;(3) on the way that time has grown more complex in this host
country born of colonialism, and which already lives in a state of double
temporality or of temporal duplicity, i.e. in the dilemma born of the weight
of history and engagement with modernity. Thus, what is called for is a study
that draws on multiple perspectives, one which connects various viewpoints
on the paradoxes of Guiana, aesthetic constructions that belong to the realm
of the literary, and Haitian-Guianese views and analyses based on the typical daily routine of an immigrant worker. This study offers an analysis of
time and place in Guiana and establishes a context for the observations and
accounts of Haitian migrants reported here, observations testifying to the
personal investment of these individuals in everyday Guianese life as they
make their way toward integration and recognition.

Unpicking Time: Routes

Cayenne, Monday, November 24, 2008: It's 5 A.M., the time Dieula[1] gets up every morning. She is leaning distractedly on the chest of drawers where there are arrayed photos of home, Haiti, which she left ten years ago. In bed, her daughter wants to grab a few more minutes of sleep and replies weakly. It's time to quickly sweep and mop the floor . . . Dieula works fast. She makes her way through the small house, with its three tiny bedrooms. Her two other children and her two nieces share two of the bedrooms. A divorcee, Dieula shares the other with her four-year-old daughter. She talks to the children, who are stretching, submitting them to a verbal shaking. Then she makes them breakfast. To save time, she eats standing up. Wolfing down bread and coffee, she looks out the open window at dawn breaking over the yard where things are beginning to stir. Usually, she showers and leaves for work between 6:30 A.M. and 7 A.M. After she has gone, the children eat on their own and get themselves off to school. She doesn't drive but has bought a new Clio (fourteen thousand Euros) so that her son can drop her off at work. Her son, however, is not as amenable as he once was. She does not care for his friends and fears he will turn out badly. Often, she takes the bus. There's a line linking Cité Bonhomme to Montjoly and the ride cost 3.60 Euros.

Since she has been in Guiana working tooth and nail, time has lost it torpor and has become highly strung and structured. The demands of time that guide her days give her a sense of security. In the mornings, she leaves between 6:30 A.M. and 7 A.M., but today she has to leave earlier. Today is the first day of the strike over the rise in gas prices and the general high cost of living. They won't settle until they get answers, and want the government to find them—so Dieula has heard on TV and the radio. There will be roadblocks everywhere. Cars will not be allowed to pass. On the radio, people are talking excitedly. The fight is on and culprits have been identified: Commissioner Laflaquière and Minister Jégo, the oil companies, SARA (the oil refining company) in Martinique, and behind them the French government and its terrible machinations. "What's going to happen?" wonders Dieula. "What about work, the family? Will they be able to shop for food? Will the children be able to go to school?" She admits to doing most of her shopping with the Hmong, who provide the Guianese markets with rice, fruit, and vegetables at prices much lower than those of anything imported from France. Occasionally, she goes to a small Chinese-owned store, or to Match, a big chain store, but mostly she consumes products from Guiana, like yogurts from Macouria or the Guianese brand of juice, *Caresse Guyanaise*. However, it's time to go. On the radio, someone is screaming in Creole: "We'll show them we're no macaques." Then all she can hear are snatches out of context and, anyway, she has no more time for daydreaming. She sets off on foot. The eight kilometers do not daunt her, nor does the work. Asked about frustrations, trials, and failures, she replies with a dazzling smile: "Nothing comes without effort, you know. And I just cannot live without working."

So, Dieula sets off to work along roads smashed up by tropical rains, along with quite a number of others who are rushing along. At the Méthon bakery, *Le pain de Sucre*, people stand in line. Children are rushing home with warm sticks of bread in their arms. There are many pedestrians and cyclists. Dieula's sister, who lives in the same neighborhood, is also heading to work and waves to her from the other side of the street. It's her baby sister, who came from Haiti after she did. She lives with some nieces and two friends in another part of Cité Bonhomme. Dieula looks absentmindedly at the fronts of the familiar houses. Because of crime, they all have bars on the doors and windows, pretty much like everywhere. Bars like fingerprints, symptomatic of a diverse flood of immigration impossible to stem. "It's normal, people are afraid," says Dieula. "I'm afraid too, but I have nothing to steal, not a thing. Almost everything I possess at home was given to me by the people in whose houses I work." She means, above all, clothing for her and her children, but also furniture, utensils, and knick-knacks. Does she think Guiana is a rich country? She pauses briefly to think before responding: "It depends. There are lots of fine cars, fine houses, but not everywhere . . . This is Cité Bonhomme and it's not a rich neighborhood. But, in general, I don't think people are unhappy . . . Life is good in Guiana, everyone says so and you can see it . . . It's an easy life." But isn't this easy life a costly one in day-to-day terms? Dieula can't really say but points to her female bosses's complaints about the price of carrots, camembert, and pears. Admittedly they can't seem to give up buying them. As for clothes, beauty products, or pharmaceuticals, they usually buy them in France where, according to them, the prices are two or three times lower. Do these women travel much? "Yeah, quite a bit . . . They go to France to see family, or to the French Antilles, or Brazil." She adds, laughing, that these women are always complaining about the price of air fares. It would seem that flights in February are already booked, even in first class where a ticket costs 4,000 Euros round-trip. Haiti? She goes back from time to time to see her parents. If only she could have had them come to Guiana, it would have been easier and less of a burden! As for herself, she will die in Guiana. What would she go back to Haiti for? Anyway, her children were born here. The blue sky is clear by now and the heavy cotton balls of cloud are moving further away into the distance. Dieula makes good progress, arrives at the crossroads by the stadium, and turns her back on Cayenne as she turns onto the road to Baduel.

The road, which is usually bumper-to-bumper with cars all the way to Cayenne, is strangely quiet, and seems almost wider. There is not a single car. The strike has broken the rhythm. The passive tension of the body carried by machines has temporarily been replaced by productive, muscular energy: people on foot or bikes. This break with habit has brought mighty shows of force, shouting, complaints, threats. In a collective delusion, there suddenly appears to be no such thing as a consumer, and all self-centered energies have been marshaled into lockstep, into one movement. Everyone rushing today seems closer to one another. It is almost a great egalitarian moment of social mixing. A little beyond *La Palette*, a store for home improvement, a cyclist offers Dieula a ride on his rear carrier. She accepts but the bike is not up to much and, after wobbling along a few yards, they are forced to give up. They laugh and then each sets off again at their respective pace. Along the road there are houses on pillars with fine wrought metal security bars completely fencing in their ground floors (such work made fortunes for the first ironwork companies in Cayenne). It would take a now-sweating Dieula about an hour to get to the Suzini intersection, where the protester barricade has been set up: trucks, chairs, banners with slogans, and strike pickets. For Dieula, it is like crossing a little border, which reminds her of her first difficult years in Guiana. She exchanges a few words with an old Haitian gardener carrying his grass trimmer on his shoulder. She bumps into him from time to time: "That's Mr. Jean. I don't know how old he is . . . perhaps sixty, perhaps more . . . he rents out his services to the villas along the road and sometimes works with his son." Gardener, housekeeper[2]: these have almost become identities for Haitians.[3] As for her cousin, who is also a housekeeper, Dieula has to admit that she is not conscientious: "She's always breaking things, then acting stupid in front of her boss as if to say it was not her fault. They think she is dumb, but she's not dumb at all. She just pretends to be and takes advantage." Acting stupid so as to confirm the boss or authorities in their power and avoid sanction; isn't that the timeworn tactic of the downtrodden, of all domestic servants? It has often been caricatured in literature and movies, this feigned humility, absurd hard-headedness, groveling in body and language. It is a way of attuning oneself to the other through a sort of bivocalism, of entering into his system of reference in order to say and do things he may or may not expect, but always things that fit with a judgment he has already made. Who cannot recall in the movie *Life is a Long Quiet River* (1988) the stubborn denials of the pregnant Marie-Thérèse, swearing to her mistress that she has never been to bed with a man? Who can forget Maryse Condé's Haitian character, Désinor, putting on his fat negro act in order to shock the Creole middle classes of Rivière au Sel, but secretly reassuring them that they are not like him? (Condé 1989: 198) Désinor and Marie-Thérèse could speak with their own voices—the voices of truth—but they would be exposing themselves pointlessly. Speaking in the voice given by the other is a much more prudent policy, allowing suspicions of duplicity to be suspended. Dieula makes quick progress under the increasing heat of the sun; still about forty-five minutes to an hour of walking to go before she arrives at her first workplace in a small residential neighborhood of Montjoly.

Usually, one has to pay attention on the sides of the roads because the shoulders are unpaved, the cars go fast, and the sputtering mopeds even faster. Dieula walks in the red dirt and the trampled grass. She has passed the Montjoly bar, a club that was all the rage in the 1970s and 1980s, a club whose heyday she never saw. There is the pharmacy on the right, the Asian shops on both sides of the road. "You take Avenue Saint-Ange Méthon and you'll see the villa Musette, where I work . . ." Madame Musette is a civil servant. She is not at work today. The strike gives her a break and allows her to garden. She is proud of her garden, which is both very blooming and very well taken care of by a taciturn Haitian gardener. Occasionally, she admonishes him and shouts directions in a mixture of French Antillean and Guianese Creole, with a few Haitian Creole words and expressions thrown in. Then she smiles sweetly: "See how beautiful these flowers are. Do you know why? In truth, it is very uneven around here. This land was filled in by prisoner laborers in order to provide somewhere for the Martinican refugees after the eruption of the Montagne Pelée.[4] Those refugees were mainly farmers who would put their animals out to graze around here, which explains the richness of certain tracts and the vigor of the plants . . . Oh yes! What you can see here is a flowering of both the work of a wave of forced labor and of Martinican migrants looking to start a new life." For one or two minutes, as the flowers are admired in silence, the forces of the repressed past of Guiana, a place of both guillotine and salvation, crystallize in the present. The splendor and the flowers of Madame Musette's garden, are they not an instance of the "auratic phenomenon" described by Benjamin? Is she not suggesting that the auratic dazzle of her garden supposes something beyond the *hic et nunc*? Aesthetic bedazzlement, a moment subtracted from time where all histories are consigned. The aura, which bears witness in the present to crystallized forces, goes beyond memory and trace since its momentum comes from an origin that is always in the process of being realized. Metamorphosis of time. "Guiana is a pretty garden," sang the traditional Guianese music group, Les Oyampis, in the 1970s. But whose sweat has watered this garden? Madame Musette receives guests on her veranda, seated on a chaise longue covered with gaily-colored cushions. A friend, Monsieur Jacques, who has also been immobilized by the strike, comes to visit. He does not know Dieula: "No, I don't know the young lady you are referring to. I could get to know her, true, since dependable people are always hard to find and keep. It's also a very common first name, you know . . . ?" Madame Musette has every confidence in her employee. "Dieula? She has worked for me for at least ten years. Before her I had Perséphone, lazy like you wouldn't believe. Dieula was recommended to me by a fellow French Antillean Rotarian. They were people with a house and needs similar to mine. I must say the woman was particularly demanding because she thought Dieula often did not go fast enough and had problems understanding. They returned to Martinique and I took Dieula on trial for a month. She was a perfect fit."[5] Dieula's boss is full of praise. From their first meeting, she was won over by the solidity, frankness, and above all loyalty of the young Haitian woman: "She was apparently capable of taking on housework and cooking. Moreover, I must tell that, unlike the average Haitian who says, 'yes, yes, I'm used to it, I know what has to be done,' and only messes everything up, Dieula was careful to find out exactly what I wanted and asked for a work schedule (Monday this, Tuesday that . . .). And, when I asked her to do some cooking, she told me straight out that she had never done any, but that if I showed her, she would do her best, and she did! . . . So, yes, I straight away trusted her, which is the most important thing for me. What is more, I wanted her to come every day, but she told me Fridays would not be possible because she has been working for years for another lady and could not leave her, even if the pay were better! I thought to myself that it would be fantastic to have someone so loyal. On the other hand, I had no hand in having her made legal. She was already legal and I pay social security for her. Later, she herself applied for naturalization and she is now French." Madame Musette has a rule: respect everyone's freedom and, above all, do not discourage those who are willing. She is aware that the Dieulas of this world are more than rare and that there are many parasites, but it is difficult to separate the wheat from the chafe. In her view, Guiana is still seen as an Eldorado, and not merely by Haitians and Brazilians. Even if the system is open to abuse, "whatever people say, we need immigration and there is enough room for everyone in Guiana . . . to develop the country." But at this point, Dieula's boss catches herself, to the approval of Monsieur Jacques. Do we really want the country to be developed? How much development? To the point where it becomes a parody of modernity like in the overpopulated French Antilles, with traffic jams, huge parking lots, the obsession with profit . . . And what about the metropolitan French, the *métros*? And their potential or real aid? She is, of course, referring to white civil servants about whom she is skeptical. The metropolitan French are motivated by a system of bonuses and financial incentives. In general, they go from one overseas post to the next without really getting involved, or without being able to do so for any meaningful period of time. Their economic influence is not negligible. Out of forty teachers at one Montjoly middle school, there are ten Creoles. The other thirty, or at least a large number of them, are waiting to set off for new pastures, "which imbue their sleep with a golden haze," she concludes in a parody of Heredia.

To tell the truth, Montjoly would not be what it is today without the horrible events of May 1902 in Martinique. On May 8, 1902, the day that Montagne Pelée erupted, Montjoly did not yet exist. Instead, there were mostly marshes and bush, virgin land belonging to the town of Rémire. As soon as the catastrophe was announced, aid committees were formed and help began to be sent to the survivors. Across political divisions and conflicting interests, an idea took hold: the attraction of new land (which could be explored, appropriated, and converted) combined with the strong desire to emigrate could be fruitfully exploited to found a new agricultural colony. Thus, the resulting migration allowed what had disappeared in Martinique to be reborn in Guiana. In the center of Montjoly, in the old town, the streets still bear the names of immigrant families from the Caribbean: Caristan, Gallot, Lony, Méthon, and many others, who were the town's first architects.[6] Today, there are modest houses: identical lots with villas for rent built by companies or civil servants in order to provide for a comfortable retirement, as well as many cute private villas more or less hidden by the vegetation. Does Dieula know that before her, other Creoles settled here, driven by a sense of adventure, despair, or a desire to start afresh? One day, they stood back from their bleak everyday existences, heeded the contradictory voices vying for prominence within, and allowed themselves to be swept up by a new rhythm that pushed them toward the crossing. With this, they dared to make the journey. "When I came across," continues Dieula in Haitian Creole, "I turned my back on wasted time. Over there, I was moving but it was as if I was standing still. Here is different, it's bam, bam, bam bam . . ." She punctuates her words with cutting hand movements. So, it's a question of rhythm. It's as if leaving was necessary because, whatever she might do, there was no possible resonance over there between her rhythm and that of her surroundings. Deleuze and Guattari are right when they say that "every environment is vibratory." (Deleuze and Gattari 1980: 384) If any confirmation were needed, another Haitian, Dany Laferrière, provides it in an account which in a few pages lays out his experience, multicadenced by different locations and different languages: Port-au-Prince, Cayenne, Manhattan, Brooklyn, N'Djamena, Paris, Montréal, São Paulo, Dublin, Guadeloupe, and Mexico. The cadence of French is with him wherever he goes: "its song is," in his words, "the rhythm of my blood." (87) But that is not the most important thing. What counts is the leaking of the different narrative layers in one another, the blurring of borders between the sites where he travels. Passing from one category to another, from one code to the next (from Port-au-Prince to Cayenne, from Guadeloupe to Mexico etc.), particular intonations and anachronistic sensations emerge at different levels of multisensorial coordination. The way Laferrière organizes the strata of his account lends more force to his interventions and the rhythmical disparities. Each name-code, like a musical key, initiates a rhythmic variation, a system of resonance. There is also a resonance with the song that pulses within him: "Each city has its own sound. When I close my eyes in Mexico, despite the fact Spanish is different to Creole (while all the same being close to French), I often have the feeling I'm in Port-au-Prince. (87) In Port-au-Prince, his niece drives fast while talking at the top of her lungs on the telephone: "She talks about work, her boyfriend, above all about music, moving from English to Creole like you would change gears." (89) In Cayenne, Laferrière dives into the noise of downtown: the rhythm of tropical rain, the city's homeless, the bright skirts of the young girls from Paramaribo, the rowdy laughs of Dominican women, the explosive exhausts of young Brazilians on their fast bikes, and "that young man with a blackbird under his arm that he teaches to hum folk songs."(90) And he often, if not always, notices in himself a kind of harking back to an unchanging origin that lies beneath them all: Port-au-Prince. In Mexico City, when you close your eyes and concentrate on the aspect of the language, you could think you were in Haiti. Or, if you open your eyes in N'Djamena, the aspect of the city recalls Port-au-Prince.

Clearly, aspect is not the same thing as appearance, but rather an internal disposition, the way in which a language or a city manages to breathe. From our earliest moments, isn't our inner life of desire structured by variations of resemblance and dissemblance? Arriving back in Cayenne, says Laférierre, the rhythm of the rain on the corrugated iron roofs "transport[s] me back to a world I thought lost." (89) "What is ultimate is thus the relation between sensation and rhythm, which places in each sensation the levels and domains through which it passes. This rhythm runs through a painting just as it runs through a piece of music. It is diastole-systole: the world that seizes me by closing in around me, the self that opens to the world and opens the world itself."(Deleuze 2003: 37) Asking Dieula about rhythm in her daily life sends her back to dance and music. She laughs when carnival dances are mentioned to her: "My sister dances, but I don't dance in the street or discos. Honestly, that's not my thing, but I do like music. Not the sort my son listens to, though. Traditional music, the *Konpa.*" Sure she hums reassuring motivational melodies, sure she sometimes dreams as she looks out at the landscape. Does she sing Haitian tunes to fortify herself? Yes, all the time: while doing housework, sometimes while walking. Singing her music, her cadence, is a way of getting into the rhythm of what she is doing and also of getting back in touch nostalgically with her previous home. And when she speaks, does her language have the same rhythm as before? Yes, if she is speaking to compatriots. Otherwise, she puts together a mixture of French, Guianese, and Haitian Creole, which she has a hard time savoring or mastering. It is impossible to avoid contamination between languages. Even the ladies she works for are obliged to use Haitian expressions to be understood. In the 1900s, the French Antilleans also came with their music, their accent, and their Creole began to leach into Guianese sentences and phrases. Music, for instance, was at the heart of everything, including the success of the *Le Cric-Crac* supper club, which has since become a disco in a large hotel complex run by Maurice Méthon, who today is quick to pick up his saxophone in order to play a *biguine* from the old days. Of course, *Le Cric-Crac* is the relatively recent result of investments by this descendant of an inhabitant of Saint-Pierre. In the beginning, dances took place around feast days:

The band was rather small, but we used to enjoy ourselves. The singing instrument might only be a simple beak flute or an accordion, a very common instrument in the placers (gold mine sites). Accompaniment took the form of the ancestor of today's drums, comprising a metal cylinder with holes in it, which was filled with pieces of lead (*le chacha*), and a drummer who marked the beat by hitting a plank or bamboo branch with a pair of hardwood sticks. Later, the accompaniment would be reinforced by the presence of two further instruments, a banjo and violoncello. Progress would be even more marked when, on the occasion of the city festival, the mayor would send to Cayenne for a band comprised of clarinet, trombone, banjo, guitar, violoncello, and drums. (B. Lony 1995)

The rhythmic complexity grew, strengthened, became increasingly dominant, and created a new relationship, not only with dancers and music-lovers, but also with the surrounding community. This document from another son of a refugee from Saint-Pierre first of all attests to how the music, but also the other rhythms of schools, feasts, elections, herders, farmers, and fishermen have contributed to the coherence of the New World; the way in which the process of "quotidianization" (Bégout 2005: 523) took on consistency, the way in which the community marked its territory and appropriated it. Progress is evident not only in the shape of this dance band—which would grow, show, and perform—but above all in the territorial consolidation of which it is a sign.

In Montjoly, as temporary migrant workers began to settle down, distribution of plots of land took place. Bernard Lony talks about the construction of the church and the generous labor put in by the carpenter, Doctorée Moges. Then he recalls the abusive expropriations under the Vichy regime and the stubbornness of Méthon Saint-Ange, Rémire's mayor, in demanding that the abuses not be admitted. At that time, the community was united and people helped one another. Of course, there must have been tensions, but nothing comparable to the general loss of common cause that exists today. Can time wipe everything out? All of a sudden, doubt inhibits the involuntary outpouring of memory, giving way to an evaluation of what has been lost. What has been lost? How else can it be measured but by reference to a feeling of strangeness and geographic disorientation? B. Lony walks along the same streets of Montjoly looking for people and details. He stares at the people he meets for an uncomfortably long amount of time, smiling quietly. "Is that so-and-so's son or daughter? . . . Where is the Kapok tree, the bench . . . ?" A Proustian drive carries him away in search of that lost time that made him and that has disappeared somewhere beneath the present: "What I have to say will only deal with the small village where I was born, where I grew up, and which I really enjoy going back to, despite the fact that

I always feel a little choked up at how different it is from when I lived there not so long ago." In the maze of streets and new buildings, he feels as though he is in a wilderness, like the brush that grew there before, and he realizes that all of it started to sprout long ago, and there occurs to him the question he never could ask his father: "What could have possessed those families to travel the two thousand kilometers separating Martinique and Guiana at a time when it took at least ten days by boat?" Leaving blind, taking the leap without knowing. "Do we know why people emigrate?" one of the Caristan brothers wonders out loud to himself, another child of Martinican immigration. (Cornuau 2002) The question is a simple one and reveals not only how the events of the past are useless in making sense of the past, but also that they may even be a hindrance. The huge catastrophe, despite its extent, may not have been sufficient reason for the departure of the French West Indian founders. Similarly, there are Haitians that, despite the severe poverty, remain in Haiti. The question obviously remains a rhetorical one, for only the imagination can supply the necessary narrative once the memory has been interrogated. However, if the Montjoly of today was neither the motivation nor the intention of those who left the ruins of Saint-Pierre, it is paradoxically the answer to the question *why* that resurfaces in the face of the last century. All the possible reasons have fed into the productive power that has triumphed over obstacles in order to preside over the construction of this place. Even though French Antillean and Haitian immigration have little in common, historical logic suggests that the Haitians of today will be the Guianese of tomorrow. Is it right to speak of a resemblance or an anachronistic affinity between these two migrations?

A few years before the catastrophe in Saint-Pierre, French West Indians arrived en masse during the gold rush between 1880 and 1916. (Mam-Lam-Fouk 1987: 85) Having made a quick fortune, some of them settled down. Rodolphe Alexandre, who has studied what he calls the "Antillean question" of that time, explains that Martinicans succeeded in maximizing their competencies in the construction and business sectors linked to goldmining. (Alexandre 1999: 63) Integration was not easy. Before the arrival of the refugees after 1902, the proponents and enemies of the Antillean community waged war in the columns of two newspapers, *L'Oeil* and *Le Bon droit*. Should French Antilleans be allowed only limited access to political office? Should French Antillean business undertakings be encouraged in Guiana? Mocked as *Mennen-vini* (literally "those who have been brought"), "carpet baggers," or "plant used in witchcraft," explains Alexandre (Alexandre 1999: 62), French Antilleans found it hard to gain a foothold. Finally, the "Antillean question" had a bloody epilogue in the form of the 1928 uprising following the death of Jean Galmot, during which six Martinicans were killed, some in lynchings. Édouard Glissant makes passing reference to this French Antillean colonization and its consequences in his *Discours Antillais*: "So, what about Guiana? An infinite realm we think of as overflowing with water and woods. The Guianese want the Martinicans and the Guadeloupeans to leave them alone. We've done quite a bit of colonizing over there" (Glissant 1997: 450).

Long dependent on them, Guiana is connected less and less—in terms of administration—with the French Antilles. However, for Biringanine Ndagano, this potential autonomy with regard to the Antilles has to be put in perspective. Wishing to pass unnoticed, French Antillean interests have simply gone underground: "The French Antilles recognizes the supremacy of Paris, but Guiana bears the brunt of dual domination by Paris and the Antilles, for, in various circumstances, it falls under the influence of Martinique or Guadeloupe, or of both islands at once. The Guianese economy, for instance, is controlled by a few local families and by the Antillean *Békés*. The dominance of the Antilles in Guianese affairs, which has been occluded by critics of colonialism—obsessed by the historical role of skin color—is as insidious and effective as the power exercised by Paris." (Ndagano 2000: 18) Everything seems to hinge on how the Guianese choose to live and confer value through their presence, their "weight," their involvement—things that will make them not only consumers, but social actors too. But who are these Guianese? The Guianese poet Élie Stephenson long ago claimed that the Guianese are a "population of different races placed side by side, sharing with each other neither heart nor blood, as they crouch together over the vibrant earth." (Stephenson 1975: 84–85)

This Monday, November 24, is the first day of a strike that will strangle and endanger the Guianese economy. Of course, this strike has almost nothing in common with the food riots and acute Haitian poverty that produced earth cakes designed to fill empty stomachs and the scandal of *Restavecs* or *Lapourças*, children sold or given away into slavery. But can we be so sure? It is a strike born of exasperation with the world downturn and the loss of buying power locally. Of course, the crisis is global, but the effects are always local and here they are made more acute by monopolies and a scandalous lack of price controls. Saying that the strike has almost nothing to do with the trade engendered by major migrations is to suggest all the same a certain relationship between the ways that two countries can be, to a different extent, undermined by their dependence on the capitalist machine. In his *Introduction à une poétique du divers*, Glissant underscores this point: "The present poverty in Haiti and the type of dissatisfied ambiguity that exists in Martinique, two completely polar opposites, both result from the same initial state of affairs: the slave trade and the uprooting of people from Africa." (Glissant 1996: 87)[7] Everything began with the huge capitalist folly that aimed to absorb by means of its mercantile structure and its speculative apparatus societies it deemed inferior. Since that scandalous original equality, the whirlwinds of history and political and economic gambles, with their unexpected consequences and necessities, have brought one population to its knees with no choice left but exile, and another to an ambiguous contentment with a vague claim on a providential state structure that is always called on to make things better and blamed for things getting worse. If things have become intolerable for the Guianese, Martinicans, and Guadeloupeans, what can we possibly say about the people who provide their cheap labor and are ready to do anything, even run the gauntlet of hostility and petty fascism condemned by Michel Foucault? Indeed it was Foucault who well understood that "the major enemy, the strategic adversary is . . . the fascism in us all, in our heads and in our everyday behavior, the fascism that causes us to love power, to desire the very thing that dominates and exploits us" (Foucault 2001: 134). Ordinary fascism, the sort we have internalized, does not depend only on emotional rewards and bonuses. It is structural. It emanates from accepted hierarchies and imperatives linked to our desire to conform. In his *Nègre tricolore*, Ndagano quotes this anecdote told by the Guianese writer Serge Patient: "My grandmother used to tell us, once again, that when slavery was first abolished, one of the Blacks who had been freed went up to his old master and said: 'Now that I am free, that I have money, I would like to buy slaves.' He was told: 'You have got it all wrong. Slavery has been abolished. There are no more slaves. You are free.' So, he answered in Creole: 'Ki m'a foutu liberté-la, si mo pa pouvé acheté esclaves?' [What sort of freedom is that if I can't buy slaves?]." (Ndagano 2000: 17) We can laugh at him and call him a fool and an opportunist, but the "tricolor Negro" is not all that dumb—he aspired to freedom from a system of drastic prohibitions and he finds his desires once again frustrated. Of what use is his freedom if it stops him from having slaves? What use did suffering the neutralization of all his desires serve? To have escaped from the antagonism of free/not free to that of competition if the market is no longer open to him? Better still, how else can he show his status as newly free and nouveau riche other than by becoming a master? He does not really know what to think of a freedom that reins in his desire for social advancement, a freedom that is paradoxically restrictive. He observed and understood that power involved subjecting others to one's will, that social status was less a matter of owning material goods than, as Deleuze crudely put it, being part of a group of "people who want to be a pain in the ass to other people, who have the chance and even the 'right' to do it." (Deleuze 2002: 366) The remark made by Patient's Negro is to the effect that this status entails the right to such behavior. Without the right, the status is devoid of meaning. He has yet to understand that subjugation has changed form, that he can still buy a workforce and exercise this right but no longer in the same way as under the *Code Noir*. It was perhaps from the moment of this enormous initial scandal pointed out by Glissant—a scandal that was, however so profitable that it was found repugnant by only a small few—that the world began to take on a different meaning. The moment that the triangular trade began to show signs of running out of steam, that this huge machine laden with greed and longing for power and wealth began to flounder economically, it became necessary to ask what the theoreticians and first speculators had gotten wrong and to look for alternatives. The desires of the rich and powerful are always cynical, and it was less a matter of breaking with a practice than of seeking greater efficiency. The regime of desire was the first to be put in the spotlight. How to unleash the slave's desires and offer him other investments, that was the question. "Black or ebony, the slave lives from day to day. He only works to fulfill his needs; as soon as his material existence is assured, his modest desires met, he rests. In order to spur him to work, to engage him in the cultivation of his soil and his woods, civilization (and this is sad to say and admit) must give him new appetites, passions, weaknesses, even vices. It is a matter of choosing the one that are least destructive to him."(Bouyer 1990: 305)

The big question in the case of Guiana has always been the following: how to turn it into a land of production and profit with the minimum investment possible? Unlike Guadeloupe, slavery and the plantation economy were not decisive factors. "From the beginning, this French colony in America got caught in a vicious cycle that it could never free itself from: insufficient labor meant that it could not develop, which in turn meant that it never produced enough to attract the interest of the slavers." (Mam-Lam-Fouk 1987: 41) In this narrow colonial world, important wealthy whites, poor whites, free colored people, and slaves all occupied well defined positions and relations between them obeyed strict rules. There were, however, many bridges between races and classes, according to Frédéric Bouyer, a frigate captain who traveled to Guiana from 1862 to 1863. If the unfree were subject to a regime designed to neutralize their desires, which was occasionally relaxed (Mam-Lam-Fouk mentions toleration with regard to slaves who ran away for short periods, slave strikes, and slave appeals to the courts), some of them could hope to become free and, like Patient's Negro, slave-holders in turn. "As a group, the class of free coloreds owned 28.1 percent of all slaves in the colony in 1842, and mixed-race coloreds owned most of these." (Mam-Lam-Fouk 1986: 208) After abolition, and vain attempts to retain the slaves through offering them a salary or share in profits, the colonizers turned instead to voluntary immigration in the form of Chinese, Indians, Madeirans, and Africans lured by promises of salaries and press-ganged by persuasive recruiting agents. However, in 1862, under philanthropic pressure and above all because of the Charles-Georges Affair (the scandal involving the slaving ship boarded by the British Navy in 1858) Napoleon III forbade the recruitment of Africans because it too closely resembled slave trading. (Mam-Lam-Fouk 1987: 73) Whatever the case, disease killed the newcomers by the hundreds and the landowners exploited them in conditions similar to those of slavery. "Poverty, disease, and death awaited the immigrants, who could be seen dragging themselves around town, malnourished and for the most part clothed in rags."(79) What is more, many Africans were no sooner off the boat than they would run away. The arrival of hard labor prisons restored hope by providing a ready supply of free, servile labor. "Today we have the hands that were once missing; the gaps in the labor force that the abolition of slavery created, these can now be filled by deportation. Let's put our hopes in this unknown element." (Bouyer 1867: 311) In 1867 Bouyer had a dream of rehabilitating the deportees through agricultural work that would bring about the country's development. This meant redemptive, paying work in the eyes of God, but without cost to men. He dreamt of developing Guiana by turning it into a kind of purgatorial machine. The criminal deportees, for the most part whites, had certainly been put to work, but they were also gardeners or house boys, servants in Creole households, a fact which astounded foreign observers, above all Americans who, even in 1934, were still steeped in anti-black racism at home: "It is the only colony in the world, French or otherwise, in which the black people not only are virtually in charge of their own lives, but are the employers of Whites. Nowhere else is that true, not even in Haiti." (Smith 1942: 91) Nowhere else was this the case, not even in Haiti, insisted Smith, referring to the country that was then considered by Creoles as a model of struggle and triumph. All of a sudden, in a cruel twist of fate, and as an ironic consequence of policies put in place by French authorities, Guianese blacks were manifesting a pseudo-superiority, one which unlike the Haitians they had not even fought for, by employing whites, albeit mere outlaws. Later, Smith would witness in the exasperation of a Guianese hostess at the laziness of her domestic: "How strange it was, I reflected, that in the great cities of the Far East I had heard white men yelling, 'Boy! Boy!' at unhappy native waiters, while here, on the other side of the world, I was listening to a Negress employing the same word, and in the same tone, to a white man." (130) Although outsiders might have been disturbed by the contrast in skin color and apparent inversion of roles, the fact that the Creole's servant was white did not arouse any impression that revenge was being exacted since he was a member of a non-free, criminal class. Furthermore, the boss's skin color was not necessarily an issue when it comes to managing a household runs by slaves, prisoners, or Haitians. The overall system thrived on an antagonism between groups of contrasting status: between those who held a privileged position and those who belonged to the new racialized class of despised migrants, confined to the devalued sphere of anonymous production, obviously still holding out the hope that they or the next generation would redeem themselves (a level of social redemption similar to liberation from slavery), moving up one notch in the game. Reference to the white model in order to explain the behavior of Creoles is not a sufficient explanation. In fact, nothing going on today in Guiana is a break with the long history of capitalism and of its mutations. There is a clear link between the subjectivity of the powerful and those who are merely fodder for labor (in the way that we also speak of cannon fodder). Certainly, one might optimistically if rather ingenuously see in the variety that characterizes the social fabric of Guiana the alluring symbol of *Awara soup*, as imagined by the filmmaker Cesar Paese in his film of the same name in 1995. The film emphasizes the harmony of this multiethnic society by showing a small community near Mana where 1,500 people who speak thirteen different languages manage to coexist. *Awara soup* is a local dish that contains a variety of ingredients mixed together into a sauce that has an orangey color thanks to the pulp of the palm fruit known as the *awara*. It is traditionally eaten on Easter Sunday. Clearly, this would be the symbol of a successful creolization. One still has to determine what kind of relationships might exist between the different elements that go into its creation.

The location of the largest Region of France on the northeast coast of South America constitutes an exception that is impossible to ignore. It is shot through with an undeniable atmosphere of modernity, space, and freedom. A region poised on the extreme periphery of the European Union, Guiana is an enclave of the euro zone of 86,000 square kilometers with a population of little more than 200,000 inhabitants possessing social, fiscal, and other advantages, and in sharp disappointing contrast to Guiana's economic, political, and social situation—with an unemployment rate just under 30 percent. The modernity of Guiana is not without flaws, since it lies essentially in external signs of wealth and progress rather than in real development, in entertainment and consumption rather than production. In addition, there is an important difference in the treatment of the urbanized, populous coastal territory, where the signs of wealth are fully evident on the outside in an excess show of leisure and consumption, and the rest of the country, covered by tropical forest (96 percent), where the people live according to the rhythms of traditional populations and isolated gold prospectors. One might say that the way that time is marked down there is not according to the opposition between country and city, but rather according to the contrast between "ultra modernity and extreme antiquity."(Peyrat 1999: 23) This opposition has even led to the coexistence of two different legal systems. "How, then, can one combine laws and custom in a way that does not end up giving insult to custom or breaking down the Law?" is the question posed by the magistrate Didier Peyrat. (26)

Without even casting a critical eye, the social and cultural heterogeneity, along with a multitude of other paradoxical phenomena, marks even the most naïve gaze cast on Guiana. On one hand, it is a kaleidoscope of anachronistic images, as those in the Prices's mind before their departure in 1990: "a lurid backdrop of the crumbling prison buildings of the French Guiana penal colony, the modernistic Ariane satellite-launching station, and the bustling outdoor markets where Parisians, Hmong, and Haitian are as much in evidence as Carib Indians, Suriname Maroons, and Brazilians from the Amazon." (Price 1992: 11)[8] In a different way, Peter Redfield in his book *Space in the Tropics* is able to juxtapose without difficulty the colonial penitentiary and the "colonial" Space Center of Guiana mostly populated with *métros* from metropolitan France. Once one leaves the airport, on the road leading to Cayenne, the perception often becomes flustered. A confused feeling of paradox prevails, an impression of baroque which for the Haitian writer Emile Ollivier bursts in Haiti everywhere and is the essence of his country's reality. For those who choose to pass through Matoury and take the Route de la Madeleine toward Cité Bonhomme and Cayenne, they can admire at the entrance to the city the statue celebrating ethnic diversity; a curious diversity reduced to three actors: An Amerindian, a Creole, and a Bushinengue. Is this selective memory or a conscious omission? In the middle of the Mirza circle this statue of false diversity stands in front of the fast food chain "MacDo," the modern location of true diversity that is always full.

What would then be the rules for the game of diversity in Guiana? A game in which the immigrant held in a state of endless waiting on the borders of the country wishes to enter. Why is it that one of the fundamental rules seems to push people to bar their windows as if they were suddenly in a lawless zone?[9] Why do they transform their cities into human zoos, and in the case of Guiana, into inversed prisons? What difference exists in the end between Haitian Creoles and Guianese Creoles?[10] In what way does the presence of one require the submission—whether real or imagined—of the other? The fact of affirming one's presence represents a power struggle where one is ceaselessly threatened by effacement when others enter the game. The individual enters into an endless quest for mastery through social pressuring of the other (a subtle form of oppression). These are the small pleasures of fascist domination. To illustrate this game of mastery, let us consider the case of *Le dispensaire de Maripasoula* [The Maripasoula dispensary] as described by the anthropologist Michèle Baj-Strobel. As we shall see, the ethnic interaction among the patients led to a systematic appropriation of space and invites us to consider the double meaning of the term "dispense," which can mean either to exempt oneself from something ("to dispense with") or to bestow something on someone else. The dispensary can be approached as a metaphor to elucidate *fascist* ethnic interaction.

The building has three doors, and each one of them has become the preferred entrance of a particular group, without any evidence that the system was set up in a deliberate way. The door that offers direct access to the doctor's office has been appropriated by the Amerindians. . . . The main entrance, which leads into the waiting room, is used almost exclusively by the Aluku, the ethnic group to which most of the patients belong. After presenting themselves to the nurse, who is a nun, they wait their turn and make their way to the doctor's office. Finally, the back door, which is almost hidden out of sight and leads into the pharmacy, is used by the Creoles. They speak directly to the nurses's assistant or the nun, who are both also Creoles, and then make their way to the doctor's office without passing through the waiting room. This tripartite entry system, which was observed up to 1985, shows—in a schematic way—a type of ethnic separatism established by the users and tolerated by the staff of the dispensary. The amusing thing about this situation is that each group considers itself to have the best deal. The Amerindians because they short-circuit the intermediaries, the Creoles because they deal individually with the nun in their own language, and the Maroons because they monopolize the main entrance and the waiting room, showing that they are at home and actually forcing the others to enter and leave the building through the service doors. (Baj-Strobel 1998: 47)

Picking time: Voices

1. Interview with Mister Jacques: Guianese civil servant. (Cayenne, December 2008)

Of course, I am partly affected since my present partner is of Haitian origin and I am sensitive to these matters, but I have neither the time nor the expertise to examine these topics.[11] I can only give a quick, highly personal reaction. First of all, your remarks about barred up houses . . . You've got the wrong end of the stick. There is no Haitian delinquency. Not of that type. Absolutely not! The burglars, muggers, rapists, and other bag snatchers are from Georgetown (in former British colony of Guyana), they are Brazilians, Surinamese, Guianese (oh, yes!). Haitians don't have the time. I mean they are either too busy with working to survive, or with the joys of consumption. The desperate need to work to survive that one finds in their community rarely leads to delinquency. It seems to me they are more motivated by an ambition to make the best of their lot.

Let's talk about Haitians by dividing them into immigration waves and generations:
The first wave (up until the 1970s): essentially political exiles, adults, sometimes with their families. These people did not have major problems, primarily because they had a profession (rare are the changes of career). Certain of them were intellectuals, cultivated people. Others were accountants, business people, cooks, even property owners. Afterwards, there was nothing like the major influx that would come

later. A portion of this group only transited in Guiana before moving on to the U.S., Canada, etc . . . The rest stayed in Guiana and integrated without incident (a case in point, Mécène Fortuné, founder of the *Mécènes).*[12]

The first generation (of settlers): that's where it all started to go wrong. There were people on their own, men or women, (sometimes) rarely couples with young children in search of a better life; agricultural workers, illiterate people, domestic help; above all "undocumented" people who entered without a tourist visa or simply by sneaking over the border from Suriname. They arrived in waves, creating makeshift rural housing in the suburbs of Cayenne (Larivot, Matoury, Balata), sometimes on the outskirts of coastal towns. They took all sorts of odd jobs and were employed as day laborers by unscrupulous businesses that either paid them as an afterthought, that is when they didn't simply turn them in once the job was done. They were grass cutters (not yet with mowers, but with machetes . . .) at the villas in the residential districts of Cayenne; careers for children and old folk; housekeepers. The younger women undertook to seduce the men of Cayenne by giving them what the inhibited Guianese women had always withheld . . . I leave the details to your imagination . . .

Well, the Guianese let loose: Haitian women were breaking up families, the men were idiots; the gardeners cut everything that grew, they pretended to be mental retards in order to be accepted or get what they wanted; they had AIDS, they were stealing Guianese land (Imagine! They had already planted patches of wild vegetables stretching as far as the slopes of Rorota and Baduel . . .). Their children were ostracized in class, by the pupils but also by some of the Guianese teachers (male and female), and they had a particularly tough time of it. But, highly motivated as they were, they advanced and succeeded, before eventually fleeing elsewhere, most of them. Marked by their experiences, the ones who would remain would marry within their community and keep their distance from Guianese society. From an administrative point of view, as you say, they would do better than the Guianese (school results), or at least no worse.

The second (or third, it depends) generation: it is made up the children of those I have just mentioned. They blend into the Guianese population. They have no memory of the lost country. Tradition is limited to food, music, and a little bit of the language. They are totally integrated into the country's youth (with a few exceptions). They have qualifications and find jobs (in no greater or lesser proportion than the indigenous Guianese). Racism lingers but is a thing of the past, emanating from the older antagonistic generations, and they are quite oblivious to it. They have Guianese "djales."[13] They are less motivated by social advancement, have not suffered; they are like young Guianese people, spoiled and eager consumers in a society of the same name.

The new arrivals: more come than are necessary, attracted by the success of distant relations or hearsay. Surinamians or Brazilians for instance. They are regularly arrested by the police and deported. Some go to ground. There is no longer the practice of regularizing those who have been resident for ten years. Things have gotten difficult, but the racism is no longer as violent as in the 1970s and 1980s. Once again, these immigrants are farm workers, hiring themselves out on the black market in the towns (Macouria, Montsinéry), and lying low at night in small survival groups in the woods (honestly!). They end up leaving because no one can do anything for them with these new laws. For the most part they are single (with families left behind in their home country, they provide good business for the Dominican prostitutes).

Once again, I am no sociologist. There are many other things to be said, like the fact that the Haitians have a monopoly on the informal economy in Guiana (traveling vendors of all types, selling merchandise—women's clothing, black cosmetics—imported from Miami cosmetics; the selling is done, all the same, out of vans). They do reconditioned vehicles, fast food etc . . . The famous illegal lottery, the *Bolèt*, siphons off hundreds of thousands of Euros and its agents drive around in Mercedes and launder their money through the local real estate market . . . And some have made their fortunes in private construction and live the high life . . .

Racism? Sure, all immigrants meet up with. As far as the seventeen types of Negroes identified in the book you quoted, I can only confirm that it varies by region. From the most to least harsh, there is Martinique, Guadeloupe, and then Guiana, which is least susceptible to this phenomenon because of its history.

2. Interview with Dieula, housekeeper, a divorced mother of three (Cayenne, December 2007-December 2008)

Lony: Tell me a bit about Haiti and your life there.

Dieula: In Haiti, I lived in Aquin, in the countryside, with my partner and my two children. We were poor. We had no time for anything. We grew vegetables to eat, and to sell too, and we sold sugar, soap, flour . . . Life was hard; we did not really have enough money to live and I couldn't read or write. A lot of people can't read or write over there . . .

Lony: How did you decide to leave?

Dieula: My brother had already left. He was so poor. After a while, he wrote to say things were better and that we had to leave. So, I didn't wait, I too left for Cayenne, all alone. My partner and my kids were going to come later. I thought, "It won't take long." That was in 1988. I was twenty-five.

Lony: What did you think you were in for? Did you dream of a gorgeous country where you would have more time, where life would be easy?

Dieula: Not really. I had no dreams, no. I just had to leave . . . for me, for the children . . . Life there was just a waste of time. Lots of people do nothing because there is nothing to do. I wanted to leave like the others, to find a better life, but I had no clue how it would be in reality . . . except for what my brother had told me.

Lony: How did you get into Guiana?

Dieula: It was impossible to get a visa for Cayenne. It's difficult to get into a *département* of France. The tourist visa for Suriname is easier. Everyone does it that way. You go to Suriname and then you cross by night to Cayenne. I had no papers. I went to my brother's place in Cité Bonhomme, where he lives with his wife and kids. I was scared. No, it was not an easy time.

Lony: What was life like at your brother's?

Dieula: It was "an lakou": a courtyard. That's the way you live here. There is a piece of land belonging to a Guianese person. He builds a few houses around a courtyard and rents them out cheap. There is someone in charge of the "yard," who collects rent for the landlord. Some yards have decent, solid, small houses; others are more poorly built, out of corrugated iron, but not too bad. There is a tap in the middle of the yard. That's it. In any event, there is a single meter for water and electricity, and all the residents share the bill. The housing is very simple, and a lot of people live in the houses, but it is better than back home.

Lony: Can you live legally there?

Dieula: Yes, in Cité Bonhomme, in Cité Eau Lisette, in Cogneau-Larivot. They are not very nice areas, but it's legal. Sometimes, when you have a bit of money, you look for a vacant lot. You have to put aside money for that, to do nothing else if you want to have your own house.

Lony: It's not exactly legal, is it?

Dieula: No, but some people have money, so they want their own house like everyone else. They build themselves a real cement house made of breeze blocks, without machines, with their own bare hands. They hook up the water and electricity themselves. They live well.

Lony: At some stage, there are problems, right?

Dieula: Sure. When the owner of the land notices what has happened, he reacts, but it takes time to go to court. After a while, you get an eviction notice, but you don't answer. Then they come to evict you. That's what you see on TV. The police are there to oversee and the bulldozers destroy the houses. OK, it's sad for the families, the kids cry, but that's the way it is. The Guianese are not happy about people taking their land, even if there is nothing built on it. It's better to have your own land.

Lony: You always say that you can't just sit back and not work. How did it go for you?

Dieula: I looked for any sort of work when I arrived. I didn't want to waste any time, and I found work in a restaurant straight away. I washed dishes. The boss wanted everything done above board. He declared me to Social Security and sponsored me as an employer. In 1992, the City Hall issued me a residency permit that was renewable every year. I never stopped working. I went to work taking care of an elderly lady. Then I started doing housework, cooking, like I do now. I get up at 5 A.M. to get the kids ready for school, then I go off to work until 1 P.M. I have another job in the afternoon. Sometimes my son brings me to work now that he has his license and his own car. It's far, but I can also walk. I'm used to the sun. It's hot in the afternoons; that doesn't bother me.

Lony: In the end, you became French?

Dieula: For a while, I did several jobs. I took care of kids, I minded an old person, I was a cleaning lady. In 1988, I applied for naturalization, and I got it in 2003. A long time had passed and I had worked without stop. But, that's OK because I'm not capable of sitting idle. [Laughter] . . . I get sick if I don't work.

Lony: And your partner, did he eventually come to join you with the children?

Dieula: Yes, he came in the end with the children, the same way I had, but time had passed. A long time. I had met another man from Haiti. I married him and had another child with him. I divorced him recently because he was violent. My partner from Haiti came and he settled in a different yard. Now I live alone in Cité Bonhomme. I am responsible for six people, children, nieces, cousins . . . I have to work for all these people [Laughter] . . .

Lony: How are things financially?

Dieula: Since I'm French, I get all benefits and allowances. I'm very happy. I'm in good shape. I could never have imagined things would work out this way. I earn about 1,600 Euros per month when you add up my salary, my extra work, and my allowances. I pay no taxes because my official salary is too low, about six hundred Euros. I can save and send money to Haiti. But I rarely go to see my relatives because the air ticket is expensive.

Lony: What do you think of the situation for Haitians in Guiana these days?

Dieula: Between us, people help one another a lot. There is a Haitian association created by a Haitian priest, which helps us to find work, somewhere to live, and to navigate administrative red tape. It's true that for a lot of people, it's necessary to avail of all the social benefits. Since we have lots of children, we can get children's allowance without working. I didn't go to school, but I work for my kids. I don't want them mix with bad people, getting into trouble, and going to prison. My children went to school. My daughter is at the IUFM training to be a primary school teacher. My son says he is doing a BTS diploma. The youngest is four. Unfortunately, my son is doing nothing and I'm worried he's wasting his time . . . I don't like his friends much.

Lony: Here's another question for you, Dieula. Do you have any free time now? Time to buy things you like, to go shopping? Do you go out occasionally?

Dieula: [Laughter] . . . Like to the cinema, or dancing? I have no time for that, and I don't like to dance. I work and, in the evening, I go to bed early because I have to get up for work at 5 A.M. I go to the market on Saturdays to buy food. In general, the people I work for give me nice clothes, and even furniture. Sometimes I go see people I know for a chat and a laugh. I buy stuff for the children, not really for myself. For instance, I just bought a new car that my son drives. It's almost brand new. I saved up for a year to buy it. The previous one was breaking down too often. It was too old. Or, when I want to go to Haiti to see my family, I save up for a year for the trip . . . You have to save for that sort of thing.

Lony: You spoke early about having one's own land. Do you have yours?

Dieula: In fact, there is a Haitian group that gives out land that needs improving in various towns in Guiana. I have a piece of land in Roura. I like tending it, hoeing, planting . . . when possible. I have to go there in June 24 to take advantage of the full moon. Everyone is going to go. It grows better that way.

Lony: But the full moon is June 18, I think, isn't it?

Dieula: I don't really know. According to tradition, that is the day the moon is good. Everyone is going to plant on the 24th, that's all. I'm going to ask my boss for the day off to plant vegetables.

Lony: I've heard of "bananes pesées." What are they? Do you cook mostly Creole for your employers?

Dieula: No, not really. I do what they ask. If they explain what they want, I do it. "Banane pesée" is fried green banana. It's eaten with *djondjon* rice, a kind of black rice, or "national rice." It goes with pork *griots*, which are grilled pork squares. It's dry, but we put picklies sauce, made with chopped up vegetables, over it. It's pretty hot . . .

Lony: Do you have time for family meals? How do mealtimes work? What do you eat?

Dieula: I get up at 5 A.M. I fix breakfast for the kids. I have bread and coffee, always standing up to save time. The children eat alone when I'm gone. When I get to work, I have another coffee to give me energy [laughter]. Around 12.30 P.M., I go home to eat with the children who have got out of school. I make salad, meat, rice, beans in sauce. There is bread, yogurt, fruit I bought at the Chinese-run local store . . . apples or pears. Sometimes my sister brings coconuts she has picked up, or mangoes.

Lony: Do you go shopping for dinner?

Dieula: In the evening we eat supper; that's what we call it. Not dinner. We eat creamed corn or bananas (bananas mashed up with sugar). It's on Saturdays that I go shopping at the market for fresh vegetables. On Saturdays, we also eat vegetable soup. Usually, I go to bed at 8 P.M. This is the way the day ends: supper, shower, TV, and bed by 8 P.M.

Translated from the French by Colin Keavenney

Notes

1. I wish to thank the main agent of this text, the young woman designated as Dieula, who kindly responded to my questions and supplied me with all the necessary information for this project. I also thank Monsieur Jacques and Madame Musette, who contributed their perspective to my work.

2. Numerous studies have treated the subject of migration management through gender; see for example, *Gender and International Migration in Europe*: London, Routledge, 2000.

3. According to the definition adopted by the French High Commission on Integration, "immigrants are people who were born as non-French citizens in a foreign country; they can be foreigners or naturalized French citizens." Their immigrant profile remains a permanent aspect of their identity. An individual continues to belong to the immigrant population even if he has become a French citizen.

4. At first Guiana was willing to accept 1,500 people. Because of insufficient funding only 340 refugees settled there.

5. Like Hegel's master-slave dialectic, the Guianese bourgeoisie has succumbed to the power of cheap domestic help. As was the case in nineteenth-century France, having servants is a way to proclaim one's bourgeois status by rejecting one's real origins. According to Jean Baudrillard's *The System of Objects*, this, like leisure and decorative objects, is one of the principal indicators of prestige. Bernard Chérubini in his *Cayenne, ville créole et polyethnique* speaks extensively about domesticity in Guiana.

6. I am referring to Bertrand Lony's description in *Il a bien changé le Montjoly de mon enfance* (unpublished manuscript) and to Jacques Lony's explanations in *Dans la commune de Rémire: formation et évolution du vieux Montjoly* (unpublished, quoted by Alexandre 1999: 61).

7. To evoke the complexity of the postcolonial present is to perceive it as haunted by the past and by the future that it prophesizes, yet colored with hope because of a desire to undo the past's power to determine everything, and neutralized by that hum of ambivalent self satisfaction that Glissant notes among the people of Martinique but which is found everywhere.

8. The two renowned American anthropologists Richard and Sally Price who wrote on Maroon societies were invited to participate in a project of developing the *Musée*

de l'Homme Guyanais [Museum of the Guianese People] in 1990. This project was later abandoned.

9. According to Wenger and Chaumet the crime rate in Guiana is three times higher than the average crime rate in France. (Wenger 2001: 112)

10. Lézy notes: "the Creole population is torn apart by really violent racism . . . Not only external racism and racism against Whites, Brazilians or Haitians, but also internal racism based on a very precise scale of skin tones within the Black population itself. A Guadeloupean friend explained to me that one can distinguish seventeen types of 'Negroes,' from the almost white, curly haired *chabin* to the zombie type to which he himself belonged. And it seems odd to hear school children apparently belonging to the same race calling each other 'Saramaka' or 'Zombi.'" (Lézy 1989: 117) However if the ethnic divide is recognized in French Guiana this "violent racism" is always denied by scholars and researchers.

11. The names of the people who participated in this study have been modified at their request.

12. The work of Mécène Fortuné, a Haitian who settled in Guiana several years ago, illustrates the crucial role that music plays in the integration and organization of immigrant communities. The historical importance of music to African Americans is well known; and we have also seen that music was a significant factor for the migrants from Martinique. An orchestra conductor and businessman, Mécène Fortuné speaks of himself as president of the association known as Les Mécènes, a musical group he founded and performs in. Through the group he has become something of a celebrity in the context of the Guianese carnival. Carnival is such an important aspect of life in Guiana that Ndagano claims that life there is like life in the Middle Ages, and consists of two seasons, carnival and the rest of the year: "During the carnival season, which is to say from December to March if one takes into account the period of preparation time and the aftermath, life and time seem suspended."(Ndagano 2000: 21) Over the years carnival has lost the spontaneity it had in the past, submitting to strict rules that govern the organization of parades, the order in which the costumed groups can appear, and the designation of particular places where the viewers can gather to watch the spectacle. Yet it has also seen the rise of a number of minor skilled jobs, among which the role of the costume makers (usually immigrants who can barely speak French or Creole) is certainly not among the least important. The unique tradition of the *Touloulous Ball* on Friday and Saturday evening has also encouraged the emergence of specialized musical groups, linked to one or other of the two oldest dancehalls in Cayenne, which pull in masses of costumed dancers. The uniqueness of the Guianese carnival has provided the focus of numerous articles published in metropolitan France, and it has been the object of several, mostly descriptive publications. The *Touloulous*, women disguised from head to toe and without a single spot of flesh visible to the eye can approach the men who appeal to them (who are not in costume) and can, if they wish, make the men submit to the torments of the most unbridled sensuality swept up in the gaiety of Aristotle's musical catharsis. The two dance "academies" that are all the rage are Polina and Nana. Nana is the oldest dancehall in Cayenne. Called the Rising Sun (since people danced there till dawn), it was founded by Evelina Modica who died at the age of ninety-five. The genius

of Mécène Fortuné lies in creating his group, Les Mécènes (his name, plus a sense of offering a generous contribution to the enterprise of carnival), bringing to carnival a particular rhythm, the *piké Djouk*, a variation on the traditional mazurka, which has become indispensable to the *Touloulous* and is firmly linked to the Polina Dancehall.

13. This expression means "girl" or "girlfriend" in Guianese Creole. It is the Creole pronunciation of "girl."

References

Alexandre, Rodolphe. 1999. *Gaston Monnerville et la Guyane*. Petit-Bourg: Ibis Rouge.

Baj-Strobel, Michèle. 1998. *Les Gens de l'Or*. Petit-Bourg: Ibis Rouge.

Bégout, Bruce. 2005. *La découverte du quotidien*. Paris: Allia.

Benjamin, Walter. 1979. *Charles Baudelaire, un poète lyrique à l'apogée du capitalisme*. Paris: Petite Bibliothèque Payot.

———. 2002. *Paris capitale du XIXe siècle*. Paris: Les Éditions du Cerf.

Bourdieu, Pierre. 1997. *Méditations pascaliennes*. Paris: Seuil.

Bouyer, Frédéric. 1990. *La Guyane française*. Cayenne: Guy Delabergerie.

Condé, Maryse.1989. *Traversée de la mangrove*. Paris: Mercure de France.

Condé, Maryse, and Madeleine Cottenet-Hage. 1995. *Penser la créolité*. Paris: Karthala.

Cornuau, Benoit. 2002. *L'exode des Pierrotins*. Videotape, Radio France Outre-Mer.

Deleuze, Gilles. 1981. *Francis Bacon: the Logic of sensation*. Paris: Éditions de la Différence.

———. 2002. *L'île déserte*. Paris: Les Éditions de Minuit.

Deleuze, Gilles, and Félix Guattari. 1980. *Mille Plateaux*. Paris: Les Éditions de Minuit.

Foucault, Michel. 2001. *Dits et Ecrits II, 1976–1988*. Paris: Gallimard.

Glissant, Édouard. 1996. *Introduction à une poétique du divers*. Paris: Gallimard.

———. 1997. *Le Discours antillais*. Paris: Gallimard.

Lézy, Emmanuel. 1989. *Guyane, de l'autre côté des images*. Paris: L'Harmattan.

Lony, Bertrand. 1995. *Il a bien changé le Montjoly de mon enfance*. Unpublished typed document.

Mam-Lam-Fouk, Serge. 1986. *2 siècles d'esclavage*. Paris: L'Harmattan.

———. 1987. *Histoire de la société Guyanaise*. Paris: Éditions Caribéennes.

Ndagano, Biringanine. 2000. *Nègre tricolore*. Paris: Servédit.

Peyrat, Didier. 1999. *Le juge et le lieu*. Petit-Bourg: Ibis Rouge.

Price, Richard and Sally Price. 1992. *Equatoria*. New York: Routledge.

Redfield, Peter. 2000. *Space in the Tropics*. Berkeley: University of California Press.

Smith, Nicol. 1942. *Black Martinique—Red Guiana*. New York: Bobbs-Merrill Company.

Stephenson, Élie. 1975. *Une Flèche pour le pays à l'encan*. Paris: Oswald.

Wenger, Jean, and Alain Chaumet. 2001. *La Guyane: Plaidoyer pour Cendrillon*. Moussy-le-Neuf: J-B Impressions.

Contributors

Cécile Accilien is Assistant Professor of French and Francophone Literatures at Columbus State University in Columbus, Georgia.

Paul Brodwin is Associate Professor of Anthropology at the University of Wisconsin-Milwaukee and Adjunct Professor of Bioethics at the Medical College of Wisconsin.

Sharon Eleanor Clarke is a Refugee Studies and International Human Rights Law specialist. She regularly works for the International Organization for Migration (IOM) in London.

Odile Ferly is Assistant Professor of French at Clark University, Worcester, Massachusetts.

Maud Laëthier is an anthropologist. She is currently a postdoctoral fellow at the Institut de Recherche pour le Développement (Unité de Recherche Constructions Identitaires et Mondialisation) in France.

Marc Lony is Associate Professor of French in the Department of Modern Languages at Loyola Marymount University in Los Angeles.

Pierre Minn is a doctoral candidate in the Departments of Anthropology and Social Studies of Medicine at McGill University in Canada.

Catherine Reinhardt is a lecturer of French at Chapman University.

Philippe Zacaïr is Associate Professor of History at California State University Fullerton.

Index